THE MAGICAL UNFOLDING

Eight Magical Processes for Peace, Potential and Purpose

Helen Rebello

Make Your Mark Global Publishing, ltd
USA & Monaco

MAKE YOUR MARK GLOBAL PUBLISHING, LTD

USA & French Riviera

The Magical Unfolding © 2018 Helen Rebello

Published by Make Your Mark Global Publishing, LTD

Book cover concept: Ces Loftus

Book cover final design: Andrea Danon & Stefan Komljenović of ArtBiro Network

Editor: Carol Taylor

Paperback ISBN 978-0-9992579-7-5

Library of Congress Control Number: 2018961110

Praise for The Magical Unfolding

"Helen has written an unapologetically joyous guide to getting out of the darkness so many of us find ourselves lost in at some point in our lives. Her ideas and her writing bubble with lightness and a hard won wisdom that feels so genuine and loving.

I believe Helen: there is magic to be found no matter what!"

— Jennifer Louden, best-selling author of
The Woman's Comfort Book and *The Life Organizer*
http://www.jenniferlouden.com

"If you're not sure who you are in the world, or you feel lost or stuck and want to change, The Magical Unfolding is for you.

Perhaps you were hoping for a magic wand, but we all know that life isn't that simple. Instead, Helen will guide you gently, with empathy and understanding through a series of processes to unearth your own magic.

This is not a book of theory but, as you will read in her story, Helen has learned by walking the path herself. It's a book I will enjoy working through slowly and will dip into again and again."

— Lesley Pyne – best-selling author of *Finding Joy Beyond Childlessness*
https://lesleypyne.co.uk/

"Ever had the feeling that things could be different in life, work, or relationships? This book will lovingly, and supportively guide you there.

This book provides the fertile ground for the most profound realisations about who you really are underneath all the thinking, worrying, and 'shoulds' and reconnect you to your clarity, courage and confidence.

I encourage anyone who is looking to make changes in their life, but has felt stuck or held back up to now; this book is written by someone who wholeheartedly believes what's really possible for human beings, the potential that resides inside all of us. Consider this book a delightful wake up call to the life that is possible for you right now!"

— Sarah Swanton, Founder of Happy Healthy Entrepreneur
www.sarahswanton.com

"In her powerful book, Helen Rebello takes us on a magical journey. Written with a beautiful blend of honesty, self-reflection, and loving coaching, Rebello invites us to cross the bridge with her – from a life that isn't truly our own to the life that we were always meant to live.

With soulful tools, exercises, and guidance, she shows how it's possible for each of us to embrace our lives and live them fully, each and every day. A must-read, for sure!"

— Jodi Chapman & Dan Teck,
co-creators of the bestselling 365 Book Series
https://www.jodichapman.com/

"This book is a call to live fully and be aware of how much you can change in your life. Helen's compassion for her readers knows no bounds. She will tangibly hold your hand on every step of this Magical path where you will re-discover your inner power, true self, innate resources and learn how to navigate today's chaotic world.

A warm, inspiring and often highly humorous treasure hunt in unlocking your true potential."

— Alexandra Thornton-Hopwood,
Hotelier and Indie Film-Maker
https://sidneyhouse.co.uk/

"Becoming who we really are takes courage... and Helen Rebello has courage in spades as she models the paradox between power and vulnerability in the sharing of her personal story & experience.

This is a book about the power of hope and possibility in the often complex journey of life. The possibility that comes through knowing your own true strength even, and especially, when you don't have all the answers.

Helen's powerful storytelling & teaching gently draws you in to a deeper understanding of all that is truly possible for you if you are ready to make peace with who you are and who you can become. If you are, read on."

— Sue Revell, The Mission Maven
http://magentachange.com/

"I read The Magical Unfolding over a number of days and one of the many beautiful things about it is that you can read it at your own pace, or dip in and out when you need it, so that you get the most from this inspiring illumination of how your life journey flows into your expansive future.

This book combines facts and tangible techniques with the author's personal experience, thoughts and support that reaches through the pages to hold you with no judgement and pure love wherever you are at in your life.

An array of metaphors help the content to connect with your soul, unlocking the motivation to set yourself free and grow your happiness any time you want."

— Ces Rosanna Price

Founder of Inspired To Inspire Design

https://inspiredtoinspire.co.uk/

Dedication

This book is dedicated to my husband and soulmate, Gavin. You have held me with unconditional love, patience, encouragement and support since the day we met. We are stronger together and I am honored to travel through life with you.

Table of Contents

Prologue

I was hovering nervously by the front door of my tiny flat, heart hammering, legs like jelly, eyes anxiously scanning the road left and right. Part of me was praying the taxi I had ordered would arrive soon, and the other part was getting primed to run if it didn't. One hand tightly gripped the handle of a shiny new black suitcase. The other held the letter that had set me free. To anyone observing me, I looked like I was waiting to go on holiday. In a way they would be right – I was going on holiday from my own life...

There are times in your life that stay etched in memory, like part of your soul has reformed itself around them. These times only later reveal themselves to be your catalysts and turning points – crucial signposts marking your unique journey through life. Good or bad, regretful or ecstatic, these are your important transitional moments and, ultimately, they help you become who you came here to be.

This was one such moment.

These moments may be huge and dramatic, or barely noticeable, almost apologetic whispers. They might make perfect sense because you're actively directing them; or you feel like you're stuck in a dark tunnel with no visible exit. There's no right or wrong. No tick-list or failings. No right place to start and no place so lost that you'll never find a way out. Mostly, these moments only make sense in retrospect. Because you're in them, living and breathing it - doing your best to make sense of your situation and choose your next best step.

In my case, this moment felt like pure terror. The kind that seeps into your bones, turning your legs to lead and filling your belly with butterflies. Coupled with the rising panic that made it hard to breathe and, in my head, creating multiple disastrous scenarios. This was NOT a good moment. Important moments don't always feel like you're about to conquer the world. Sometimes they feel closer to hovering over an abyss.

The truth is I was less heroine and more survivor. I was doing what I could to stay safe and escape intact from the nightmare my life had become. I had resorted to desperate measures, deviousness, and clever planning. I didn't know it then, but this was the first time I'd listened to my heart. The first time I found the courage there to do something terrifying, and start actively directing my own life, rather than let it be dictated by others.

Before I had no life left to direct, which sounds dramatic, but is true.

Prior to this moment where I hovered in the doorway between my old life and a new, as yet unknown one, I lived in almost constant anxiety and fear; trapped in the belief I was an unworthy flawed human. I was 19 years old and already well versed in how utterly unfulfilling, painful and exhausting life can be. I had left my family at 18, moved into a squat and given my heart to a man who initially gave me the attention and love I craved but later revealed himself to be violent, unstable, insecure and possessive.

Every aspect of my life was controlled. I got hit for wearing the 'wrong' clothes, showing the wrong emotions, reacting to his dalliances with other women, and daring to go out without telling him. When I went out with the few friends I had, he often followed me, watching me from afar to ensure I followed 'the rules'. I had no money, no support, and too much guilt and shame to admit what was going on. I hid my bruises in long-sleeved, over-sized clothes that disguised my 'too skinny to be healthy' frame, made excuses and created a make-believe happy life when anyone asked, "how are you?"

Systematically, over a period of 18 months, he broke me down until I almost believed I was the most unlovable person in existence and entirely to blame for every bad thing that happened.

Thankfully, deep down in my soul, there was an intact part of me that quietly rebelled and resisted. An inner strong core that couldn't be broken. An invisible driving force that was curious, brave, and strong-willed enough to change things. Even when all seemed lost and the potential repercussions were terrifying.

This is how I ended up standing on the precipice of a new life, waiting for a taxi to come and drive me to the next destination on my life journey. In this case, to a nurse's home, where as a student nurse, I would learn much about life and death, and strength and courage.

***

I share this because I want you to know there's a core, strong part of you that cannot be broken. The part that will get you through anything, even when all seems lost. It's how you get through Big Scary Traumatic things you would never have thought you could, emerging on the other side irrevocably changed, but stronger and more fully yourself than before.

No matter where you are now, what's happened in your life, or how much ground you think you have to cover, you can reclaim your right to a life you love. In truth, you're already on your path and you've covered more ground than you know.

Life is magical like that. Sometimes the magic reveals itself to you in little moments. Sometimes you only see it in retrospect… as you'll discover by reading this book.

Whether your path through your life is relatively smooth; or convoluted, painful and self-destructive (like mine), one magical day, all your twists and turns make perfect sense.

For me, that magical day came twenty-three years later when I found myself standing on a different precipice, looking out at the Sri Lankan jungle. Feeling raw, sore, and emotional, I was very similar in many ways to the girl standing on a different threshold anxiously waiting for a taxi years earlier. In other ways I was totally different, especially when the world shifted exponentially and gifted me an incredible life-changing insight I'll never forget.

I call that moment my midlife awakening and without the magically unfolding path that led me there, it would never have happened. Which is why I have to share my insights and this process with you so you are also empowered to trust your unfolding pathway through life.

There is more to you and your life than you could ever imagine. By the time you finish this book, you'll start embodying that belief as if you'd known it all along. Which of course you do… you simply don't realise it yet.

Disclaimer

Warning:

This book may induce feelings of excitement, possibility, and hope.

Please proceed only if you are prepared to consider that your life can feel full in all the best ways, without you having to change everything, stomp all over people, or become someone you're not.

How do I know? Because you've already successfully made it this far through life... you've already begun.

This book is not intended to replace professional support - if you are struggling with severe anxiety, depression, or any other emotional trauma, please seek professional help. *The Magical Unfolding* will still be here for you when you feel strong again - indeed it will supplement and complement any existing support you have.

If you're seeking like-minded souls, support, inspiration, and a more peaceful approach to uncovering magic and meaning in life, you are invited to join the free Magical Life Movement at
www.helenrebello.com/p/Movement.

I hope to see you there.

Introduction

"I have always been delighted at the prospect of a new day, a fresh try, one more start, with perhaps a bit of magic waiting somewhere behind the morning." — J.B. Priestley

An Invitation...

Would you like the energy to do the things that bring you joy, and to end each day with a smile on your face, no matter what the day sends your way?

Life can be turbulent, demanding, unpredictable, and overwhelming. It can feel like a whirlwind as you're constantly bombarded by the needs of others, distractions, noise and the never-ending onslaught of information. It's like spinning on a hamster wheel without a stop button, with no sense of control or power over the outcome. It makes you question what life is all about, how it got to feel this way and whether it's possible to change it. When life looks like this, the concept of peace and fulfilment seem like a fantasy.

Given you only have this one precious life, and you are a unique, once in a lifetime soul, wouldn't it be wonderful to be on solid ground, establish new foundations for your life and start consciously creating your days?

What If?

What if the reason you're here is completely different from the one you think? What if everything you've been told about how to make decisions and choices is wrong and it's much simpler to find your purpose than you believe?

What if your purpose is not about achievement; becoming something or discovering anything; rather, it is about fully, unapologetically embodying yourself? You as you already are – but with the magical addition of a different life-lens that shows you another way to be.

Does this awaken a sense of excitement, fear, dread, or disbelief? Or does it confirm a suspicion you've been longing to hear someone express?

Consider this...

It is entirely possible to transform and transcend the daily grind, to know what to do each day, feel motivated, inspired, energised, free, happy, courageous, and strong. You can have this – it's not for the chosen few. Once you journey back home to your core and find your own truth and answers you will begin to slowly unfold your life to a more expansive one. It's not only an incredible journey but a way of living and being that feeds your soul and nourishes your heart. You'll find freedom from the desire to please, to say yes to everything, to be all things to all people, to bend over backwards for everyone but yourself, and to burn out because you want to heal the world.

The world needs more peaceful warriors, people who have become who they came here to be. People who are awake, aware, and present. People who know who they are, what they're here for, what they believe in, and who do what honors them, while also honoring others. These new lighthouse keepers of the world will help guide the next generation to live with more peace, presence, and purpose.

Why you?

Some people may look at the subject of this book and immediately write it off. They believe they're already heading where they want to go and understand how their world fits together to make the jigsaw puzzle of their lives, so they have no desire to change anything.

But you are not some people. You're not even most people. You are a rare breed who knows they haven't figured it all out and admits it, and is astute enough to consider whether there is another way. You're brave enough to search for answers and open and curious enough to pick up this book.

How do I know that? I'm making this assumption based upon years of 1-to-1 sessions with other wonderful souls who have sensed they have more potential within them than they're currently showing to the world.

You are one of those people. One of those beautiful souls who doesn't realise how beautiful they are. Beautiful in the sense that you are life-curious, open to discovery, prepared to do some digging, make some changes and figure life out. Beautiful enough to recognise that maybe, there is a whole world of untapped possibility you haven't found yet. Beautiful enough not to settle for a life of 'less than'.

You have a vision for your future. Although you can't fully see it you know it's there waiting for you. You might not know how it feels, what it looks like, and who you will be when you've uncovered it, but you're prepared to turn it into reality. I know you are doing your best to make sense of life and the world, and you simply want to find your place in it. You want to understand where you fit in. So if you really want to know how life turns out for you, I can give you the short version right now...

Are you ready?

It all works out.

It really does, but now that you've read that, your mind is no doubt asking a million questions:

- How do you know that? What a crazy statement to make…
- How does it work out?
- What things did I do?
- Was I happy?
- Did I get to do the things I wanted?
- Did I find love?
- Did I contribute enough?
- Did I feel fulfilled?
- Did I matter?

Ironically, having the answers given to you only raises more questions. You are human. You're a curious being. You can't help but want to know more details, to dive deeper and uncover the mysteries and the story behind the story. That's where I come in; it's why I wrote this book, and why it's called *The Magical Unfolding*.

The Precipice of Possibility…

I know you want answers but I also know you're best uncovering them yourself… because whilst I might be able to make some fairly good assumptions about you based on my lifetime of working with others like you, only you truly know your own answers.

What I can do instead is show you the pathway and guide you along it until you uncover the magic that lies within your heart and soul, waiting ready to unfold for you. What you discover to be true for yourself will take up permanent residence in your heart and help you to change your world to one you love living in, from the inside out. If these words resonate with you, you'll be delighted to know that you are standing on the precipice of possibility.

The path to you living a more fulfilling life lies in a combination of factors: daily practice, habitualised routines, knowing how to get out of your head and into your heart, becoming more present and mindful, developing a more magical mindset, learning to love your flaws and celebrate your strengths, optimising your energy, discovering your SoulGoals and staying focused on your path. It's an ebb and flow - a daily dance - one that ultimately results in a more peacefully present, purposeful life.

I've distilled the essence of this approach to life into simple, achievable steps and I'm sharing them because I believe that if we can all learn to live our lives from a more grounded, calm, mindful place, together we will create a better world.

The Magical Unfolding offers an invitation from my heart to yours, to gift yourself time to explore possibility. It gives you the power to put the bounce back in your step and the joy back in your heart... one step at a time. All you need is willingness to accept that something within you is calling for change. Add to this a pinch of patience, trust and an open mind, and you're already halfway there. This process has helped numerous people around the world – it's the one I unravelled for myself and I am living proof that it changes everything for the better.

This book provides you with a clear starting point, a place to begin making small changes, because once you awaken to the fact that something needs to change, there's no going back...there is only a slow, steady journey onwards. A journey that leads you along the magical path of self-discovery, to help you unveil a life you love inhabiting.

Why you will want to keep reading this book...

I know I am not alone in having lost the equivalent of months dreaming about how life will be when (insert your brightest dreams) happens. I'm willing to bet that your book shelves (or Kindle) are just as full as mine, lined with inspirational books that promise you miracles if only you had the time to read them and the energy to act on their advice.

In these pages, I present you with a process to uncover answers to the questions you've been asking yourself. A process I've been through many times and that I live and breathe each day. It's a journey I know has the power to transform lives – in a way that is gentle, enriching, and nourishing; one I have recommended to my closest friends and family, as well as shared with hundreds of others, many of whom were my clients.

I am one of those people whom other people 'think' has it all figured out. I know this because that's what they tell me, but I can tell you categorically that I don't! What I do have figured out; however, is who I am, what I stand for, what my values are, what I am good at, what I am passionate about and love doing, how I best serve others, and where my boundaries lie. I am connected to my inherent blueprint, my soul self and my heart, and I make all decisions based on what honours those things and what doesn't.

Doing this requires an ongoing process of self-negotiation. It involves prioritising daily connection time and checking in with what is most important to me each day to honour myself and others. It is ever-evolving and demands flexibility, willingness to mess up, a healthy relationship with my ego, honesty, humour, and strong self-worth.

I am no different to you. I simply made a choice to stop putting other people's needs before my own thus, slowly eroding myself. This is a process requiring self-love, acceptance, and support. If I can do it, so can you. I know what it's like to yearn for more and I also know how liberating it is to one day realise you're exactly where you want to be.

It's never too late to start a new chapter. You can start afresh every day if you want to, until you've built new foundations that are strong enough to support you in a much more fulfilling way. This concept may be scary or seem elusive but it will never be as scary as reaching the end of your life only to regret that you didn't live the way you truly wanted.

And so, with love, I will ask you the question that changed the trajectory of my life many years ago:

Would you feel cheated if you died tomorrow?

If the answer is yes please don't get upset… it's good to recognise this and it will give you fuel for your journey.

This question appeared unexpectedly in my head many years ago, a day after losing my friend to cancer. Whilst it annoyed me greatly at the time; especially as I was so angry that my friend died before she got to 21 years old, my answer was a resounding YES and it was the most helpful question I could ever have asked myself. It was also somewhat magical, as it marked the first time I'd heard my inner voice as an adult.

I now ask myself this regularly and it's your turn to answer this question.

The secret to living a fulfilled life lies in following your heart and using your head to support you in reaching your desires. I have created the process for you to do this – you're holding it in your hands right now.

How to Use This Book

"In the midst of our lives we must find the magic that makes our souls soar." — Unknown

The Magical Unfolding helps you discover and work through eight MAGICAL processes that give you the tools and roadmap to mindfully lay new foundations for your joyful today, and your more fulfilled tomorrows. Even if you don't work through each process, you will still come away with a fundamental shift within you. The processes are a synthesis of learnings from my teachers, intuitive daily 'downloads', research voraciously gathered over 25 years, realisations from my own journey, and 14 years of practice as a transformational therapist and mentor.

This journey is a bit like giving yourself an entry level course on Eastern philosophies, mindfulness, mindset, intuition, spirituality, and productivity. To be honest, this book is the tip of the iceberg! Everything I share with you I've incorporated into my own life. Feel free to skip what you know already and notice what you resist: those are the sections you might want to consider reading again!

The book is structured into three core sections:

<u>Part One - The Myth</u>

Part One invites you to consider a different way to view your world and yourself.

Any processes that require change are best visited after reviewing your current paradigm, and glimpsing a possible new one. Your brain needs motivation, even if your heart and soul are already on board. This section gives your brain vital foundations before you dive into the process itself. Don't be tempted to skip it - you'll be missing out! This section shares how the world around you influences your entire belief system, and how it can stop you from accessing your innate potential. Exploring stress, busyness, and society 'rules', I explore the common myths we all believe and I offer you a different, more empowering perspective.

Part Two - The MAGICAL Process

Part Two is the step-by-step breakdown of my unique MAGICAL process that helps you shift from where you are now, towards where you want to be.

Combining personal stories, insights, theory, and practical exercises, this is like embarking on your very own metaphorical self-discovery journey. Whilst on the journey you will gather useful tools, meet and make peace with all aspects of yourself, uncover your uniqueness, and discover the secrets to living in a way that feeds your soul.

Designed to work through sequentially, each chapter ends with a 'summary for your soul' and a 'magical mission' to facilitate positive change and optimise your learning. You are going to be invited to actually DO things - I promise if you do, it will be worth it.

Part Three - Maintaining the Magic

It is easy to feel all fired up and inspired at the beginning of any new adventure; only to see our original good intentions fall by the wayside once we return to 'real life'.

Part Three offers support and tips to help you continue your ongoing exploration into this more nourishing and aligned way of living.

This final section shares information on maintaining change and gives you further resources to support your ongoing magically unfolding journey.

How to Extract Maximum Magic from the book

I am not a big believer in rules; however, to extract the maximum amount of magic from this book, I ask just four things of you:

1. Approach this process with a spirit of possibility, curiosity, and play. Nothing ventured, nothing gained - no-one is watching, so go ahead and indulge your inner child.

2. As you read, adopt self-compassion: no telling yourself off! This is a 'should' free zone.

3. Practice forgiveness as you read – of yourself, others, your past and present. Don't get distracted by rumination or regrets. This is now. The only time you can influence.

4. Trust in the power of small steps to help you shift. Accept that all things unfold in their own time and be patient with your journey.

We all learn differently, so honour your instincts as you read. You may want to read the entire book through first and then revisit each process, or you may want to work with each process as you read.

There are additional resources, audio, and an accompanying 8-day Unfold Your Magic course you can access for free at www.helenrebello.com/p/MagicBookResources

When there is a downloadable audio file for the process. You will see the symbol: ◁

There is no suggested time limit for this process, as we are all different and I do not want to encourage any sense of goal chasing. However, I do suggest that if anything you read gives you a strong tug of knowing in your belly, honour it by working through the relevant process before you talk yourself out of it.

Ideally, gift yourself dedicated time and space to read this book. Make regular dates with it and take yourself on a reading, journaling journey; preferably snuggled up somewhere cosy, with a cup of something delicious, and beautiful music playing softly in the background. Allow your heart and soul to feast upon the words, and may they trigger a deep recognition and memory of the value of making time to connect inwardly so you can hear their messages and start truly living your life with more peace, potential, and purpose.

I am excited for you and what lies ahead. May your path be always aligned with who you are, and may you find the courage to gently follow it.

Extra announcement for curious souls…

As you read this book, you may well wonder why I use the female perspective. This is not designed to exclude anyone; several men generously believed in this book enough to be VIP supporters of my crowdfunding campaign and they all occupy a grateful space in my heart. I write primarily to women because 95% of my clients over many years have been women, giving me more understanding of the common struggles women face. I cannot pretend to know what it is like to grow up and live in the modern world as a man, but I hope much of what I write will also resonate with men.

In truth, I don't care about your sex, race, religion, or background. I am grateful for every single soul I am lucky enough to touch in some way through my work, and if you have somehow found this book and are open to reading it, I am happy and thankful you are here.

As you read, feel free to replace any words you dislike with ones that resonate with you. Don't let mere words detract from your experience.

Part One — The Myth

CHAPTER 1
The Matrix Myth

"To live is the rarest thing in the world. Most people exist, that is all." — Oscar Wilde

Have you seen the film The Matrix?

If you haven't, I won't spoil it for you - go and check it out for yourself because it's one of the best interpretations of what I share in this chapter.

The film highlights the difference between living a consciously aware, intentional life, versus the more common, make it up as you go along, unconscious life. Which generally speaking, doesn't make you feel like the heroine in your life; where you're *thriving* rather than *surviving*. It also leads to regrets (which might well be a subconscious reason why you picked up this book).

You may already be immersed in the process of living a more intentional life; in which case, you're wise enough to know there's always something valuable to learn from someone else's version of reality. Whether this concept is familiar or totally new to you, don't let your head talk you into skipping this section.

This chapter is a bit like a virtual sandwich to digest before your magical unfolding process. It gives you fuel before you start, to boost you if you start flagging. It will also come in handy if your head starts making up stories that advise you to Put The Book Down before it's too late and things start to change.

You may need a compelling reason to do new things. One that stands a fighting chance of staying in your head long enough to push you through your own inbuilt resistance. It is part of being human and the reason I share the Matrix Myth with you is it's essential. It gives you more understanding about why you sometimes feel stuck or frustrated with your life, and empowers you to extract yourself from the myth's grip.

Even though you may not have heard this concept in quite the way I share it, I guarantee you've already fallen victim to parts of the myth without realising it. This limits your potential more than you know.

A Story About a Girl Who Was Trapped in The Matrix

When I became unwittingly trapped in the Matrix, I was totally trapped in my life too. The Matrix is insidious, weaving its way into your life before you even realise what's happened. It rewrites your life story and tells you a new one. You become imprisoned by unconscious beliefs, society's rules, and the lies your head tells you. You end up feeling exhausted from living in a constant state of fight or flight, otherwise known as stress. That state we unconsciously think is normal; only noticing its constant presence when it gets too much and we break in some way.

I was 16 years old when I started finding ways to express the stress I felt from feeling trapped in the wrong life. I was gifted with intelligence, wit, awareness, creativity, empathy, imagination, and curiosity. I was also (still am!) super-sensitive. Somehow all my positive qualities escaped me until years later; the only ones I saw at the time were negative. Even though I'd shown promise in my younger years, by the age of 14, I already believed I was fundamentally flawed.

After my parents moved I had changed schools, opting to go to one closest to me, rather than travel further to a 'posh school' where I felt I wouldn't fit in. I had done well at school up to that point and assumed this would continue in my new school. I read books that led me to believe being the new girl would make me intriguing and popular, so it was a huge shock when I discovered the pupils at my new school thought I was weird and didn't fit in.

Attributes I had never even thought about, or considered an issue were suddenly highlighted. I was rubbish at sports, had no desire to learn things that bored me and never spoke up in class. I was clumsy, had a different accent, viewed the world differently, and was called a swot because I did fairly well. I started getting bullied because I stood out as being different. I didn't even know bullying existed before I changed schools. As a sensitive teenager just wanting to be liked and accepted by my peers, I started playing dumb to fit in. I hung around with people who didn't play by the rules, started truanting and generally becoming someone I wasn't, so that life didn't feel so hard.

According to the Matrix Myth, I didn't fit the 'acceptable' paradigm. And like a fool I believed it so much that I transformed myself into a person I thought would fit in. I'm pretty sure I was a nightmare to deal with. In the words of my parents, I went from being a 'good girl' with good grades and respectable friends to becoming a 'typical f**ked up, insecure teenager' who constantly failed to make the grade.

None of it felt typical to me. Labelling it didn't make it less painful or all-consuming. In my head, I was living in my own version of hell. Partly because of all the lies my head told me about myself and partly because of raging hormones. The lies in my head were reinforced by my daily experiences and interactions with teachers, adults, and peers; serving to further convince me I was unworthy.

I didn't know it was even 'a thing' at the time, but I became a self-harmer and started subconsciously using food as a control mechanism. I'd become someone with shameful behaviors and self-destructive secrets long before the Internet came along and helped us all realise how common these issues are.

I had no idea how to express myself or control any aspect of my life. I was the eldest child and my parents had no experience with emotional, sensitive, hormonal teenagers seeking freedom from pain. They also had my two younger siblings to deal with and their own lives to manage. So whenever I got so angry or upset I wanted to cry my heart out, I instead cut my arms or banged my head against walls. Literally trying to knock some sense into myself and numb the internal pain I felt from being a failure and not fitting in.

No one knew the full extent of what was going on. My parents could see I was verging on anorexic and were trying to stop it before it got worse, but I was able to hide my scars. I became so locked into my own world of complex emotions and beliefs, I adopted a victim mindset and self-destructive behavior pattern that would dictate and limit my life for years.

My poor parents must have been beside themselves. All that promise and potential was disappearing before their eyes. I remember snippets, rather than details - but I know they tried to reach me in ways I interpreted as intrusive at the time. Every time they did, I retreated further into the Matrix

Myth's grip, entangling myself in a web so intricately constructed, it took years to fully escape.

I share this because it's important for you to see how early entrapment in the myth can start, and how subtly it can undermine who you came here to be. Even though my example is extreme, there will be elements of it you can relate to from your own experiences that might help you understand more about what was going on.

Before your head tricks you into going on a downward spiral of regrets about your own journey, it's important for you to know that my pathway makes sense to me now and I genuinely have no regrets. Instead, I have incredible insights, full acceptance, and deep compassion for my younger self and what she taught me.

If what I share in the rest of this chapter helps you untangle some of your own threads and ultimately extract yourself from the Matrix Myth, that would be incredible. When this happens, a huge amount of your valuable life force energy is released as you stop using it to hold onto misguided beliefs and regrets, giving you the energy to create magical moments in your life instead.

It's so incredibly liberating when you learn to trust and start believing life is there to support you, rather than believe the limiting influence of the Matrix Myth.

Components of The Matrix Myth

The world around us influences our entire belief system, and the negative beliefs we acquire and install have the power to stop us from reaching our innate potential. I call this The Matrix Myth because we effectively become trapped and stuck in a web-like matrix created by society's myths, expectations, conditioning, and our upbringing.

There are four components of the Matrix Myth:

1. Doing versus Being
2. Asleep versus Conscious
3. External versus Internal
4. Head versus Heart

Knowing these components gives you crucial knowledge for optimising your wellbeing, and accessing greater peace, potential, and purpose. If you don't know about them, it's likely you're using up energy, doing the wrong things, with no idea half the time why you're doing them.

Which isn't your fault.

You're a product of generations of people who came before you and believed the myth too... the difference nowadays is that it has escalated in terms of its limiting effects, because the modern world has evolved at a faster rate than humans have. We're trying to navigate our way through a constantly changing, evolving world and stay sane and balanced, with no reference points from our parents or ancestors.

This is an unprecedented time. Regardless of your age, you've witnessed the rapid evolution of more technological advances than any of our ancestors. If you're in your late 40s like me, you've seen the introduction of computers, the death of typewriters, the progression from vinyl and tapes to CDs and mp3s. You no longer need to buy physical books if you don't want to, thanks to eBook readers, and if you have limited time to read, you can enjoy books in audio form instead.

We've moved from old-style rotary telephones through various sizes and evolutions of mobile phones - from which we can now access almost anything. We've used VHS, Betamax, DVDs and Blu-ray to watch and record TV and films. Instead of only three TV channels, we can choose from hundreds of channels on TV or the Internet - many of which we don't even have to watch when they're shown.

The Internet has of course changed *everything*, in an infinite number of ways no one could have foreseen. It has become so ubiquitous in our lives, it's easy to forget there was a time when it didn't exist. We no longer have to visit a library or read encyclopedias to do research, or even use our own memory! We simply ask Guru Google for answers to all things, or delve into apps on our phone.

It's like a kind of magic.

Sometimes we forget how much has shifted. It's an incredible privilege to be witnessing these shifts - but it's also easier to feel overwhelmed and disconnected than ever before. Even having a conversation these days can involve fighting for your fellow human's attention over that of their smartphone, which can make us feel invisible and unimportant.

Research shows that even the mere presence of a face down mobile phone impacts the quality of our connection during a conversation - and without true connection, our spirit won't thrive. Depression is higher than ever before, according to the latest research from the World Health Organisation. Even though we have more access to resources, we simply haven't evolved to successfully juggle and balance so many spinning plates, and it is crippling and overwhelming us. Thankfully, there is a quiet turning of the tide.

The deep thinking, caring, awake and aware souls of the world are making waves. We've had enough of being overwhelmed and busy all the time. And there are many people creating amazing tools and resources to change this. The very same technology that entraps and depletes us, is now being used consciously by those dedicated to helping us improve our lives. You can access online videos and courses designed to create calm and balance and even establish your meditation practice alongside a virtual gathering of people worldwide, without ever leaving the house!

Doing vs. Being, Asleep vs. Conscious

When we're young, we play, daydream, create, explore, and find enjoyment in simple things. We're naturally happy and joyful - but as we mature, we start to lose these qualities. We become focused on responsibilities, reaching goals, and providing for the future; somehow absorbing the lesson that enjoyment, fun, and simply 'being' are self-indulgent. We limit ourselves, bury our whimsical creative sides, and hide our frivolity so that we can 'get serious' about being an adult. We force ourselves to fit in, rather than stand out.

Underneath our striving lies the quiet desire for a joyful, fulfilled life. We often don't realise this - or if we do, we fail to honour it. It's amazing how much time we can unconsciously spend doing things we don't enjoy, rather than free that time up to do things we really love.

Many of us make intermittent steps towards our highest goals, using our 'ideal life' vision to soothe or inspire us when we feel a bit lost. We are teleological beings - genetically wired to move towards targets - so our visions are our constant background presence. We hold onto them to fuel our daydreams and give us hope - our 'some day in the future' dream that keeps us going.

If we are lucky enough to know what we want in life and have something we yearn for, we convince ourselves the reason we're not 'there' yet is because we don't have enough knowledge or the right information. We think we need more time, money, energy, or resources. We tell ourselves we must lose weight, get fit, buy the right handbag, or get the perfect car.

We berate ourselves for feeling stuck, appeasing ourselves with stories about what holds us back. We believe other people have more choice, luck, better upbringing, or more opportunities. We blame our past, gender, race, or genetics, telling ourselves that successful people with a similar background are either freakishly lucky or have a hidden superpower.

Depending upon your life experiences or where you live, some of those things *are* of course actually true. Especially the bit about superpowers... as you'll know by the end of this book. The bigger truth; however, is that we have more choice than we know, and we all have the internal power to extract ourselves from the mythological definitions of ourselves we've acquired.

What stops us is the Matrix Myth.

That and our misguided belief in the 'Land of There'; a magical place where all dreams come true; maintained by inner whispers from our head that berates us for not getting 'There' yet. I believe the roots of our discontent stem from an underlying, inherited belief that we are not quite good enough and that in order to have worth we must be constantly 'doing' and striving, rather than do what we actually want to do or what we are really good at. We've forgotten who we came here to be, because we live in such a noisy world full of nonsensical rules about what makes us worthy and beautiful.

We make the mistake of thinking that in order to feel better about ourselves, we have to push, achieve, bend, and squash who we are. We apply layers of 'stuff' to make us feel more appealing, attractive, and secure, even when we become self-aware, emotionally intelligent adults. We do it because it's a programme we've unwittingly installed. And it takes constant awareness and practice to shift it and write a new one.

The truth is, it's pretty scary throwing away the rule book and stepping out onto an unknown pathway. There's a deeper truth though, the safe pathway you think you know is the one that's slowly depleting you. Your current paradigm is more harmful for your future self than you know, but it's well established, so it is best to approach your extraction from it with awareness, gentleness, and self-compassion.

Awareness is powerful - and one of the fundamental ways to create the changes you desire. You don't know what you don't know - which is why I am sharing this myth with you. Gentleness and self-compassion help you approach change from your heart. When you approach change from your heart, it limits your head's ability to take over and keep you stuck. Your head really hates change because it thrives on familiarity, and it will rise up to defend you when it thinks you might be considering adopting a new paradigm.

Later you will discover ways to pacify it, but to side-step your head and gift yourself some awareness right now, I invite you to consider these questions:

1. Have you ever asked yourself how you've got to where you are right now in your life?

2. Have you considered what drives your decisions each day, what keeps you going and moving forwards, even when it's really tough?

From the moment we're born we learn what is acceptable, how to behave, what the norm is and isn't. We learn from those around us and we're rewarded or chastised according to the actions and decisions we make. This is just how it is. It isn't wrong, it's how all living creatures learn and evolve. We watch, we learn, we try. We either fail or get hurt, or achieve what we were aiming for. So we repeat our actions.

Often we don't even ask ourselves why. We simply do what we do. Rinse and repeat. Ad infinitum.

It's completely normal to go through life barely pausing or stopping to consider the path you're on. You haven't somehow missed the point or failed if this is where you are in life right now. We are the sum of those that came before us, which generally means we've inherited a strong work ethic and a belief that striving is the best way forwards. As children we are rewarded for hard work, and most parents want nothing more for us than to 'do well' and start out high on the ladder of life.

Society glorifies 'doing' rather than 'being' and we adopt the same approach to our life without realising it. We are programmed to seek accolades; learning early on that when we do well, mind our manners, get good grades, or come first, we get rewarded. Our brain really likes the feel-good dopamine chemicals that come with rewards, and it seeks more and more of them in a constant self-fulfilling loop. This is why we become drawn to ticking things off a 'success' list and acquire our perfectionist tendencies. We are led by our head and our body's desire for feel-good chemicals. Thankfully, developing awareness of this empowers us to change the pattern; although we need more than awareness alone to shift patterns we've had our entire lives.

I've had clients tell me they keep themselves busy doing unimportant things at times; even when they're tired and don't really want to do them. They say they actively avoid taking time out or stopping, even when they know those in their life would applaud them for it. Like me, they've learned from their parents and society to equate worth with achievement and they feel guilty if they stop working and filling their time.

This is a natural response. We haven't evolved to want to stand out or raise our heads above the parapet, and we want to fit in. We're trained to want to stay under the radar and do things a certain way. We don't want to rock the boat; although rather confusingly, we're also taught to strive. We don't want to drift through life and never achieve success; but at the same time we've been taught not to get too big for our boots. It's complicated isn't it! It's no wonder our heads rule our lives and we get so overwhelmed.

What happens as we get older? We become so familiar with the unwritten 'rules', we stop questioning them. We work on autopilot, saving up our dreams to visit at the end of the day before we drift off to sleep. We're all so busy keeping up with life, we don't have time to think, and if we're honest, we don't really want to ask those scary questions that might cause us to make big life changes. After all, where would we find the energy to follow through and get the courage to do what scares us?

The truth is, it's physiologically easier for our minds to work on autopilot; it consumes less calories and our brains are wired to preserve resources and keep us alive. It requires much more effort and energy to change our paradigm; so we're working against our own physiology before we've even begun. There are so many subtle influences controlling our behaviour. I hope you're beginning to see how easily you can end up sleepwalking through life. It happens to us all. It's part of the human journey.

Don't let this distress or disempower you. I was once a sleepwalker, too. If I can beat my brain, shift my state, and my life by becoming more aware and making daily conscious choices, so can you.

External vs. Internal, Head vs. Heart

When we're young, we're generally taught to rely on external rather than internal information to inform us. This makes sense, after all, how would we know about the myriad of worldly things those with more learning and experience know, and how would we learn without our peers and teachers? Have you ever noticed though, that there are times when honest observations made by young children make so much more sense than those expressed by adults?

As we become older, we start learning more on our own but we still approach life very much from the perspective of our head. The whole school system is set up this way and as a result we get disconnected from our instincts and intuition, eventually leading to us making decisions based on what we think we 'should' do, rather than on what truly nourishes us.

The majority of people I've worked with over the past 14 years have been so busy focusing *outside* themselves and on everyone else, that they've totally forgotten how to listen to themselves. They rarely hear or trust their inner voice because it seems silly, indulgent, and delusional.

Most of us are so 'plugged in' to the Matrix Myth that days, hours and weeks pass by in a blur. We don't even realize how many precious moments we have wasted watching everyone else live their life, whilst we disconnect from our own. Our default setting is to live in a reactive way to external inputs, letting our day be drawn at random by the needs of those around us, or what the world dictates to us. We effectively put out fires and serve other people's agendas. Choosing everyone else over ourselves, and serving them from a depleted well because we don't serve our own needs until we've attended to everyone else's.

The biggest lie the Matrix Myth instils in us all is that we're not good enough. Consequently, we look to others for our validation or knowledge, always feeling empty because we're subconsciously trying to fill a hole. We think we are broken; not realising that all that's broken is the belief we're not enough already, exactly as we are. Since we were young we've been fed messages about needing to do or be 'more', not because our caregivers wanted us to feel this way, but because that's how society is set up. It is an outdated instinct from the days when only the strongest survived.

We subconsciously absorb a multitude of messages daily, aimed at keeping us feeling scared, disempowered, small and needy. Big corporates, organisations, religions and political parties seed their own agenda into your world so subtly you barely notice it. You're tracked on search engines and social media, fed news stories and advertised to, appealing to your underlying basic human desire to fit in and not miss out.

Because you're human, you have a natural desire to understand and fit into the world around you. You seek answers and make patterns, ascribing meaning to things based upon your own beliefs and experiences. Most of this happens in your head and creates underlying tension between who you see yourself as, and who you think you 'should' be according to your subconscious beliefs. The inner desire to close the gap between our real self and the self we think we 'should' be is what drives us. It is led primarily by our Ego, who lives in our head and wants to be loved and stay alive. As this is the Ego's primary agenda, it tries to rule our world, keep us safe, help us stay under the radar and fit it, or beat 'the competition' so that we survive.

Living from your head contributes to a constant state of 'flight or fight' as you subconsciously try to keep up and fulfil other people's needs. It becomes 'normal' to feel exhausted and repeat the same day, every day, and call it life. If we're not careful, we become like grey ghosts, totally disconnected from the head down, living as a shadow of our former self. We only wake up when something slightly different happens and we are forced to change our habitual pattern; such as someone daring to sit in 'our' seat on the train. I know this because I was a grey ghost for a while, luckily not long enough to become conditioned into thinking this was normal.

To this day, it astounds me every time I get on a tube at rush hour, and everyone is head down, plugged into their phones, exhausted, grey and oblivious to their surroundings. Effectively plugged into the Matrix. Honouring a myth they unknowingly bought into that told them to get up each day, earn money to buy shiny things they have no time to use, or pay towards a house they don't enjoy, to become worthy. It's such a normal way to live in the modern world, we don't even stop to question it… even though it often feels unfulfilling, exhausting, and stressful. More of a *should* than a *must*; however vital it seems.

Honouring your head rather than your heart creates discord, which ultimately leads to chronic stress or disease. If you live in a way that doesn't fully honour you, eventually the part of you being ignored cries out to be acknowledged. It might take the form of headaches, worry, depression, anger, backache, illness or any number of other physical or mental complaints. Generally they shift from niggles into a more permanent state, which is often when we finally hear our bodies, and start looking for solutions.

The truth is you cannot build a truly fulfilling life when you compartmentalize yourself and deny yourself what is truly important to you.

Denying yourself what brings you joy eventually creates fragmentation; leaving you feeling scattered, ungrounded, unfulfilled, and weak. Your inherent spirit will feel squashed and unexpressed, and it will revolt. It will whisper to you in your dreams, quietly nag at you whilst you're working, and eventually manifest as something louder and challenging to stop you in your tracks.

You simply cannot suppress it when your inner spirit rises up to have its say. No matter how many drugs and distractions you use. It wants to be honoured in the same way you honour your daily cup of tea or coffee. It's incredibly patient, but also very persistent, no matter how disconnected you are from your own body. In my case, it took something major to wake me up and honour my inner voice the first time. Since then the wakeup call has assumed many forms, including me needing major surgery. Twice!

Yes, I am a slow learner! But I finally learned that living from both your head *and* your heart enables you to tap into two incredibly powerful resources. When you unite these aspects of yourself, you become a fully embodied, powerful soul in a human body. Get them talking nicely to each other and add in small steps, with powerful practices, and positive daily habits, you will unlock the door to a life that feels infinitely more magical and meaningful.

You cannot control the external world, the randomness of life, or the circumstances you're born into. You cannot predict the future, make sense of senseless occurrences, or protect yourself from your mortality. You can, however, control your internal world in terms of your responses, beliefs, interactions, choices, decisions, presence, and awareness. No matter what you believe right now, you can change your life by changing your awareness and extracting yourself from the Matrix Myth. Before you do though, you need to know how the subtle stress of living in the grip of the myth is affecting you; because the more informed and aware you are, the more empowered you become.

What I am about to share with you is an interpretation of stress that helped me revolutionise my own internal and external world, and has since helped many others do the same.

On Stress - How the Matrix Myth Affects You

"Tension is who you think you should be. Relaxation is who you are." — *Chinese proverb*

The modern world is a virtual playground, full of life-liberating gadgets, endless information, virtual realities at the touch of a button and a plethora of opportunities. However, despite this instantly accessible abundance, stress and anxiety levels are increasing and it's become the norm to be overwhelmed and to simply survive, rather than thrive.

The constantly switched-on world that was meant to liberate us has effectively trapped us, as it has become normal to respond to texts, notifications, and emails as soon as possible, even when on holiday. We have effectively trained ourselves to become like Pavlovian dogs, responding to pings from our phones and gadgets, because subconsciously this makes us feel wanted, important, or distracts us from boredom.

We're always waiting for the next text message, email, 'like' and the next notification. We're not fully present because we're constantly on alert, and as a result we fail to notice the joy in life. We feel guilty for not replying to people immediately, or worry about forgetting if we don't, or stress about the emails sitting in our inbox. With our systems on constant high alert, it's no wonder we're totally exhausted, because it's unnatural and exhausting to live in a state of perpetual stimulation. And yet, for most of us, it's become the norm. We've grown almost numb to the fact we rarely switch off, even though physiologically, we're not wired to survive if we don't take time to rest.

A Brief Sojourn Into the World of Stress Chemicals

Your kidneys have two very important glands sitting on top of them, called the adrenal glands. They're important to your survival, because they switch on when danger is present, flooding your system with adrenaline. This enables you to react before you've even fully registered danger. Adrenaline is hugely powerful. I've experienced its positive effects many times, the most memorable was when I was 16. I was with my boyfriend and I fell down some steps, badly hurting my ankle. I had no idea what I'd done to it at the time, but I knew I was in trouble and needed help. There were no mobile phones in those days, and even though I knew I'd hurt myself, I was too embarrassed and shy to stop and ask for help from strangers.

It was early evening and I was in town, but the nearest phone boxes a car could get to were still a 10-minute walk away on a normal day. Although my ankle was rapidly swelling and my foot was at a very strange angle, I decided the only logical thing was get to a phone box to call my dad. Clearly childhood lessons about not trusting strangers had done their job a little too well!

Somehow, with the help of my boyfriend, we got to the phone boxes in what felt like record time. I walked there, feeling a strange euphoria and virtually no pain at all. I managed to call my dad, get safely home, and make it to the settee. I was so buoyant, we decided there was no need to go to A & E; as the Myth tell us, who wants to make a fuss after all. Instead I lay down and as the adrenaline wore off, and pain started kicking in, a state of exhaustion sent me to sleep.

The next morning it was a whole different scenario as I was in intense pain, my ankle was a fetching shade of blue and twice the size it should be. The sense of euphoria that got me safely home was long gone, and it became clear I had probably broken my ankle. Long story short; after falling and then walking on a seriously injured ankle, I ruptured my Achilles tendon, as well as several foot ligaments and broke my ankle so severely, I spent the next six months on crutches. I remember having to do my exams doped up on painkillers at the back of the school hall, with my leg propped up. To this day, I can't bend my ankle fully forwards or flex all my toes.

That's how powerful adrenaline is. Pretty impressive, isn't it.

It is indispensable when you need to get to safety, but can you imagine how damaging it is to spend your whole life living in a constant state of adrenaline stimulation? Unless you want to experience continual burnout and adrenal fatigue it's really not advised. Unfortunately this has been the reality for many people I've worked with over the years, especially those with chronic fatigue, anxiety, or depression. Their system literally 'jangles' when I put my hands on them, and not in a good way.

"Being relaxed, at peace with yourself, confident, emotionally neutral, loose, and free-floating – these are the keys to successful performance in almost everything." – Wayne W. Dyer

According to research published by the UK government in 2017, 80-90% of all disease is stress-related. We all know how prolific stress is, over 80% of Brits in that survey said that they felt "life's moving too fast" and 50% said they struggle to switch off. The outcome is a permanently achy body, an overwhelmed, agitated head, and an inability to maintain focus or get things done. We interpret this as meaning we're a failure. We all relate to how negatively stress affects our system and energy levels, but it can be hard to address it and do something about it. I've been there. So badly at times, that twice in the past, I've been on medication to deal with anxiety and panic attacks.

The good news is that understanding and de-mystifying stress helps us to notice and highlight our own stress-related patterns. From that place of awareness, we can start making changes that give us back our sense of control. Even something as simple as noticing our breathing helps us shift our state and take back control of our energy.

Stress is not *all* bad. We need a certain level of stress to help our bodies maintain equilibrium, in fact our nervous systems are designed to facilitate this. The problem is that in the modern world our systems must deal with constant stimulation, which has resulted in us being constantly in fight or flight mode. Most of the time for the wrong reasons - meaning we overreact to the most innocuous things, as we've become like a tightly coiled spring ready to pop.

There are many other chemicals that contribute to the stress response, such as cortisol and its counterpart Oxytocin (the happy hormone). It is a fascinating subject that I've studied deeply; for the purposes of this book, you simply need to know that the response to stress is a very real physiological response impacting your entire system. This means you can use tangible methods to change it.

This is not a popular opinion, but I believe we all have far more control over stress than we think. It starts by realising we're living in a heightened state of adrenaline and then becoming more aware of how the way we live contributes to it. Many of the processes you'll discover in this book will help you become less stressed as a by-product of living more consciously, and letting go of patterns that no longer serve you.

The Stress Siren

I would like to introduce you to someone you may think you haven't met, but will soon realise you know intimately....

I call her the Stress Siren.... and she's more cunning than you know.

She winds her way into as many facets of your life as she can...sneaking insidiously into pockets of your day, disrupting your thoughts, trying to drag you down negative pathways and calling to you to tense up, stress out, and worry. She serves you well sometimes - but mostly she's training you to react rather than respond - and she hates change. Which is why I thought this would be the perfect opportunity for you to get a start on taming her; before she gets wise to your desire to change your life.

Stress is NOT to be underestimated; long-term it can be hugely damaging. At the same time, it is not to be feared or deferred to because a large percentage of its power begins in our mind. That Stress Siren of yours? She merely presses the trigger, then she sits back and watches as you allow your mind to do the rest of her work for her. I've realised, from countless conversations with clients and friends, that we all share a sense of being 'controlled' by stress, rather than the other way round. It's as though the Stress Siren runs the show, whilst you watch from the sidelines as your system takes the strain.

To counteract this, I'd like to share a way to view your Stress Siren differently, which will make her less powerful in your mind. After all, the more power you give her, the more power she'll take. I've learned, and will repeat many times in this book, that *where your attention goes, your energy flows*. This is true for all things, but especially so for stress. Think about it, if a stranger asked you to follow him blindly down a dark tunnel, you're hardly likely to say yes. So why allow yourself to be drawn into a dark hole by the Stress Siren?

I would guess it's because you haven't stopped to catch yourself in the act of giving her all your attention. Now, she has loomed so large in your mind that she's taken all the power, and dragged your adrenal glands along with her for the ride... In other words, if you feed the Stress Siren by dwelling on her messages and allowing her to become dominant in your mind, guess what's going to happen? She sucks up more of your life force energy and uses it to further feed her agenda.

We really hate it when we don't have dominion over our own world, and the thoughts this creates in our head provides the Stress Siren with further fuel. We create a 'push-me, pull-me' effect, one I describe as pushing water uphill. If you spend your energy trying to change what is beyond your control or going against your own natural flow, you use up your energy more rapidly than you know.

I know this because it's what I discovered about myself; I was so stressed at one point I got panic attacks just by heading to my own front door. I could create my own inner world of stress, panic and anxiety in seconds, by letting my Stress Siren take over and lead me down the path of scenario-building panic, in less time than it takes to boil a kettle.

These days, I've minimised stress in my life so much that other people think I'm the calmest person they know. Maybe I am, or maybe I simply learned the art of letting go, not trying to control things I couldn't and honoring myself far more than I used to. The biggest shift in my ability to manage stress came when I discovered Shiatsu, a Chinese therapeutic practice and holistic approach to wellbeing. During a three-year training course, alongside learning the theory and practising the art of

Shiatsu itself, I embarked on a hugely powerful self-development journey.

As I studied more about Eastern approaches to wellbeing, I started to appreciate how many aspects of life impacted my health and energy levels. Realising the many stressors I had control over, I slowly began to make conscious shifts in those areas. Over the course of the training, as I let go of trying to control things I couldn't, I began inhabiting a body that felt less like a permanent stress zone, with tight shoulders, IBS, migraines, and anxiety, and more of a happy, calm, and spacious place to live in.

Nothing discernibly changed on the outside, but on the inside I noticed that slowly the tightness eased, my posture improved, my energy increased, I slept better, was more flexible and felt more at home in my body. Long-term health conditions I'd come to accept as inevitable, slowly disappeared. And then one day, I realised I hadn't had a backache, headache, or panic attack for ages.

The most important change in my life and what underlies everything I've since taught others is this one simple premise, summarised by Stephen Russell, AKA the Barefoot Doctor:

"Change the dynamic inside and the dynamic outside changes to reflect it."

All you need is the willingness to accept that something needs to change, and the energy and mindset to do something about it.

Your Porridge Pot of Energy

If you want to create change in your life, no matter how big or small, you must find the energy, motivation and willpower to make a start.

Getting started and moving our intentions from an idea into action is the hardest part, and it requires a spark of ignition to get you going. You will struggle to find this if your energy is already depleted because your adrenals are burned out, which is why stress is so important for you to address.

The Mind and Body are not viewed as distinct and separate entities in Traditional Chinese Medicine (TCM). The 'body-mind' has a mutually dependent relationship; mental stress will create physical symptoms; and physical stress will result in psychological symptoms. We can all relate to this; when you're stressed, your shoulders start making friends with your ears as they tighten and rise. This relationship is now backed up by modern science. It means you have the power to shift your mental state by changing the state of your physical body - for example through exercise, yoga, or meditation - and vice versa. You'll explore this as you progress through the book.

First, I want to share the porridge pot analogy with you because it's the most powerful way I've ever found to understand the effects of stress and how our choices help shift it. It will also give you more insight in to how the processes help you enhance your energy and therefore your life.

Our underlying energy, known as original chi (or qi), is finite according to Chinese Medicine and stored and distributed by our kidneys. Pronounced 'chee', this energy is responsible for our vitality and life force. Although finite, it can be boosted and optimised by taking in good quality food, breathing good quality air, and doing practices such as chi gung and yoga.

Known as our Essence, original chi represents our constitutional, underlying energy. It is the energy we're born with - and the amount we have is dictated by our parents and birth circumstances. Some of us are born with an abundance of this energy, whereas those who had stressful birth circumstances, or parents with weak constitutions, tend to be more susceptible to illness and exhaustion.

We essentially have a big reserve of 'porridge pot' of energy we're born with, that we use up at different rates depending on how we live our life. Different activities, choices, illnesses, and emotions use up, or boost our energy at different rates. It's a bit like a phone battery, which runs out faster if you use your phone to watch videos, and lasts all day if you hardly look at it.

We all have days when we're exhausted before dinner time; and energised days when we're fired up and we achieve a ridiculous amount of stuff before lunch time. Those energised days feel like gifts, whereas the more 'energetically challenged' ones feel like you're dragging yourself through mud all day, waiting for bedtime to arrive.

Imagine that each day you wake up with your own porridge pot of chi energy to use as you choose.

Although the pot is refilled every morning thanks to sleep and rest, it must still be used wisely if you want fulfilling days and a longer, happier life. If you spend too much time on things that don't nourish you, align with your values, or serve your best interests, you are giving your precious chi energy away, leaving little left for what you truly love. Some days your bowl is fuller than others because you're looking after yourself and you're less stressed; but even on a good day, once it's empty, you're done for the day and need to rest. It is your choice whether to use your underlying energy up quickly by constantly pushing, striving, and living an unhealthy lifestyle - or spend it wisely on what serves you best.

In TCM theory, when you get stressed it depletes your Kidney energy, which impacts the distribution of your essence, affecting your nervous system and hence all the body's processes. This correlates with what we know about the impact of stress on your adrenals (located on the kidneys) and offers a different perspective on why excess stress limits us so much. As the Kidney energy channels run up your back, it also offers an explanation into why it is so common for people with stress and/or depression to suffer from backaches.

Learning what stimulates and depletes your own chi energy means you can start making informed choices, increasing your vitality, strength, longevity, and mental wellbeing. When your chi energy flows more freely, your body functions better, your mind responds to stress more effectively, and you have more energy available to fulfil your potential.

The MAGICAL process gifts you the power to start making these informed choices. No matter what your current situation is, there will definitely be positive changes you can make if you reassess where your time and energy goes. Once you develop greater understanding of the impact your choices have on you, you can make different choices and do things differently. It is never too late to start using your energy in a way that serves your needs first, so you can serve others from a full bowl.

A Quiet Call to Arms

This chapter serves as a quiet call to arms, offered in the spirit of love and compassion. It highlights how much of your daily life you may be living unconsciously through no fault of your own, why this is important, and how it might be impacting you.

Before I move on, it's important to offer some reassurance. If you're anything like me and many of those I've worked with over the years, waking up to smell the virtual coffee can bring up all manner of emotions, most of them not very enjoyable. You might feel guilt, fear, regret, anger, or anxiety. You might want to run away and hide, or bury your head in the sand.

All this is normal.

The realisation you've effectively been asleep for part of your life can disorientate you, as the ground you thought was firm, shifts beneath you. Do not for one minute think you've done anything wrong, you've failed, or you're broken. Don't listen to the inner voice that tells you you've wasted your life because you haven't. One thing I've learned is that there are no wrong turns, only lessons learned.

One day, your path will make sense. The past has passed; the only time you have is this moment, right now. In this moment, you can choose to do something different that changes your trajectory to a more nourishing one. If it doesn't work out, you simply change direction, armed with new and useful information.

We all secretly believe there's an alternative virtual version of our life where future us makes different choices and we no longer get in our own way. Long before the film *Sliding Doors* came along, I used to wonder if there was another version of me making better choices in some other paradigm. I know I'm not alone in that.

We all talk about Path A and Path B and believe we'll reach a point where everything makes sense and we achieve what we want in life. It's why we listen to talks, read books, take courses, go travelling, and look for new careers or jobs. The hope inside us resolutely refuses to dim and we love feeding it. It's why you've gifted yourself this book and why I wrote it. I believe in hope and I believe in finding ways to share that hope with others... especially you.

By reading this far, you've started laying the breadcrumb trail towards your Path B... and you have taken a big step away from the Matrix Myth.

If you desire change, so that your future self can live in the Path B paradigm, you have to fully face your current reality. You must metaphorically look it in the eye and be brave enough to see what you dislike and want to change. Whilst it may feel a bit like there's a landslide underneath you, you are simply getting ready to clear away any precarious rubble; so you can build firmer foundations.

Rest assured you aren't starting again and no part of your life so far is wasted. You're simply reversing to gather your energy, ready to make a running start on your more aligned path, with the benefit of new insights to help you.

As Joseph Campbell so wisely said: *"The cave you fear to enter holds the treasure you seek."*

CHAPTER 2
Meet the Real You

"I wish I could show you when you are lonely or in darkness the astonishing light of your own being." — Hafiz

As a child I was a happy, shy, and curious daydreamer. I loved life, exploring and delighted in losing myself in stories, especially those that sparked my imagination. I adored *Alice in Wonderland* for its jumble of characters and quirky world, and to this day I'm known for my ability to lose myself in another world of my own creation. As a result, I inherently see the world differently, including seeing the light within everyone and their pure child-self in their faces, regardless of how old they are.

This chapter invites you to meet the real you – the you that I would see if you were standing in front of me – not the you that *you* see in the mirror.

Having established in the previous chapter that through no fault of your own the world you see is not the full reality; you are about to discover that the same is true about how you see yourself. Before you can proceed further into your personal journey, this is a vitally important pausing place, because your magical unfolding will be so much richer if you do it from the perspective of seeing yourself as you truly are.

Why is This Important?

By the time I was 15 years old, I had already forgotten about the joy and wonder of the world.

By this tender age, I had the awareness of an adult in a teenager's body. I didn't know until years later that I am an empath, I simply knew I was different and therefore got bullied at school. Having spent most of my life to this point acutely feeling the pain of everything and everyone around me, I concluded that the world was a negative, hurtful place, and was best avoided. I had no idea that it was unusual to see right through everyone, notice everything, and feel unkind words cutting deeply into my being. I didn't know that the things I was told about myself weren't true. All I knew was that it was downright painful, noisy, and unkind in the world, and that none of the things I picked up on were 'supposed' to be mentioned out loud.

Because that's not what we did in my world. Children after all, 'should' be seen and not heard. And so, I remained silent. Inwardly I quietly rebelled and raged. Externally, I had already learnt the art of appearing untouched by others, realizing that reacting added fuel to their fire, and therefore my greatest weapon was to hide my feelings.

Little did I know then that silence was to become my default behavior until into my 40s, and that suppressing my voice meant that I suppressed the full expression of myself in all senses. I had no idea that it was impossible to fully experience and extract joy from life without this expression. It wasn't until I started my Shiatsu training in my 30s that I realized where I had been burying my unexpressed emotions and I learned how damaging that was.

You probably know that science has proved that energy cannot be destroyed – it can change form, but it is still energy in another form. Emotions, as powerful as they can be, are simply a type of energy in motion (E-Motion). Emotions therefore, cannot be buried and they don't go away. They accumulate and then transform – in my case, into disease and depression.

Here's something you probably resonate with...

I got so wrapped up in believing the myth that the world had told me about myself, that I forgot my lighthearted, life-loving child self, and instead believed I was flawed. The original Me that I saw did not correspond to the Me that others saw, and so I buried my true self deeply in a safe box marked 'delusions'. I wouldn't open that box again for years – but what I would see in later life, is that almost all other adults carried a similar box – whether they knew it or not. A classic case of what we see mirrored in others is what we most need to see for ourselves.

Now that I've seen inside it more clearly, I call it the Broken Box.

Why We Build Boxes

We build boxes primarily to keep us safe. We don't even know we are doing it. We build them instinctively, starting to hide things in them in early childhood. Our boxes then define us, shape our world, and give us meaning. We put all sorts of things in them, building walls out of our beliefs, society's rules, and the messages we get from peers and parents. We use them to decide what acceptable behavior is, and what isn't, and this becomes the basis of our belief system.

As a small child, I really liked boxes.

I used to pray to the Lord of Breakages to tamper with the various big things in the house, so that my parents would have to order a new big thing - which would of course come in a wonderful big box that I could hide in. I liked boxes and small spaces so much that I built an entire world of my own in the various hiding places in my house. It meant I could escape from the real world, and instead spend time in one I preferred.

I know that I am not alone in this love of having a place of my own to hide in. Amongst children, this is common. Animals do it too, especially cats, who like nothing better than finding small spaces to fold themselves into. The problem is that whilst 'folding ourselves in' might protect us, it also limits us and stops us from living with full expression.

Our boxes affect how we see the world, how we view others, how we view things we're scared of, and how we view ourselves. When you think about, it is incredibly clever of our subconscious minds to build boxes for us. It's an inherent survival instinct we adopt without realising it. It helps us to stay under the radar, stay alive, and fit into the tribe. As an adult I perfected the art of living in boxes of my own making so well that one day, I woke up in someone else's life, wondering how I got there and who on earth I was.

Our boxes give us somewhere to store our dreams, secrets, and resentments. They also reinforce our limiting beliefs, keep us trapped in the lies and stories we tell ourselves about what our life means and who we are, and they give us a place to dump all the emotions we don't like expressing. The type of broken box you have depends entirely upon your unique experiences and your belief system. There is a whole subconscious operating system protecting your box, keeping you safe from imagined danger. You are not only dragging around boxes you don't know you have, you're also being held back by your invisible safety committee.

I believe we are born with all the inner wisdom and tools we need to travel our individual paths - and that somewhere along the line, as we become conditioned, learn life-lessons, acquire layers of protection, and devote our energy to others, we forget who we truly are, why we are here, and how we can access our inner knowledge and power. Your safety committee has taught you to fear change and feel safe with familiarity. You undoubtedly resist doing anything new or challenging as a result and it can appear so much easier to cruise along as you are, and keep your life predictable. You are not to blame for this – research has demonstrated that we all have little compassion for our future self – and that is why we so often fail to change our habits.

Now you have more insight into why you built your boxes and what keeps them there, the most important thing for you to realise is that you are not your box. Your broken box does not define you and without it, you will feel so much lighter. Knowing that is wonderfully empowering, because once you've felt this truth in your heart, it makes it so much easier to choose to put the box down and step away.

You are not a fixed entity and you have infinite capacity to change and transcend the confines of your box. The trick is to do it bit by bit, so that your safety committee barely notices, leaving you free to step away with your original self-intact and unencumbered by the weight of suppression and outdated beliefs.

Your Broken Box

The following list aims to help you identify what delusions might live in your broken box. Knowledge is power and identifying what you keep inside your box empowers you. Later in your magical process, you'll learn how to disarm the box too. I invite you to dig out your self-kindness hat. Put it on, and breathe slowly as you read.

Do you (or does that little voice inside your head) agree or disagree with any of the following statements? Notice how your body feels when you read them.

a) I am enough.
b) I am NOT broken.
c) I have not failed.
d) I am unique.
e) I am a miracle.
f) I matter.
g) I deserve to be seen and heard.
h) I am allowed to ask for what I want.
i) I am allowed to rest and do nothing.
j) I do not have to look after everyone.
k) I don't have to be busy to gain respect.

I invite you to notice what you feel in your body because this is a gentle way to start noticing what is going on subconsciously in your system. In the best case scenario, you might have read all the statements above and agreed with every single one, but even if that were the case, I wouldn't be surprised if you noticed a little flutter, a tightening, a quickening of breath, a mini-argument in the back of your mind, or any number of other subtle responses.

It might be that you agreed or disagreed with some, but felt nothing in your body at all. That's okay. There are no rules, no rights or wrongs, and no need to tell anyone your true responses. This is the first step of changing your reality; noticing what you believe, feel, or think about are all great places to start. You will be invited to explore your responses more deeply when you get to the second part of the book.

For now, it is enough to simply realise that you have been carrying boxes around with you containing all the feelings and thoughts you buried to stay safe, and the lies about yourself you unwittingly acquired from others.

May The Real You Step Forward

"A fundamental concept within biodynamic craniosacral therapy is that we are self-regulating organisms. Enfolded within the flesh of the body is a blueprint, or recipe, for life – called the original matrix or original health in biodynamics. It is an inherent knowing or a wisdom of the body." — *Steve Haines and Ged Sumner*

Whether you are aware of it or not, you contain a light vibrant energy that you can use to support you at any time. Your mind might resist this because it's hard to explain, but it exists and is there already. It is simply a matter of learning how to get out of your head so you can connect to it. You'll discover a way to do this later in the book; a way to connect to your own potential.

To help your brain understand this concept, consider that the word potential derives from the Latin word *potentia;* which means power, might, force. It describes 'that which is possible' given the right conditions. Scientists know that everything in our world is energy; your potential is simply your stored energy, the bits you have locked up in your boxes. Once you start liberating this energy, you'll begin experiencing a very different reality to your current one, because even the simple act of changing your perspective creates an exponential shift in your system.

Let me remind you that you are not a set of 'labels'. You are not a collection of rules, thoughts, mistakes, achievements, or acquirements. Whatever you have been told, you are perfectly imperfect, *exactly* as you are. You are not broken, you haven't failed, and you do not need fixing. The point of this personal discovery process is not to fix you. It's to help you reclaim all the bits of yourself you've disowned or lost along the way, so you can live a more congruent and complete life.

You are a unique, beautiful, capable, limitless soul encapsulated within the vehicle of your incredible ever-healing body. You came here with an inherent gift, and you owe it to yourself and to the world to uncover what that gift is, so you can share it. You were born with a distinct perspective, skill set, inherent constitution, and a totally unique blueprint. Your blueprint has a special combination of gifts, insights, flaws, weaknesses, and strengths and is utterly beautiful in its rarity. Like your one-of-a-kind fingerprint, it will never appear again. It contains your inherent wisdom, your guiding light, and everything that makes you the miraculous being you are, and no one else can express its truths.

We are aware of this blueprint on some level when we are very young, accepting it without question and simply acting upon our instincts. We know what we need as a baby or toddler, and we are generally good at making our requests heard by crying or talking. As we grow up however, and we start absorbing the truth of others, we lose sight of our blueprint, stop asking for what we want, and forget how to listen to our inherent wisdom.

Everything in nature has a purpose, even if we don't always understand it.

If the smallest insect and the biggest tree have a purpose, why would you imagine that you are any different? Recognising that you, in your uniqueness, are as significant and vital to the world as any other life on earth is crucial to identifying your soul's desires, and living your best life. Once you realise this, and start fulfilling your purpose, you'll move into alignment with the Universe, and life will flow more smoothly.

One of our biggest limiting factors in following our dreams is that when we set out on our individual life path, most of us make decisions based on the approval of others. We subconsciously adopt behaviour and beliefs based on our upbringing and start living someone else's perception of life - not our own. How you see yourself and view life also plays a massive role in how likely you are to fulfil your potential. You have no doubt heard the phrase that your thoughts create your reality? I used to think that was rubbish, but now I realise it isn't as esoteric as it first seems.

If you believe your life is a struggle, it will always appear to present itself as that and you will spend your time overcoming challenge after challenge. If, however, you believe life is a glorious adventure to be engaged in, the more it will become that. The very same situations might occur, but the way you interpret them will be very different. We all know people who have achieved incredible things despite difficult circumstances, and also those who seemed to have everything, but totally lost themselves in depression and debt. You can call it luck, but more often, it is about personal attitude, perspective, and beliefs.

Knowing that is powerful... because it means you get to choose your perspective each and every day. Knowledge really is power. Especially self-knowledge.

You can wake up each day feeling excited about life, knowing you can choose how you respond to whatever unfolds. It's pretty simple, we only think it's complicated because we have bought into societal myths that say we have to look, act, or feel a certain way. Trying to conform to that feels impossible, so we never meet our own expectations.

A fundamental aspect of my work is to see the 'child self' in all the adults I work with, so I can subtly and safely communicate directly with that part of them. It cuts through the grown-up facade, right to the essence of who each person came here to be, and that part never disagrees with pure truth when it hears it.

You still are that gorgeous, original 'child self' at your core and I invite you to remember that fact when life feels heavy or serious. Sometimes simply remembering what you loved as a child and seeing how that has helped shaped you as an adult reconnects you to the core part of you that has never gone away.

You are here to experience life as your true self, not a constructed version of yourself. You may have added scars, traumas, and layers of learning, but essentially you are that same core version of you. Many of those scars are to be celebrated as important parts of your story and it's never too late to let unnecessary, over-protective layers fall away so you can invite your original self to re-emerge. I can tell you from my own experience, once you do, the delight and promise of each day greets you exactly as it did as a small child – and it is a delightful way to live your life.

"You must learn to get in touch with the innermost essence of your being. This true essence is beyond the ego. It is fearless; it is free; it is immune to criticism; it does not fear any challenge. It is beneath no one, superior to no one, and full of magic, mystery, and enchantment." — Deepak Chopra

Even though there is a part of you that understands this blueprint concept, it can seem very strange to your logical mind. So it doesn't undermine you, invite it to think of an apple core. Within the core are seeds, which contain all the information needed for the apple to grow. The surrounding area grew from the information in the seed. It is unapologetically an apple. Whether perfectly round or oblong, it doesn't pretend to be anything else and it couldn't be if it tried.

The core blueprint is a tangible thing I've been privileged to feel in each individual I have worked with. Sometimes it feels strong and fully expressed; more usually it feels fragmented or weak. In those cases, the person I am working with says they feel low in energy and scattered in their life. Those who are more present and joyful tend to have a very vibrant core blueprint, it pulses with life and is easy to feel from the moment I put my hands on them.

This core blueprint is located in a vessel known as the central channel in Chinese Medicine. Said to be our most powerful vessel, it acts as an energetic reservoir from which all our energy channels (meridians) flow. It has powerful correspondences in many Eastern traditions and relates to our central nervous system in Western terms (which controls all our functions and is extremely responsive to external and internal stimuli).

Having felt this myself so many times, there is no doubt in my mind that the more we free up our innermost selves by releasing the boxes around us, the more space our systems have for us to live in full, expansive expression. Both physically and mentally.

Interestingly, when we are in the embryonic stage, our core starts on the outside as our neural tube, which contains our central nervous system and our heart. This then folds in on itself, as the rest of our body forms around it. What was on the outside therefore ends up on the inside, becoming our central core, so it's no wonder we learn to wrap things around us to keep us safe.

CHAPTER 3
The Actual Matrix

"There are only two ways to live your life. One is as though nothing is a miracle. The other is as though everything is a miracle." — Albert Einstein

You have discovered the real you. In this chapter you are going to discover the real matrix of life.

The world, as you know it, forms only part of the true picture. In this chapter you will discover that there is so much more to the world than any of us truly know. Before you read on, I invite you to remember those boxes you discovered in the last chapter. Now is the time to leave them on the floor, park your cynicism at the door, suspend disbelief, and conjure up your inner curious child.

Have you ever wondered why some people seemingly flow easily through life and appear to be so annoyingly 'sorted'? Have you ever spent ages really trying to make something you want happen, only to give up, let it go, and then somehow it happens almost magically without you even trying? These things cannot ever be fully explained. Be honest, if they could, you'd be a bit disappointed. Magic loses its allure when you know exactly how it's done...

"Whether we realize it or not, we are all dreaming the world into being. What we're engaging in is not the sleeping act we're so familiar with, but rather the type of dreaming we do with our eyes open. When we're unaware that we share the power to co-create with the universe itself, that power slips away from us, causing our dream to become a nightmare. We begin to feel we're the victims of an unknown and frightening creation that we're unable to influence, and events seem to control and trap us. The only way to end this dreadful reality is to awaken to the fact that it too is a dream — and then recognize our ability to write a better story, one that the universe will work with us to manifest." — Alberto Villoldo

Having summarily dismissed the version of reality we all inhabit as being a myth, it seems only fair to offer you an alternative perspective.

Once you reach the end of this chapter, it is totally up to you what you do with the information. Throw it out, keep some, or save it to revisit. I hope it at least gives you something interesting to muse over... at best it will set you free. Like it did me, even though I'm part scientist! Wouldn't it be wonderful to know that the world is not as fixed as it seems, and you have more control over life than you've previously been led to believe? Your infinite potential awaits you when you open your eyes to see it.

The Day I Saw the Actual Matrix

It was Valentine's Day 2013, and after almost 24 hours of travelling, my lovely husband and I finally arrived in the Sri Lankan jungle. We were exhausted, sweaty, and I was almost bent over with pain. Ten weeks earlier, I had undergone the sort of surgery that changes your life forever. The sort that isn't really conducive to long periods of sitting on a plane or to yoga retreats in the middle of the jungle.

I was there to heal, rebuild, restore and recuperate; with the magical powers of yoga, clean healthy food, and our wonderful hosts that knew us well. The yoga retreat marked the end of a significant period in our lives and we were there to make peace with what had happened and move on to the next chapter together.

I used to be a Sonographer; which unfortunately meant I knew my diagnosis and its eventual outcome a long time before I reached the point of this surgery. It was a matter of 'when' not 'if'. A bit like having a ticking clock inside me, counting down the years until I went under the knife. Despite having abdominal surgery to remove fibroids a few years earlier, my uterus was so disease-prone, that needing a total hysterectomy was an inevitable, non-negotiable option.

What was less inevitable was how complicated and long the surgery was when it eventually happened at the age of 42. Which is why, despite doing what I could to prepare prior to the operation, ten weeks on I still felt sore, weak, emotionally raw, and fragile. The convoluted journey, being forced to sit for long periods, and the anticipation of what was to come heightened my state. In retrospect, it was a very similar condition to when I escaped from my violent boyfriend 23 years earlier. A discombobulating mixture of physical pain, emotional angst, deep fear, bubbling excitement, legs like jelly and tears I refused to let flow.

Unused to feeling vulnerable, I had quite deliberately placed myself somewhere I couldn't run from because I knew I had a lot to process. Our wonderful hosts Jools and Helen knew that too, they were part of my recovery plan before the surgery date was even set. I had nowhere to hide, no distractions, and the perfect conditions to further heal.

We had ten days; each day representing each week that had passed since my surgery.

The Universe is funny like that.

After a decade trying and failing to become parents, encompassing multiple surgeries, miscarriages, an ectopic and IVF, it was time for us to finally close this chapter and begin a new one. As well-adjusted as we were already to being on path B - the 'childless by circumstance' path - the hysterectomy had brought up a whole load of residual emotions neither of us saw coming. We had never made not having children a big thing. Most of our friends, clients, and colleagues had no idea what we had experienced. It wasn't something either of us wanted to become defined by and we preferred focusing on the many positive aspects of our life together. We also didn't want others to feel awkward around us, especially as we were the only people in our circle without children. In order to move on and save our sanity, we had consciously drawn the line on becoming parents when I turned 40.

We knew we were lucky in many respects, because not having children meant we were free to simply be.

In truth, however, that didn't mean there wasn't part of me that didn't still harbor quiet hope each month. The same part that wondered what I was here for and why I mattered if I wasn't able to do something other women could do. The part that wasn't entirely sure what my purpose was. The part the hysterectomy shut down once and for all.

I remember lying in bed after the surgery and crying almost constantly for two days. I was unable to hide my tears like I had managed to do so well for most of the previous 42 years. I felt alone because I didn't know anyone else in my situation, who would understand. I remember how angry I was when my male consultant told me 'feeling low' was normal and how it felt like the indifferent dismissal of something so colossal.

I was depressed about the inevitability of an early menopause, because despite my best plans to avoid this, I also inadvertently lost one ovary. It was only a matter of time before the remaining one gave up trying to do it all alone, and I felt angry because I 'accidentally' found out this had happened during handover from recovery. The nursing staff forgot I had an obs and gynae background and could understand 'medical speak'. It felt like the last hammer blow of a body that had never played nicely.

I felt cheated, less of a woman, and a failure in life. In my head, I had not fulfilled society norms and was forever doomed to be the weird one who didn't fit in to 'girls' night' out with friends who always ended up talking about their children. I felt I had failed as a 'well-rounded' Shiatsu practitioner, failed my parents and in-laws by not giving them grandchildren - and even worse - that I had let down my lovely husband. I felt incredibly guilty that because he chose me, he wouldn't get to be a father. In short, I was hormonal and emotional (which I now know was entirely normal!) and I needed help to process what this operation fully represented.

I had foreseen this to some extent and for the first time in my life, I had reached out and asked for support before I even had the surgery. I received an abundance of love and notes from many friends and clients, all of which were gratefully received. By the time I got to Sri Lanka ten weeks later, I had healed on so many levels, but unbeknown to me, a whole new level of healing was about to begin.

I spent the first few days battling with physical pain, feeling ashamed because I could no longer 'do' yoga, being annoyed with myself for still being angry, and trying desperately to suppress tears. I had lost 'sense' of my body below the waist, couldn't feel my feet properly, and consequently struggled to feel grounded. I was facing many fears — fear of vulnerability, of hurting myself, and having nowhere to hide like I usually did when I was hurting. Being physically cut across my abdomen for the second time in only a few years, left me stuck in my own head. I had disconnected from my energy below the waist and the emotions buried in my pelvis couldn't go down; so they were rising up to be addressed.

After a decade of Eastern-based training and personal development, I was unravelling deeper layers of 'stuff' I didn't even know existed. I felt a bit like I 'should' be over it all by this point; something I now know to be laughably naive! Thankfully, despite my Ego wanting to appear strong, I knew the only way through was to stop fighting with myself and let things unfold.

Slowly but surely, as I stopped resisting and trying to control everything, I began reconnecting to myself again. Small step by small step, I sat with the uprising emotions, let the tears flow, said a final farewell to motherhood and started rebuilding again, with the help of the lovely souls around me. It is incredible what can change and shift in a short time, given the right circumstances.

On the day I saw the real Matrix, we were guided by our lovely teacher Helen to work with our purest desires for our time on the retreat.

We each picked words representing what our heart most called out for... my word was Presence. I craved peace; for my head to be quiet and less busy, and my sense of my feet to come back to me. Helen intuitively gave us each different focuses to work with, guiding me to simply stand in Tadasana, the yoga mountain posture. Using minimal words, she led me to the edge of the deck, turned me away from everyone, and advised me to imagine sending energetic roots deep into the ground. This was a posture and focus I had done thousands of times over many years of yoga practice, but never before on the edge of a deck, with limited sense of my own feet, very little to hear, and nothing to see ahead except trees and mountains.

I stood still, stopped trying to feel my feet and imagined connecting my energy up to the sky and down to the earth. As I gazed softly beyond the forest to the distant mountains and reconnected to the space around me, I focused only on my breath. As I quietly grounded, and my sense of the others behind me receded, my body softened and the noise in my head diminished. I lost any sense of my internal struggle and in turn was rewarded with one of those unexpected and rare moments of stillness. The incredible sense of pure consciousness we all glimpse sometimes... but can never hold onto.

As this happened, the world, slowly and unforgettably transformed.

One moment, the view in front of me was of the trees and mountains beyond. The next, a silvery, liquid-like, exquisitely fine matrix slowly formed between the trees and into the ground; connecting everything. As I unwittingly entered an incredible parallel world, I felt a sense of acceptance and peace at depths I had never experienced. The world shimmered with vibrant richness and colour. In that moment, as I perceived the true inter-connectedness of all things, I finally, somewhat magically, felt my feet.

I had no awareness of thoughts, expectation, judgement or fear. The moment was as real as the skin on my body and the hair on my head, and my eyes and ears were clearer than they had ever been. In that moment, no matter how weirdly wonderful what was happening seemed, I felt deeply held, supported, and loved by a bigger presence I inherently knew I was part of. By getting grounded and feeling my feet, I quite literally connected to something huge.

In truth, there are no words I could possibly find to convey the incredible nature of that magical moment to you. Everything I previously thought important simply melted away, as I was gifted a glimpse of the actual matrix of life and the universe. It took only moments. Moments are sometimes all you need to experience something magical. That, and the ability to get out of your busy head.

Even though part of me inevitably doubted what I saw and felt, in that moment, I understood the bigger picture of life and my place in the world. Even though it made no sense to my logical mind, I inherently knew I mattered and that my purpose here was simply to be me, unapologetically and unreservedly.

In that magical moment I stopped clinging to my desire to control things, let go of the need to try so hard, and leaned into a sense of trust that I would always be held with unconditional love by something far greater than my mere physical self. I realised everything happened for a reason I didn't need to understand, and that everything would always work itself out. Even if it took a lifetime. All I really needed to do was get out of my head and into my heart, lean back, and enjoy the ride.

It was a rare and precious moment in my life that has changed all my subsequent moments.

Some would call it an enlightenment experience. For me, it was an incredible gift for which I will always be thankful; one that woke me up and gave me back a sense of perspective. As weird as this experience may sound and as inaccessible as it may seem, if I can experience something this profound, anyone can. I had several years of energy training and yoga under my belt by this stage; but I was still just a woman, standing in front of a jungle, expecting nothing but somehow being gifted a glimpse of *everything*!

An Opportunity to Pause

This seems like an opportune moment to invite you to pause.

You might be feeling any number of things: fear, annoyance, disbelief, confusion or bewilderment through to reassurance, excitement, wonder, hope, and joy. Your head may be spinning with questions, or you may be feeling vindicated, as you read things you have quietly believed for years.

Take a breath.

Pause…

No matter how you feel, or what stage you are at in your life, all your reactions and thoughts after reading this, are normal. There is no right or wrong, nothing to fear and no need for regrets. You have been invited to view life through a different filter for a while. At any time, you can choose to dismiss what I have shared as stuff my mind made up... and if you do, you are wise indeed.

My mind is no different than yours. If it wants me to believe in something enough, it will present me with an endless supply of arguments and stories to back itself up. Whilst I have no doubt whatsoever about anything I've shared, we all have cognitive bias; as much as I try and minimise that, you are still reading *my* interpretation that you then interpret through *your* own filter. This doesn't mean it isn't real; it simply means you'll attach your own meanings and opinions to it, and you get to choose whether to integrate what I share for your future self or not.

You are right to question anything you haven't evidence for, but before dismissing things too quickly, remember you can't physically see electricity, yet you know for a fact it is there. You don't know what force makes your heart beat, and yet as you read this, it faithfully continues to serve you.

Magic is often closer than you think.

I have found there is a blissful sense of freedom that arises from realising you can view the world a different way any time you choose. In much the same way as you temporarily inhabit an alternative world when you're immersed in a compelling film or book, at any given moment you can decide to look at life through a different lens.

Once you realise you can alter your own experiences by altering your perception or viewpoint, it automatically reconnects you to the inherent power you already have. The power you unknowingly gave the Matrix Myth. The power that once accessed, gives you the strength to stay grounded in any of life's storms. Once you accept this, you will never feel stuck again.

This of course, can feel scary, rather than enlightening. If you're honest, there is a sense of safety and relief that arises from deciding you don't have any control over anything. It gives you an understandable excuse, a good reason NOT to change. I know this because I unknowingly clung to that belief for years - and sometimes I still momentarily revert to it.

I call it Justification for Abdication.

It's worth knowing about because it can arise at any time, no matter how worldly-wise or evolved you are.

We all have this tendency, because it feels far safer and easier to cling to what we know than embrace the unknown. It is part of your human wiring, so it's normal to resist letting this go; which is why I invited you to pause for a moment. It gives you a chance to notice and name any resistance you might be feeling and let yourself process what I've shared so far.

Before you move on, remember you can pause again any time you choose.

As you read, let go of any concerns about whether what I share resonates with you. You will interpret things your own way, but as you keep reading, know that what you need to know and remember will stay with you, and percolate and form new connections in your mind as needed. Anything else can fall away… and that is perfectly okay.

At all times, remember I am on your side. Nothing I share in this book comes from a place of criticism, a sense of superiority, or the implication that you need to become more than you already are. It is worth re-iterating again and again that you are enough, exactly as you are. You always were and you always will be.

Why Does Knowing About the Actual Matrix Matter?

When I saw the actual Matrix, I know I was visually accessing the Universal energy field that forms, surrounds, and connects all things. It is always there and as science has taught us, energy cannot be destroyed. This field is not generally seen by us, because we are not tuned into its frequency. It is a bit like having your radio tuned into certain stations - when you are tuned into a play on BBC Radio 4, you won't hear the music playing on other stations. If you change the dial, you tune in and can hear different channels, it is simply a matter of shifting your frequency.

In much the same way that the vibration from music you love can physically be felt as it resonates with your system and touches your emotions, you can shift your own energy frequency, so you are better able to discern subtle vibrations and direct your own energy. You aren't accessing something that appears once and can never be seen or felt again, *you are tuning into something that is always there*, but which you often miss, because you're busy living life on a different frequency.

It seems magical, mystical, esoteric, and spiritual, but it can also be viewed logically to some extent. A deaf person can interpret sound waves without actually hearing them. We all feel and filter more things in every moment than we consciously know. We don't recognise it because thankfully we have evolved to do it automatically (or as I often say, automagically!).

Can you imagine smelling ALL the smells, seeing every little tiny nuance and detail of everything, or hearing every single conversation, creak and footstep around you? Can you imagine the sensory overload this would cause and how little energy you would have left if our brain didn't automatically filter it out? If you were consciously aware of every sensory input and cognitive function happening each and every moment, it would feel exhausting and totally overwhelming.

We have labels for different degrees of this sensory overload already; one we all know is Autism. I believe we all exist to some degree on the same spectrum, what differs is how our individual processing system communicates sensory inputs to us and how we interpret them. Some of us have more control over this than others, and for those with severe autism, their ability to communicate what they perceive in ways we all understand, is limited. Possibly because their cognitive awareness is switched on so highly, they have no energy remaining to apply to things such as verbal communication.

In the past, when I was highly stressed and anxious, my system was so tight, I had no awareness whatsoever of subtle energies; I was lucky if I even heard conversations around me. Most of my energy was focussed on getting through the day, which I achieved by shutting out the world. When I've been immersed in practices that create a deep sense of calm and space such as at a yoga retreat, my ability to access subtle things such as hearing my inner voice or sensing other people's energy more acutely increased. Nothing has changed externally. What is different is my perception, how expansive and quiet my system is, where I have directed my energy and what my current focus is at that time.

Your life force energy changes as your system softens and eases, or tightens and compresses. It changes in response to where, what, and how you focus your attention. Your nervous system shifts in different physical and emotional states. The energy that flows through your veins, arteries, nerve pathways, muscle fibres, and tissues, flows more easily and functions better when you are relaxed and at ease.

We're not fixed solo entities, we expand or contract in relation to what or who is around us. And therein lies our capacity to access far greater levels of energy and potential. If I can shift from a fixed, scientific Western viewpoint and a body that was once tight, stressed, and rigid, to one that is more expansive, aware, open, and healthy, so can you.

It starts by shifting your sense of what you can influence and adopting a more empowered and open attitude towards change.

The Magic of Energy and Epigenetics

"There is a vitality, a life force, an energy, a quickening that is translated through you into action, and because there is only one of you in all time, this expression is unique. And if you block it, it will never exist through any other medium and will be lost." — Martha Graham

I want to show you how to use the MAGICAL processes to optimise your energy and shift your state from compressed to expansive. You could think about it as moving along the spectrum somewhere from chaos to calm, stressed to expressed, yin to yang, fear to love. The same energies with different names; constantly moving back and forth, impacting your system and shaping your experience of the world.

Rather than them shaping your experience of the world from the outside, you'll explore ways to control them and build your world from the inside out.

You are going to become a kind of magical energy alchemist. In many ways you already are, you're simply not fully using your inherent power and potential. To give this some context, below I expand further on Eastern Energy. There is no way I can do justice to this organic way of viewing life without writing a separate book on it - if you want to learn more - there are links to recommended resources at the end. Learning about this perspective of energy changed my world, it explains so many things Western science has no answers for (yet!).

Whilst we can logically grasp the concept of energy from a scientific perspective, there are more esoteric and spiritual energy concepts that we can only learn through practice or training in Eastern disciplines such as aikido, yoga, or chi gung. For thousands of years, these types of discipline have been practiced by people wanting to stay strong, fit, and healthy. These practices teach ways to optimise your life force energy through movement, mindfulness, and meditation. When you have free-flowing life force energy, you feel a sense of lightness, and a deep contentment and connection with life.

There is a reason these ancient energy practices not only survive to this day but are increasing in popularity; it is because they are effective and give us respite from the stress of modern life.

As much as our Western minds struggle to understand the intangible concepts of universal and life force energy, scientists are now proving the existence of things known to Eastern philosophy for years. Our knowledge changes constantly. We now know the heart emits a powerful energy field, a phenomenon known as heart coherence. We know that the gut has a powerful communication neural network known as the gut brain, and that human consciousness has a demonstrable effect on water molecules thanks to the work of Masaru Emoto.

These are fascinating and ongoing areas of research, that have contributed to the scientific field of Epigenetics, which studies the impact of our thoughts and behaviors versus genes on our wellbeing.

The word Epigenetics derives from Latin; translating as 'above the genes.' This area of science has overthrown the long-held belief that our genetic expression is a fixed entity that cannot be changed. Whilst there are some things that are fixed and pre-determined, our lifestyle influences our wellbeing far more than an inherited predisposition. In effect, Epigenetics is a scientific exploration of nature versus nurture.

"You may have a genetic predisposition to a disease, but the environment you bathe your cells and genes in determines how those genes are expressed. This means that there are lots of potential versions of you." — Frank Lipman M.D.

There are many examples of genetically identical twins who in later life have very different physiological and mental wellbeing; because they have been subject to different external factors that outweighed their identical DNA. There is also research showing that if children of cancer sufferers are adopted by healthy parents who never get cancer, those children are more likely to stay cancer-free, because of the healthier lifestyle they adopt. You can regard these research findings as representing how well your life force energy flows.

Whether or not you think about it this way, it's proven that we influence our wellbeing with our lifestyle choices and change our genetic expression by the decisions we make. We can use this knowledge to inspire us to adopt healthier practices such as mindfulness and motivate us to improve our wellbeing through movement and nutrition. Epigenetics also gives us hope that if we have 'lost the genetic lottery' and are predisposed to certain diseases, the outcome is not an inevitable conclusion if we do what we can to maximise our health.

There is so much scientific research emerging that correlates with Eastern knowledge; which demonstrates how much science has yet to discover. Theories thousands of years old, once dismissed as rhetoric, are substantiated with each passing year. We have no idea how much untapped potential we really have, which is very exciting. What we do know is when we let go of old paradigms that have their basis in rigid science, we open our world to wonderfully expansive, empowering possibilities.

After working with hundreds of women over the years, I can definitively state that your body contains dynamic flowing energy that shifts and changes constantly. I was once a sceptical soul with a science degree, and was well into the third year of my Shiatsu training before I felt this energy. When I finally did, it was emanating so powerfully from my friend's neck, I literally jumped back in shock!

This life force energy is known by various names; Prana in Indian philosophy, Chi in Chinese philosophy and Ruach, the breath of God, in the Old Testament. It runs through channels known as meridians, which supply your organs, keep your blood flowing, your nervous system firing, your muscles toned, and your digestive system lubricated. There are twelve meridians; ten are linked to vital organs and two are linked to libido and brainpower. As you learned earlier, you also have extraordinary channels, one of which is your central channel, representing your core potential.

Your body is a bit like a city; with busy areas, highways, processing plants, energy chambers, and peaceful zones. Each part is interconnected and impacts the others, in much the same way as a broken-down lorry can cause a traffic buildup slowing the flow of traffic in another part of town. For example, a physical blockage such as a tight neck disrupts your concentration, causes headaches, and eventually tightness throughout your whole system. If you are worried or stressed, you tense up physically, and this leads to backache and ultimately your immunity decreases. A blockage in one place can affect the whole system. This is not only related to your energy channels, it is also because your body is physically held together by a web-like matrix of connective tissue, called fascia.

Fascia surrounds everything in your body and is interconnected throughout your entire system. Tightness in the fascia in one area, will ultimately create tension and tightness elsewhere, which is why a tight left shoulder can actually be caused by a misaligned right foot. When fascia is healthy, it benefits your organs, blood vessels, lymphatic system, and nervous system, so it is easy to see how when stress tightens your fascia, it affects you physically, mentally, and energetically.

Start thinking of your body like a house or container, which your life force energy flows through and around. If the dense part (your physical structure) is misaligned or constricted, the lighter energetic part cannot flow properly.

When your body is unrestricted, your chi energy flows more freely, your body functions properly, your mind responds to stress more effectively, and you have more energy available to unfold your unique potential.

"He who tries to separate the body from the mind or the mind from the body distances his heart from the truth." —
Kahlil Gibran

As weird and wonderful as this may seem, if you're not already on board with the fact that your mind and body are interconnected and cannot be regarded as separate entities, it is time to ask yourself why you are holding onto this belief and how well it has served you up to now. Maybe, just maybe, there is something in the ancient beliefs after all. There is so much more to you than meets the eye and you have more power over your mind, body, and spirit than you know.

Soul and Spirit Energetics

Traditional Chinese Medicine philosophy (TCM) is complicated, fascinating, and nuanced. Whilst it can seem irrelevant to our modern lives, it is a holistic, empowering approach to wellbeing that is more relevant than ever, as we try to find balance in a constantly switched-on world.

TCM attributes different spiritual and psychological aspects to each meridian and its corresponding organs. They believe each organ has a very distinct character, which is disturbed if the organ or corresponding meridian is affected in any way. The organs work in pairs, with each meridian having two paired organs that complement each other in terms of their function. One example is the kidney and bladder organs, which are both related to the water meridians. In each pair, there is a yin and yang organ. I like to think of the yang organs as being the processing organs; moving body substances around, whereas the yin organs are the manufacturing and storage centres.

As well as having distinct functions, each yin organ also houses one of the five spirits. These are the Shen, Hun, Po, Yi, and Zhi, living in the Heart, Liver, Lungs, Spleen and Kidneys respectively. Balance of each is considered fundamental to your mental wellbeing. In fact, when all five aspects are in balance, they are said to vibrate with the almighty power of the Universe itself (known as the Tao). From the smallest cell, to the skin layers, to your energy centres known as chakras, Eastern traditions believe you are an ever-changing, somewhat magical bundle of energy.

TCM aims to maintain a state of dynamic balance in your system by optimising your energy channels and strengthening what is called the Three Treasures. These are your Jing (essence), Qi (energy) and the Shen (spirit). They are said to be fundamental aspects; giving you mental, physical, emotional and spiritual strength and wellbeing.

Jing is your underlying porridge pot of energy, keeping you strong and healthy and providing firm foundations when in balance. Qi is the liquid energy moving through your system, nourishing everything, keeping your mind and body working well. Shen is your inner light, your mental and emotional intelligence, your personality and your spirituality. When the Three Treasures function well you are better able to adapt to change, your porridge pot of energy is full, you are calmer, more grounded, and more resistant to disease and illness.

If they are imbalanced however, you are said to be 'dispirited' because in TCM terms, you cannot have wellbeing in one area without having it in others. Or in other words, you could have the fittest looking body because you work out daily; but if you're working out at the cost of your personal relationships or you're not eating well, you still won't feel 'on top of your game'.

You can think of the words Soul and Spirit as aspects of your entire energy field. You can also attach any other meanings to them you like, whether religious, spiritual, factual, or purely energetic. Whatever your view of soul and spirit as entities in their own right, there is no doubting we all have different aspects to our characters and they are beautifully explained by the ancient concepts of spirit energies and their associations.

For example, in TCM philosophy, your Liver is responsible for an aspect of your being called the Hun. You may well have heard this word before; for most of us it conjures up the image of a warrior or tribal nomad. The opposite is true in TCM; the Hun translates as Ethereal Soul and closely corresponds to the Western aspects of the soul most of us are familiar with. It is considered more of a dreamer than a fighter.

The Hun gives us our ability to access a sense of direction and purpose. If it is healthy, we have more clarity about what we want and who we are. It's a bit like our compass or guiding light.

When we are awake, the Hun is said to rest in our eyes, helping us see where we're going and make aligned decisions. Think of how someone's eyes shine when they are excited or feeling on top of the world; their eyes literally come alive as you see the light of their soul. When we're asleep, the Hun dictates our dream state, if it is imbalanced, we experience interrupted sleep or intense dreams. No surprise that whilst writing this book (therefore planning and making decisions, which relate to Liver energy), my sleep was more interrupted with vivid dreams than it has been for years!

The ability of our Hun to see a clear direction ahead is affected by the health of our liver. In TCM terms, an overindulged or unhealthy liver is likely to cause us problems in terms of knowing what we want or accessing a sense of direction in life. It will be too busy processing food and emotions to have energy left for clear decision-making or visioning. No wonder then, that in a world where so much of what we take into our body and our senses is toxic and overwhelms our system, it is common for many of us to have no idea what we want in our life.

As far as Eastern and Western spiritual traditions are concerned, we are souls contained in a human body, and our soul cannot be destroyed. When I use the word soul throughout this book, I am talking to the part of you that is indefinable, that drives or nudges you to do things that make no logical sense, and the part that lights up your eyes when you are excited.

It is not used in a religious sense and it does not matter one iota whether you believe this aspect of you is your heart, soul, consciousness, creative streak, inner voice etc. What matters is you recognise there is something incredible and unique about *you* that no-one else can bring to the world. Something you cannot fully explain, but in your brightest moments, you *know* exists. Feel free to change this word to one that makes sense to you as you read (or suspend your disbelief for now).

Embrace the possibility that you are always supported, and part of a greater oneness. This opens your mind up, offers you a more liberating way to view the world and sets you free from the need to control and bend things to your will. As you are about to discover, there is a far easier, more fulfilling way to live life.

INTERLUDE ONE
On Magic....

Magic is in the small things,
The stuff we take for granted
The daily gifts of life.

Moments that make us smile,
Connecting with another soul,
Warm coffee on a cold blustery day.

Butterflies, sunshine, and rainbows.
Being present and simply noticing.
Seeing colours, eating fresh food.

Honouring your heart,
making friends with your head.
Indulging your curiosity.
Expressing your creativity.

Unfolding and becoming real.
Trusting the Universe and trusting yourself.
Living with appreciation, compassion, and love.
Owning your worth and playing your part.

Embracing the daily dance of life
Making peace with clouds
And seeing magic in the shadows.

Part Two — The Magical Process

The Bridge Between Two Worlds

Have you ever walked across a flimsy looking bridge suspended over a raging river, and then frozen momentarily in the middle because you're scared of heights and it feels impossible to make it to the other side? You look behind you, trying in vain not to look down; and then realise it's no easier to go back than it is to move forwards.

In that moment you have are two options that feel equally impossible. As your head fights with itself and the river beneath you crashes and swirls violently over jagged rocks, you are quite literally stuck between a rock and a hard place. Your only options are to somehow turn around in the small scary space, and retrace your steps or take a step forwards, and keep repeating that action until you have made it to the other side.

One choice will make you feel like a winner, the other is more likely to make you feel you've failed.

You are a winner regardless of your decision; because it required courage for you to step out onto the bridge in the first place. In the eyes of those still standing fearfully on the precipice, you are a heroine.

It takes courage to explore anything new, and you wouldn't be human if you didn't feel fear or resistance every time you faced a challenge (even something you do regularly). I bet you've discovered though, as I have, that when you face your fear, it often melts into a little puddle of nothingness. Fears built up as huge monsters in your head are unable to maintain the illusion when you see them as they truly are.

Helpful hint: bear that in mind as you read on.

I wrote earlier that you are standing on the precipice of possibility; this precipice is located on the edge of the Bridge between the two worlds you were introduced to in Part One:

On one side is the old paradigm world, governed by the Matrix Myth.

Then there is the Bridge with the pathway between the two.

On the other side is the new paradigm world; the place where Magic happens.

The Old Paradigm World

This is where the majority of people live and work under the rule of their head. On this side, you live within the comfort zone limits set by society and your unconscious beliefs about the world and yourself.

You may feel like you're stuck, overwhelmed and stressed, and your life is limited by forces greater than yourself. This side is the disempowered, fear-led side, where you don't get too big for your boots or stand up too tall.

It works for most of us as long as we lower our expectations and bury our dreams. We subconsciously maintain this self-delusion by numbing ourselves with food, spending money on 'stuff', wearing masks hiding who we really are or want to be, and gathering accolades in various forms.

The Bridge

You generally stumble upon the Bridge after something makes you realise you have to stop, slow down, and change things. The 'something' may take many forms, and visit many times before you take notice of it.

Generally, this occurs when either your discomfort outweighs your fear of change; you are driven by an urgent need, or you become so aware of the fragility of life you are filled with a burning passion that won't be quenched unless you honour it. This is when you'll start looking for ways to live life differently, more authentically, and without knowing it, you move towards the Bridge.

Once on the Bridge, you may fall off and have to climb back on, you may move forwards, backwards, from side to side, or forge straight ahead. The Bridge can feel long or short, winding or straight and you can feel lost in the middle when you lose sight of the other side.

Once traversed, however, you start feeling magical and life becomes infinitely more meaningful.

The New Paradigm World

This is where the awake, aware minority live, free from the Matrix Myth. Over here you live and think outside of the box, in the zone where magic happens.

You have embraced the concept of Universal connection, and respect all forms of life. You have learned how to optimise your energy so you flow more freely through life. You are empowered and accept full responsibility for your health and wellbeing; meaning you are less triggered by others, or events outside your control.

On this side, you still feel scared sometimes; but you act in spite of fear, knowing this is how you grow. You follow your heart, using your head to support you in living intentionally and mindfully. You accept you will mess up at times, knowing it doesn't matter if you do. It's all part of the bigger game of Life and you are happy to be part of it.

When you honour the call to step onto the Bridge and you choose the unknown path, you'll find courage and love will meet you on the other side.

It's both exciting and scary... alas, you can't have one without the other.

The MAGICAL process happens on the Bridge; so with every step you take forwards, you get better at balancing, and are less likely to fall.

Once you have worked through the process and reached the other side, you will have left behind the Matrix Myth and started adopting a more Magical Mindset. This equips you to navigate life with more grace, balance better between fear and courage, and proactively choose whether to take one step forwards each day into growth, or move backwards into safety.

Either way, you are a winner.

Because you, lovely soul, faced your fear and stepped out onto the Bridge in the first place.

What Will You Discover on the Bridge?

For your future to be the one you dream of, where everything has fallen into place and you're happy and fulfilled, you have to start consciously following the breadcrumb trail every day, starting now.

The MAGICAL process invites you on an unfolding journey across the Bridge to discover those breadcrumbs. At times it will be fun, inspiring, and enlightening, and at other times it will feel scary, you'll feel resistance, and you might want to run away. This range of emotions is completely normal and shows that you truly care about this journey, believe you are capable of achieving what you want, and you're making positive shifts towards it. Feeling a range of emotions is not only a natural aspect of change, it's also a wonderful feedback mechanism and I'll show you exactly how to use your emotions to inform you. I will guide you through your entire journey – gentle step by gentle step – so you never feel alone and you have the tools you need to stay true to the intentions you set for yourself.

I invite you to view this as a possibility process – it's called the MAGICAL process because that's what it is – it is a magical unfolding journey back home to yourself. It's perfectly safe because being fully back in connection with your inner self is the safest place you can be. It's your only true compass in the world – the one place you can rely on to always travel with you and to inform you every step of the way of what works for you and what doesn't. I am not talking about big changes. You will make subtle inner changes that no one else will initially notice, but which change how you respond to the world, how you design your days, how you set intentions and maintain boundaries, how you process stress and find calm, and how you make proactive decisions from the core of your being.

You will start operating from the inside out, from a new place of strength, your original blueprint. Reinventing your life story, one small step at a time - by learning how to live and think outside the box - in the more peaceful, purposeful place, where magic truly happens.

The MAGICAL process will help you to create a life you love. One that enriches, nourishes, and empowers you.

I wish you a joyful journey. There may be ups and downs, some twists and turns, but it will all be totally worth it!

"You don't always have to know exactly what you're doing, or where you're going. You just have to be willing to take the first step. Sometimes clear and powerful. Sometimes with blind, unwavering faith." — Lisa Nichols

Back to the Precipice of Possibility...

"A woman in harmony with her spirit is like a river flowing. She goes where she will without pretence and arrives at her destination prepared to be herself and only herself." — Maya Angelou

Part One: The Myth gave you context for your journey, so your brain started adjusting to the idea that perhaps a new paradigm will serve you better than the old familiar one. For your brain to see the point of stepping out onto the Bridge, you needed to take the first step of showing it that the world it thought was real might not be so real after all. This makes it more open to considering alternatives; which is fundamental to any change.

Now you truly are ready to stand on the precipice of possibility and your magic can slowly unfold.

Whilst the concept of unfolding your own magic may seem disconcerting (even if you are already well versed in personal development), this is where things get exciting! None of us really inhabit a life in which we fully thrive until we throw out what we know and open our minds and hearts to new possibilities. You now get to explore the MAGICAL processes that took me from being the head-led person - who once let someone else take over her life in all the worse ways - to the heart-led person who transformed her life to one she loves waking up in each day.

By the end of Part Two, you'll have those processes too, and your time in the Matrix myth's grip will be well and truly over.

You are extracting yourself from the Matrix Myth and trying out a new paradigm. It is a little like uninstalling a life-long programme and over-writing it with a new improved one you can't see yet, which requires trust, patience, and faith.

I know life gets busy and you may struggle to find time to work through each process. I want to remind you that you can take your time. There is no time limit on becoming who you were born to be or living in a way that feels more peaceful and purposeful. If you work through every process, it will shorten the time it takes you, but it will still be an unfolding journey that continues your entire life. This is not a prescriptive 'one-size fits all' regime, it is a self-discovery journey helping you rediscover the magic in yourself to live in a way that is aligned with who you already are.

The MAGICAL process is sequential; each step builds upon the preceding one once you have established your foundations. No self-development journey is linear, each one organically twists and turns in spirals, as you evolve, learn, revisit old lessons, and discover new ones. That is why spirals have been used for centuries to represent life's journey in indigenous tribes worldwide. We have to unfurl delicately and unfold slowly, at our own pace.

As you explore each process, you will revisit familiar concepts, discover new ones, be invited to explore practical exercises and try new strategies on for size. I invite you to honour yourself as you read; we are all unique, and different approaches appeal to different people. Walk away from anything that doesn't resonate with you, and embrace what does. No excuses or justification needed. Simply ensure that before you dismiss anything that seems like common sense or you think doesn't suit you, your inner fear fairy isn't leading you astray from something potentially transformational.

If you work through each process as suggested, you'll get out of your head and back into your body, access more peace, shift and optimise your energy, and start uncovering your sense of purpose. You'll become more mindful and learn tools for life, to support you any time you feel stuck or disempowered. In much the same way as you brush your teeth daily, many of the tools are best slowly incorporated into your routine. In the final process, I share the strategies I have used to establish my daily positive habits.

Each chapter in Part Two is presented the same way to help your brain assimilate the content. Changes won't magically occur just by reading, some will, but for effective change, you will have to do something new. It will be worth it, because you'll boost your confidence simply by honouring your own intentions. This is often one of the hardest challenges we face when trying to make changes, so in Process 1 you will equip yourself to better honour your intentions.

I am not delusional enough to believe everyone who buys this book will even read it; never mind work through to the end. I also know it is rare for a book alone to change your life. What I do know is that the right book, read at the right time, with the right words for you in that moment, can act as a catalyst for change that lasts a lifetime.

It would be wonderful if this process did that for you; if not, it will definitely offer you new perspectives and life-enhancing tools.

As Oliver Wendell Holmes so wisely said: *"A moment's insight is sometimes worth a life's experience."*

To which I would add: *"even if it doesn't appear to happen straight away."*

To accompany the MAGICAL process, enrich your experience and supplement your learning, you are invited to explore the accompanying resources and Unfold Your Magic online course at www.helenrebello.com/p/MagicBookResources These can be used alongside each process, or revisited after you have read the book.

Life School

You don't need to be scared of your dreams.

You've been training for them your whole life. Learning the lessons of the ages.

In the best training camp there is.

It's called Life School.

Where you've learned about courage, compassion, fortitude, peace, understanding,
spirituality, pain, love, death, confidence, strength and adversity.

You've transcended challenges and done things you wouldn't ever have imagined.

Old you is so proud of you now. Old you can't believe what's magically unfolding.

This is your new paradigm. Now is your time. You are the solution.

You and your virtual army of women alongside you.

And so it is. You've got this.

CHAPTER 4
Process 1
Unfold Your Cape of Possibility

"Once you realise that the road is the goal, and that you are always on the road, not to reach a goal, but to enjoy its beauty and wisdom, life ceases to be a task, and becomes natural and simple, in itself an ecstasy." — Sri Nisargadatta Maharaj

Welcome to Process 1! I am so very happy you've made it this far. You are clearly ready for a life-enhancing adventure.

This is your less glamorous, no less vital, preparatory step. In order to get the most from your journey, you will have to step away from your Superwoman persona (the one that tries to be all things to all people). I know the persona feels familiar, and you may feel safe in it, but I have a different one for you to try out.

I invite you to imagine you have sent your Superwoman persona on holiday for a while. She hasn't done anything wrong - and you may not even think she is particularly super - but in order for you to truly embrace what is possible for you, it might be good for you to try a new persona on for size. If Superwoman hangs around, she might feel a little threatened, so best to unfold your new Cape of Possibility once she has gone.

As you would expect from the name, your Cape of Possibility comes with pockets for all the tools you will

90

discover on your journey. The tools in this process help you believe anything is possible, which is a good thing, because Possibility weakens the power of Procrastination. Even if you're really good at being Superwoman, procrastination is an inherent aspect of your human brain wiring, so overcoming this is a great place to start.

No heroine embarks on a mission into unknown territory without the right outfit, appropriate tools, and a few strategies in place; not if she wants to reach her destination. In this chapter you set yourself up for the best outcome by pre-arming yourself with some magical mindset tools. They help you overcome the biggest obstacles to getting starting; so that you move forwards on the Bridge. This process helps you set firm foundations you can use not only now; but for life, whenever you start something new.

In Process 2 you will learn how to build upon the momentum you are about to gain.

Sound good? Cape ready? Let me set the scene...

My Story — Waking Up

There is no better place to begin than the start... even if you don't know where the next step is.

There are times when the need to step up and stop life-cruising shouts at you so loudly that you can no longer ignore it. Sometimes you see it coming from miles away. Others it takes you completely by surprise.

In my case, it came as something of a shock the first time it happened, but looking back I realise the buildup was subtle and drawn out over many months. Mainly because I had no idea I even was life-cruising. I thought I was just doing what we all do - living life and responding to things that come at you in the moment. No matter that it looked like a car crash, with constant drama and fights. That was just life, as far as I was concerned. I had made some bad choices, but what could I do other than get on with it and soldier through.

It wasn't as though I believed I deserved any better, and I certainly didn't see the point in self-enquiry back then. Even though I wrote a journal in secret, something I only saw the point of much later. Our souls are clever at getting us to do things like that almost without us realising it. At that point, I was 19 years old and this was my first Path A/Path B turning point, when I reconnected with my inner brave warrior and hatched the plan that eventually helped me escape from the violent situation I lived in with my first long-term boyfriend.

Looking back, I remember quite clearly that until this point, I always had a sense of 'waiting' for something to happen. Something magical, that would mean my life had properly begun. It sounds totally illogical; after all I had already lived 19 years, messed up at school, left home and started disastrously 'adulting'. In my head; however, none of this really counted. It wasn't like I actively 'decided' to make these things happen - they were a glitch, something I had to live through until the fairy tale life I had read about in countless books appeared. All I had to do was wait and then a knight in shining armour would appear, ready to direct me and make good decisions for me.

No wonder I buried myself in distractions, such as cannabis use, to escape the stark contrast of my actual reality. No wonder I felt like a powerless puppet, whose life looked as it did thanks to the actions of everyone else. In my head I was simply responding to the crappy hand of life I had been dealt, whilst waiting for an external rescuer. The true definition of a victim mindset.

It had not yet occurred to me I had to make things happen *myself*.

No one tells you when you're growing up that you get to decide and choose and you have options outside of those offered to you by authority figures. Even though by unconsciously opting out of my parent's 'preferred' life choices of becoming a doctor or similar, I had effectively chosen an alternative. I now wonder how I even found the courage or momentum to raise my head so I could see through my own delusions, never mind hatch a plan that saw me pretending to be so 'normal' I somehow got a nurse training place.

Turns out I am a pretty good actor and world-class at hiding things. Which was a good thing in this case, because my boyfriend had no idea what I was up to. If he had he would no doubt have held a knife to my throat, which is what he had done the last time I did something he deemed subversive. Thankfully, I took a series of small scary steps that led to my escape, and to me being given a residential training place. It was a fresh start with the added bonus of a new career, somewhere to live, money, and social acceptability.

The catalyst that led to this point was unremarkable. There was no blinding flash of clarity, no moment of inspiration, no wise mentor sharing their insights with me. It was more a slow burner; a series of personal transgressions that ate away at my core. It was simply a matter of time before I reached the point of no return, where my heart took over and had a very big word with my head. There was only one way to go unless I gave up entirely. Which something inside me wasn't prepared to do. No matter how powerless I felt.

As painful and hard as it was, the good thing about getting to that stage is it helped me unearth a level of inner strength and courage I never knew I had. It woke me up to the realisation that I needed to create my own plot, rather than wait for a rescuer to create it for me. I saw it was up to me to change the story and choose a new role. The nursing role I chose turned out to be the wrong one - and the violent boyfriend somehow found me - but at least I made a choice and began. It beat staying stuck and never even trying. From that day, only one man raised his hand and hit me, and I ended that relationship without hesitation on the spot.

To change the trajectory of my life, all I had to do was decide to do life differently.

Then take small steps towards changing my own paradigm. It doesn't matter whether it worked out or not, what is important is I chose me. And in doing so, I set in course a chain of events that ultimately set me free from feeling like a victim of life, and becoming a magical creator instead.

Head-Led Challenges Of Process 1

The blossoming field of possibility is scattered with the dying weeds of resistance and fear.

There are some very common challenges we have to transcend and make peace with before we can truly transform. It's one thing having a sense of what we need to change, it is knowing how or where to start that effectively cripples us. Mainly because we're scared of making the wrong move or looking like an idiot (because clearly looking like an idiot means you are doomed!).

You have no doubt set out many times with pep in your step and joy in your heart, all fired up to change things... only to find yourself back in Dead-end Alley, with a head full of self-criticism and a heart heavy with 'no-can-dos'. If this describes you, you have my FULL permission to let yourself off. It is really hard to make changes, to reach for the dreams you long for.... unless you are a challenge-overcoming heroine.

Which is of course, where the Cape of Possibility comes in.

Think of your Cape of Possibility as being an outfit you wear that can help you face these challenges with more awareness and confidence. They will always be there trying to stall you, but your Cape gifts you belief in the bigger Power of Possibility. Maybe this time, with that power, you will break through your procrastination barriers. You are already more courageous and capable than you realise; the Cape merely shields you from the Fear Fairies, whilst you learn how to trust in your own abilities.

I am a great believer in the power of naming things, as it helps your brain to understand and demystify them. By naming your possible challenges, you also become better equipped to notice when they sneak in; which is powerful because it disentangles your conscious mind from the subconscious part that stops you taking action. Therefore you are less likely to get in your own way.

What you will notice about almost all these challenges is that they arise from your head. The most common challenges we all face are caused by fear manifesting in various forms. They cleverly disguise themselves as something else, to convince you they are insurmountable. They might feel real, but they are usually 'thoughts appearing real', derived from the lies your head assimilated from the Matrix Myth.

I have separated them into recognisable categories. As you read, I invite you to pay attention to your reactions, because they will tell you everything you need to know about what your biggest challenges might be. Even if none of them apply to you, I guarantee that by reading them, you will think of plenty of your own. This is a good thing, information truly is power. Hidden shadow monsters under your bed are revealed as illusions once you turn on the light, but we all know how scary they are until we learn they don't exist.

It might be useful for you to make a short list of your common challenges after you have read this section. You know whether that is something that feels useful for you or not, so honour your instincts.

You will discover solutions to overcome your challenges in the next section.

Challenges you might encounter:

1. Time Based Challenges

AKA: 'I'm too busy / I don't have enough time (in your day or in life) / It will take too long - I want change to happen right now.'

Whilst these words may well be true to some degree, telling yourself them is definitely not going to help you move from where you are to where you want to be. These head-led words keep you stuck and shut you off from the power of possibility. Very few of the many things we fill our time with are truly so important that we cannot shave some time off, do them less often, delegate, or shift how we perceive them. The question is, what is it you're so busy doing, does it fill you up, and why are you doing it? We will return to these questions later.

Instant gratification can also trip you up. I've seen this time and time again with my clients as well as myself. So many stressed souls love the instant changes of feeling calm and grounded during and after their session. They then struggle to implement the small shifts I recommend that would take them a bit more time, but see them accessing this state more often. The reality is your biggest changes happen slowly, like a seed unfolding slowly into a beautiful flower. Often we don't notice until one day we realise we have broken through our own boundaries to truly blossom.

As the philosopher Brian Johnson so wisely said: *"Saying you're too busy to check in with your highest Self is kinda like saying you're too busy driving to stop for gas. That's just not smart and *definitely* not gonna help you live a life of meaning and bliss!"*

2. Resistance

AKA - excuses, fear, procrastination

Have you ever made a declaration to yourself that tomorrow morning you are going to get up early and do some exercise or meditate… and then the next morning, you felt so much resistance you actually ended up getting up later than usual? We all experience times when even though part of us really wants to do something, the other part resists and digs its heels in. This part will win almost every time without some strategies in place.

I call this 'doing the resist-dance'. It is an entertaining dance between two parts of yourself you will encounter whenever you want to do something new, scary, or different. It will present itself in any number of guises, such as excuses, justification, distraction, or an apparently urgent need to clean the house, or search online for new shoes you don't really need.

The good news is that it is a sign that you are on the cusp of change. It is a normal response from your primitive brain, which merely wants to keep you safe. It doesn't always know change is good and it certainly doesn't want you to raise your head above the parapet. You might get shot... or you might leave your primitive brain behind as you see through its messages, which leaves your brain feeling impotent.

Steven Pressfield has written some wonderful books about getting over yourself and taking action, and this quote for me, sums it up perfectly: *"Rule of thumb: The more important a call or action is to our soul's evolution, the more resistance we will feel toward pursuing it."*

3. Fear of Change or of Failure

AKA - being overly attached to what is, thinking safety lies in staying the same, that comfort zones are fixed, or you can't change.

Fear in all its forms is the biggest dream killer we all face and is unique to each person. What gives me internal shivers is not the same as it is for you. It is also not fixed and can change very quickly once you start challenging it; the problem is we don't know that until we release ourselves from its grip.

Fear of failure ranks up there highly as one of the biggest blocks that prevents us from even trying new things. It is not surprising. From an early age we get praised for achievement, whereas there are no prizes given for trying and failing. We learn quickly how stupid we feel when we give a wrong answer in school; how everyone looks at us when we don't catch a ball in rounders (or baseball), or how rubbish we feel about ourselves when we come last in a race. This imprint stays in our subconscious, tripping us up before we start, without us even being aware of it.

I could write an entire book on fear of change, and the countless ways I've seen it manifest in myself and others. As with procrastination (which is often fear wearing different clothes), fear is a totally normal response. Again, it's due to your brain wanting to keep you safe, and it is an evolutionary response you cannot do without.

Fear is a powerful agent that serves us well when we really need to escape danger; the problem is, we experience fear on a daily basis and we misinterpret it as meaning 'back away', play safe, and we shut the fear down as soon as possible. Unfortunately, playing it safe effectively means 'stay put'. A wise strategy when hiding away from real danger in a safe place; but not so wise when you're hiding from your personal growth and fulfilment.

As Bob Goff, author of *Everybody, Always: Becoming Love in a World Full of Setbacks and Difficult People* stated: "*Playing it safe doesn't move us forward or help us grow; it just finds us where we are and leaves us in the same condition it found us in.*"

You can think of fear as the phenomenon that arises whenever you are about to step over the line of your comfort zone. As you will have discovered already, whenever you do something new or scary, this line shifts and expands, and the fear subsides. It's just another one of those sneaky boxes we mislabel. Even if you've already taken small steps on your daily path towards living in a way you love, it doesn't mean you'll never again feel fear or doubt. When fear trips you up, it's okay. The fact is embodying courage is a daily practice. And absence of fear is a lie. And can be foolish.

We simply have to make peace with that, and recognise that fear alone won't kill us.

4. Guilt

AKA - the martyr complex: shoulds, musts, ought-to's.

Are you one of those generous, heart-centred women who feels guilty if you sit down for five minutes, especially when others around you are busy doing 'stuff'? Does this still happen even when you're absolutely shattered or you have a very good reason to rest (such as a health condition)?

There's a sneaky little pest I call the 'pulling your weight' pest. He lives in the guilty trap and cannot wait for you to fall into it... especially if you're a woman who will always help others. He is close friends with the shame monster. Their messages of guilt and shame, are installed early in life when we get told off for what is deemed unacceptable behaviour, such as focusing on ourselves or putting our needs first.

Guilt seems to be an inevitable part of the human picture. Most humans care about others and see indulging themselves as being selfish in some way. This has been passed down to us through generations of ancestors to keep us safe. Like the challenges above, it arises subconsciously from our heads and can be viewed as representing positive qualities, once you know how to manage and transcend it.

We all know the saying about putting on our own oxygen mask first, but we are fighting with an inner desire to put ourselves last and everyone else first. The worst people for doing this in the Western world, in my experience, are mothers struggling with an unhappy or sick baby. They will seek help for the baby immediately; but continue to drive themselves into the ground. In many Eastern cultures however, it is normal to treat the mother in order to treat the child. I have witnessed this truth many times; when working with a mother whilst their unhappy baby is in the room, then watching as the baby relaxes and quietens at the same time as the mother. It is magical and never ceases to amaze me.

I love this quote from Geshe Michael Roach, in his book *The Diamond Cutter*: *"There's no word in Tibetan for 'guilty.' The closest thing is 'intelligent regret that decides to do things differently'."*

Sounds like a much more empowered response than beating yourself up, doesn't it?

5. Self-doubt

AKA: 'Who am I to do this / I cannot do this, I will fail / I should stay as I am'.

Unless you got very lucky, you probably weren't brought up believing it was possible for you to be or do anything you dream of. You probably weren't told it was allowed or acceptable to focus on yourself. You no doubt worry about seeming ungrateful or delusional to go after what you want, and you doubt your ability to do so.

You feel this way because you're a wonderful kind soul, with a good heart and you don't want to upset people. You've unwittingly accepted less than helpful society 'rules' that have you believing you're wrong to want more for yourself. Your inner 5 year old doesn't want you to get picked on, so she sometimes persuades you to play it safe.

You may also be battling with a fixed mindset you don't even know you have. This means you give up before you've even started because you don't believe you can change. I was once told by a client that she 'couldn't change' because she wasn't positive like I am, and therefore I wouldn't be able to understand why she couldn't get unstuck from a life she hated.

I used to limit what I disclosed about myself in sessions, because it is about who I am working with, not about me. On this occasion though, it felt highly appropriate to tell her that I was once the most negative person out there - mainly because that was the environment into which I was born so I didn't know any different. Moaning, seeing the worst in others, suppressing my real feelings and believing I was a victim of circumstances, got installed as my default. No one knows better than I do that once you realise these are all lies your head makes up to keep you safe, you are empowered to remove them before they gain traction. Do this often enough and you rewire your brain to see the silver lining, not just the cloud. Sharing this gave her hope and sowed the seed of possibility; thankfully her life looks and feels extremely different today.

Carol Dweck is a leading researcher in the subject of motivation and has written extensively about two perspectives called the Fixed versus Growth mindset. She says: *"When you enter a mindset, you enter into a New World. In one world - the world of fixed traits - success is about proving you're smart or talented. Validating yourself. In the other - the world of changing qualities - it's about stretching yourself to learn something new. Developing yourself."*

From my experience, I know they are merely at different ends of the same spectrum. If I can change my Eeyore pessimistic, victim viewpoint and become more like bouncy Tigger crossed with Pooh Bear, anyone can.

6. Delusions

AKA the 'need more information' story, the 'it takes XYZ to change' story, the 'Guru' story, the 'it looks like this' story.

A very close cousin of Procrastination and Self-Doubt, this challenge is one that manifests in various forms again, all stemming from your head's attempts to keep you safe. A lot of people I know who are into self-development are the worst people for thinking they need to have all their ducks in a row, or they need everything sorted before they can begin.

You may think you must gather more information before you can press the start button, that you need to be more special, or you need to be a certain type of person before you can move towards your desires. Your head will tell you only gurus are able to attain a certain state, and you cannot be one of them because you are not equipped to climb up onto the pedestal you put gurus on.

It is incredibly common to beat yourself up for not being 'There' yet the mystical land where all your dreams come true once you find the path, lose the weight, learn ALL the things, and tick the right boxes. Your brain will tell you lies like all yoga teachers are skinny ex-dancers who never get stressed, therapists have special healing abilities, and meditation is only for Zen monks. No wonder you think it's delusional for you to even dream of reaching these dizzy heights.

Your brain may also ascribe erroneous meanings to feelings you desire, putting them in a special box that makes them seem elusive for normal humans. One example is something John C. Parkin wrote about peace, in his book *F**k it: Be at Peace with Life, Just as it is*: *"Being at peace with life doesn't necessarily mean being peaceful, and it certainly isn't being passive; it means embracing life in all its colours."*

103

Adopting this mindset is what brought me peace in my life. Also, as your brain is listening whilst you read, I would like to reassure it there are no gurus as such. Self-proclaimed ones I've met are generally a bit messed up and those that I view as being guru-like would be horrified if I ever actually called them that! There are incredible, heroic, and inspirational people, who have achieved incredible things - but they have worked diligently, usually suffered many setbacks and still consciously maintain daily practices and habits to stay in integrity.

We're always a work in progress. If we waited until everything was perfect before we showed up, we'd wait a lifetime. Which is a dangerous game that can lead to regrets, don't let your brain convince you otherwise.

7. Wanting it to Be Easy/Expecting it All to Be Too Hard

AKA — 'this hurts, I want to stop' / 'I won't start, it will be too hard' / 'I will push harder so I get through this more quickly'.

Change often feels hard before it feels easy. We like to convince ourselves that this is not the case, and we can outwit the norm, by uncovering a magic wand that fast-tracks us to the promised land. We don't like the fact that in order to get different results, we have to push through an initial barrier that can feel like climbing our own personal Everest.

We think the ongoing journey will always be hard, so to avoid the pain of that, the voices in our head tell us lies that keep us stuck. We have quite naturally evolved to associate pain with threat to our life; therefore we avoid it. Ironically, we simply adapt to the pain we experience already, papering over it or accepting it as inevitable.

Change doesn't need to look or feel a certain way, and once you get over the first hump, it is often easier than staying put. There is no precedent to set, no shortcut, no diversion around the hard stuff. Pain doesn't always represent a threat to your life, it sometimes means you're growing and developing new muscles. You know this, but your sneaky mind delights in telling you to give up when the going gets hard, conveniently forgetting the pain you're already feeling that makes you yearn for change.

No one finds change easy in the beginning, and no one gets to take a shortcut by pushing harder. You cannot shove your way into change and the only way through is to accept the struggle that comes up when you push your own boundaries. None of us progress without 'doing the work', and even if it becomes easier over time, you'll always have to do some work to maintain the changes and win the internal war with your own head.

This is yet another battle between two aspects of yourself, and as Barry Michels and Phil Stutz say in their great book, *Coming Alive: 4 Tools to Defeat Your Inner Enemy, Ignite Creative Expression & Unleash Your Soul's Potential*: *"A great life is not one without injuries. A great life is one in which you risk great injuries and overcome them when they happen, again and again. The more willing you are to risk getting hurt, the more you'll have the expansive, opportunity-filled life you want. If you remain small because you're terrified of hurt, failure or rejection... you'll live a limited, disengaged, fearful life."*

Heart-Led Solutions For Process 1

"To abandon the familiar ways in which we've grown accustomed to thinking about life in order to embrace new paradigms will feel unnatural in the beginning. Frankly, it takes effort—and it's uncomfortable. Why? Because when we change, we no longer feel like ourselves. My definition of genius, then, is to be uncomfortable and to be okay with being uncomfortable." — *Joe Dispenza*

Just because you don't yet see yourself as the person you dream of being - the one who no longer lets fear stop them from living on their terms - doesn't mean you're not that person inside already.

Even though it will initially feel uncomfortable and self-indulgent to move towards living in a way that fully expresses all you truly are, this doesn't make it wrong. You might feel like an imposter in your own skin as you put on the Cape of Possibility and start making changes... but let's be honest, don't you often feel like that anyway?

The question is, which character would you like to be from now?

The one created by the Matrix Myth or the Real You?

If both feel like you're making it up, you may as well choose the Real You.

Now you know the challenges your head could use to try and trip you up, I want to reassure you that your subconscious mind only wants the best for you and is not your enemy. Every time you consume information, your helpful mind sets to work, filtering and filing it into good/ bad, safe/dangerous categories. The overriding question in your mind is 'will this keep me safe or kill me?'. It will base its conclusion upon prior evidence, past experiences, and the desire to stay safe, known as your subconscious beliefs.

Your subconscious can be an ally. You simply have to know how to pacify it. As you move through each Process, you will find numerous ways to do this. As you discovered from reading my story, no matter how unaware you are of your underlying beliefs or how challenging your past experiences, you can still transcend your own limits. You start by embracing something small, but hugely powerful. Something subtle enough not to awaken the dozing subconscious guard in your mind. Luckily, I know just the thing…

Solution 1: Embrace The Six Letter Word That Changes Your Life

The only way you can change anything is to embrace the six-letter word that changes your life.

That word is CHOICE.

Choice derives from the French verb *choisir*, which according to the Etymology Dictionary, means to choose, distinguish, discern, recognise, perceive, see.

You know this word, but this doesn't mean you always recognise or act upon it with discernment. *Knowing* you have it isn't the same as *remembering* you have it. We like to tell ourselves we are stuck and have no choice, which effectively disempowers us. This is because those pesky fear challenges get in your way more often than you realise. Once they've made themselves present in your conscious mind, they convince you that making a choice represents something huge, and therefore scary.

There are lots of things in life you genuinely don't have choice over, but the fact is, you DO have control over most of the everyday choices you make. Whether you realise it or not, in every moment, you either consciously make a choice, or you don't; in which case, you have subconsciously chosen NOT to choose. Either way you are making a choice. So you might as well do what you can to make more of your choices conscious ones that *support* you, not unconscious ones that *diminish* you.

The more present and aware you are, the more this is possible.

> *"Everything can be taken from a man but one thing: the last of the human freedoms — to choose one's attitude in any given set of circumstances, to choose one's own way." —*
> *Viktor E. Frankl*

The key to making choices that lead to change, without arousing the suspicions of your subconscious, is to make them very small and approach them with an attitude of play and experimentation. I highly recommend choosing to tell yourself something along these lines as you make moment to moment choices: *'if this is for my highest good it will work out, if not, I will have learned something valuable'*.

You can change these words to ones that sound more like you, but essentially, you want to take the pressure off yourself.

This will pacify your head, because you take away the risk of 'needing to succeed and do well'. Your inner protector will always cajole, worry on your behalf, and lie to you. By keeping your actions small and defining them as being merely 'no risk' experiments, your mind will play so nicely with you that one day you will realise you have achieved what you want, without your head getting in the way.

Right now, you can choose what you tell yourself, whether you listen to your head or your heart, how you respond or react, whether you take action or stay stuck. You can choose to have faith in yourself, to have patience and trust, and to accept that life changes in small steps. In every moment, you can choose a different option. The power lies in your hands. Small step by small step, you can slowly, but surely shift your relationship to life and to yourself. It will happen so subtly, your head will barely notice what's happening, and by the time it does, you will be happily celebrating the day you decided to make the best choice of your life.

Which in the case of Process 1, is to choose YOU... and keep moving forwards in small steps with self-compassion.

Even a slowly dripping tap will fill up a bowl given enough time.

Solution 2: Accept

"I believe that I am not responsible for the meaningfulness or meaninglessness of life, but that I am responsible for what I do with the life I've got." — Hermann Hesse

Acceptance is another well-known word containing infinite amounts of magical power.

I first learned this when I had my second 'inner voice' experience in my late twenties. I was a student radiographer by then and living with my boyfriend, who was a fellow mature student. We were in the middle of an argument over something when I became aware of a sense of déjà vu as I realised I had repeated this scenario many times. It was as though I was watching myself play a role in a film, and a pretty pointless one at that. In that moment, the words I heard from somewhere in my system were: *'The secret to life is acceptance'*.

Those words are so simple and yet also profound. It was another one of those catalyst moments, where I realised how crazy it was for me to waste my energy fighting over something I couldn't control or change. The biggest loser in that scenario was only ever going to be me.

When you accept the things you *cannot* change, you release all the life force energy you used trying to fight them. The same can be said for accepting the things you *can* change, rather than resisting or denying them.

Here is a summary of what you must accept in order to move forwards from your heart, rather than your head:

a. **Accept Possibility**

Accept the possibility that your way up to now might not be working and you might need to change things. This might include giving up your time and energy to distractions such as reality TV or social media feeds. Accept the possibility that small steps slowly change your life, imperfect action is better than none, you are ready for change, and you can do this.

b. **Accept Responsibility**

Accept that you are responsible for yourself. There is no knight coming to save you, because you don't need one. You were born to be response-able. It is in your DNA; you know how to respond in a more healthy, autonomous way to life. You may just have forgotten that once you got absorbed into the Matrix Myth. This is your journey; you are answerable only to yourself.

c. **Accept Inevitability**

Accept that challenges are inevitable when you embark on change; but they don't need to keep you stuck. Accept you will experience the resist-dance and want to run away. As you evolve and learn, old patterns will come up and bring with them emotions. Accept that as you transcend your comfort zones, you will inevitably feel discomfort. It can be useful to identify your emotions as they arise; labelling them and then thanking them for showing you that you are shifting your energy.

d. **Accept Unconventionality**

Accept that to get where you want to go, you must embrace a spiraling journey from your head to your heart that you cannot create in a formulaic way. It will not always make sense, it cannot be predicted or mapped out, and you will not see the way ahead until you reach the next step. This means you can let go of doing things in the 'right way' and take the pressure off.

As Joseph Campbell so wisely wrote: *"If you can see your path laid out in front of you step by step, you know it's not your path. Your own path you make with every step you take. That's why it's your path."*

Solution 3: Pack Your Self-Care Tools

As you learn new concepts, you will inevitably be in your head a lot of the time because that is where you consciously process information. Being in your head where the fear fairies live, can bring up old patterns. Rather than resist these thoughts and give them more energy, apply this solution instead:

Be kind to yourself.

The following list of self-care tools will help; gather the ones you want and put them in your Cape pockets right now:

- The tool of patience.
- The tool of trust.
- The tool of self-compassion.
- The perfection-releasing tool.
- The take it less seriously tool.
- The magical breath focus tool.

As you move through the process, allow yourself to enjoy what you discover. Learning does not have to be serious and you'll take far more in if you're relaxed and open. Let your shoulders go, breathe, and smile!

If you find any of the challenges threatening to take over at any point, your biggest self-care tool is your breath. Pause to breathe deeply and slowly for a moment or two whenever you feel the need… fear is really just excitement without the breath. You'll learn more about that soon, but for now, if you feel fear rising, check whether you're subconsciously holding your breath. Whether you are or not, breathe slowly, deeply, and consciously. It will help.

Solution 4: Identify Your Personal Anti-Procrastination Mantra

As an inevitable part of any new endeavour, your head will try to tempt you away from change with the lure of procrastination treats. In order to be pre-armed against this thinly disguised attempt to keep you stuck and safe, I invite you to create an anti-procrastination mantra. All you need to do is identify a meaningful phrase that empowers you enough to break through your mind's initial attempts to stop you.

It can be anything you like, but it needs to be a phrase that you are prepared to believe might be true, that fires you up when you say it. Something may have popped into your head immediately - if it did, trust it and use it - no matter how it sounds.

My phrase is *'I can and I will, watch me'*.

This is not the most eloquent phrase, but I have never been able to shift it since it appeared in my head. Having reflected on it since I started using it a few years ago, I now realise it represents a prevalent theme in my life. Namely, if you tell me I can't do something, I will prove I can. In younger years, this definitely came from my ego; but these days it comes from me trusting my heart over the opinions of others.

I use this phrase daily when I'm working on anything I find challenging, especially if it means overcoming fear of being seen, showing up, or expanding my comfort zone. It fills me with a sense of internal fire, reminding me my mission is bigger than my fear. Like many of the tools I share, it seems simple; but that doesn't mean it isn't powerful. The trick is using it!

Solution 5: Act

"To go far you must begin near, and the nearest step is the most important one." — *Jiddu Krishnamurti*

Having made a choice to choose you, you must now ACT upon it, because your inner human drive to evolve and seek meaning will not go away.

I've lost count of the number of times clients have told me they will *try* to incorporate something new, or they will *try* to honour their decision to do something different. As someone who has stumbled many times, and seriously contemplated leaving this world, I can categorically state that there is no *try*. Every time I've stumbled I managed to rise and shift myself from being stuck by taking one small action at a time.

Once you have made a conscious choice from your heart to make a change, you WILL find a way to honour it and act upon it. No matter what your circumstances. No matter how scared you are.

If you say you will *try* to do it, the intention will 'sort of' be there, but won't be embedded enough to overcome the resistance that arises when you think about it. You won't make it a priority. Then life will happen, you'll get busy and forget about it until something triggers your memory. Then you'll tell yourself off, use it as evidence you're a flawed human, make excuses and repeat the cycle. At some point, you will likely abandon it altogether.

In the meantime, your life stays the same, nothing changes, and your head says you are not an action taker and you have no willpower. None of this is true, you simply haven't identified a compelling 'why' behind your decision, and you haven't yet learned how to use your brain to optimise your willpower.

Conversely, something magical happens when you take action, especially if approached from the perspective of experimentation, rather than 'must succeed'.

Your mind interprets it as proof that you are brave and determined, and it starts changing the story of being stuck that it tells itself. Over time, as you repeat the pattern of taking action, your mind starts believing you are a courageous warrior, worthy of self-respect. Your confidence increases with every conscious step taken, your comfort zone expands and the self-defeating messages get weaker and weaker, losing their power to keep you stuck.

Action negates fear. Life changes. You learn, explore, experiment, and evolve.

Inaction breeds fear. Life stays the same. You feel stuck, unworthy, as if you have failed.

Life will align for you as you choose to commit to the process. You might not see it at first, but it will. It is simply waiting for you to choose *you* and act.

Once you take your first small step, you have set the wheels into motion. Newton's first law states that an object at rest will stay at rest unless an external force acts upon it. Once the object is in motion, it takes an external force to stop it. You have to work so hard to start, once you do, it is hard to stop. You've built up momentum. Which makes it very easy to build confidence. So easy, it almost seems too good to be true.

Solution 6: Redefine Your Perception Of Goals

"If you deliberately plan on being less than you are capable of being, then I warn you that you'll be unhappy for the rest of your life." — Abraham Maslow

To help you honour your intention to act, what if you could take the pressure off yourself for the next few chapters, by letting go of the traditional idea of meeting goals? You will explore goal-setting approaches at the end, but for now, what if you could let go of any sense that you need to achieve a set of things or you 'have' to do things? What if your only goal throughout this process was to start getting out of your head and more into your body? What if your goal was to get better acquainted with yourself and start making friends with who you discover yourself to be?

Maybe we aren't here on earth to do anything other than fully inhabit ourselves and be who we are. That is elusive enough to occupy us all for an entire lifetime.

Have you ever considered goals from that perspective before? I don't know about you, but to me it feels liberating. If it doesn't feel like that to you, feel free to create your own To-Be goals. No one is watching or judging, so take a moment to indulge your heart.

You are not letting yourself off the hook entirely. That might let your head win; and as something made you pick up this book, that would be a shame. Even if it was only curiosity, there is still always something to learn from everything you come across. You might gain new perspectives, discover inner strength and determination, and even if you only learn what you *don't* like, it is invaluable.

To honour this, in the next section you will find your magical mission, which is a very easy writing exercise. Approach it from the perspective above and you'll find it feels a lot more joyful than if you approached it from your head's desire to tick off goals.

"Your life is an occasion. Rise to it." — Mr Magorium (from the film Mr Magorium's Wonder Emporium.)

You are worth it and in Process 2 you will start believing that even if you don't right now.

Process 1 — Summary For Your Soul:

Your life doesn't magically change overnight, it changes bit by bit and the cumulative effect of those small changes one day adds up to a massive change.

Your desired future lies in the daily small steps you take, and when those steps are in alignment with who you are and what you want, they will powerfully move you towards your dreams.

Your life is lived right now, and today is all you really have. Be present in each moment, delight in each day, be grateful for each breath, and live with awareness, knowing that everything you do is in alignment with your soul.

Walk your pathway mindfully and soon you'll realise that your today has become a place of wonderful potential, of appreciation and inner joy and contentment.

Process 1 Self-Affirmation: I trust and embrace each step.

MAGICAL MISSION — Create Your Declaration Of Promise

You have just discovered lots of information and tools to help you disempower the possible fear-led challenges that could stop you from reaching Process 2. If you are feeling overwhelmed, please know that the easiest way to overcome any of these challenges is simply to *become aware* of them.

When you wear your Cape of Possibility, you magically unfold the power to take the next step. Mainly because even if you don't always believe it, you had the power all along.

Before you move on, I invite you to undertake this magical mission to consolidate your learning, imprint your intentions on your brain, and reinforce your commitment to yourself.

The Declaration of Promise

This is an invitation to create your own declaration of promise – one I highly recommend saying yes to - no matter how many times you have done similar things, or how pointless it might seem.

This is a simple, free-flowing writing exercise, which need not take any more than 5 minutes. In fact, if you take too long doing it, you can be fairly certain your inner perfectionist has taken over.

This isn't about perfect writing or setting up your ideal space; it is about making a promise to yourself. Writing it down will activate the part of your brain responsible for recording important things. This will serve you well later on.

Start by gathering your supplies: you need a pen, paper or your journal, or even a beautiful card if you have one. If you love creating a sense of ritual or ceremony, feel free to add in things you love, like candles, music, flowers, or cosy cushions. This is an occasion to be celebrated; however, make sure you don't get sidetracked by trying to make everything 'just so'.

If you're in a coffee shop, grab your favourite drink. If you're reading this in a park, take a moment to notice the view. If you're on a packed train take a deep breath to centre yourself.

Wherever you are, take a moment to ease your neck, shrug your shoulders and let them go, maybe even have a stretch. Take a couple of slow conscious breaths in and out to drop you out of your head and into your body.

Then ask yourself this question:

If anything were possible, how would you love the next six months to unfold for you?

You are not looking for anything you don't want or anything you want to stop. The idea of this is to identify something you can move toward, rather than something you want to move away from.

Don't think too hard. If you find yourself labouring over an answer, let it go, move about a little and then see if you can identify a feeling you'd like to have instead. Maybe you just want to feel more peaceful, more comfortable in your skin, or happier when you wake up.

If nothing comes up, try asking your brain what it would say if it knew the answer. This is a great way to circumvent your brain's inner perfectionist!

There is no right or wrong answer. No need to judge what comes up and no need to for a 'perfect' answer; the one you 'think' others would understand or a more virtuous one.

Let yourself freely write your response without censorship and see what comes up. You might surprise yourself.

Having identified something (even if only a very small thing!), give yourself permission to spend a moment daydreaming about yourself six months ahead.

What does it look and feel like to be the person you don't yet believe yourself to be? What would the most positive aspects be? Why do those matter to you?

Feel free to write or draw any aspects of this as you see fit. Or not.

With your thoughts and feelings in mind, I invite you write the following Declaration of Promise to yourself, and then sign and date it.

Something powerful I cannot explain happens when you do this… what I know for sure, is you have nothing to lose.

Using either the same page, or a fresh one, write these words:

I, *insert your name* will embrace possibility, stay open, suspend disbelief, and commit to following the Magical Unfolding pathway wherever it takes me. If my vision is meant for me as I see it today, I trust that it will unfold. If not, I trust I will discover a more aligned, fulfilling one.

Finally, sign and date it and inwardly smile at your future self, safe in the knowledge that she is proud of you and who you are already.

Keep this safe to revisit and expand upon later. If your dreams are within, they contain seeds that can be grown by you…. all you have to do to ignite their power is decide to do something different.

And you have just done that. Let the magic unfold…

CHAPTER 5
Process 2 — Motivate Yourself
Own Your Miraculousness

"Do not let your fire go out, spark by irreplaceable spark in the hopeless swamps of the not-quite, the not-yet and the not-at-all. Do not let the hero in your soul perish in lonely frustration for the life you deserved and have never been able to reach. The world you desire can be won. It exists.. it is real.. it is possible.. it's yours." — Ayn Rand

The time has come to motivate yourself by diving a little deeper below the surface.

You met the real you in Part One, but I expect part of you doubted my words, maybe even ridiculed them as you read. That's the part suffering from what I call the Self-Worth Delusion. In this process you are going to start dissolving this delusion with love, before it sabotages you and stomps all over your dreams for yourself.

The Self-Worth Delusion is so sneaky, most of us don't even realise how often it stops us from moving forward, because it has managed to disguise itself as being the ONLY reality. I wouldn't be surprised if you have stopped even noticing the inner voice constantly asking 'who on earth do you think you are', or 'who are you to do this?... because maybe you no longer attempt the kind of change that makes that question appear in the first place.

Without self-worth in place it is almost impossible to honour commitments to yourself, never mind feel motivated. In this process, you will discover how much this delusion limits you and what you can do differently to change it.

One of the biggest issues we all encounter when embarking on anything new is staying motivated long enough to get past the first hard bit. The Motivation Equation, created by a research scientist called Piers Steele, explains this. He discovered that in order for you to follow through on your intentions, two positive factors must be in place and they must be strong enough to outweigh two negative ones.

The equation is $M = E \times V / I \times D$

Motivation = Expectancy x Value, divided by Impulsivity x Delay.

In other words; you have to believe your desired outcome is possible and you are capable of achieving it (expectancy) and you *really* want it (it must have huge value to you). In my experience, in order to truly believe this, you have to value and believe in yourself. Knowing your self-worth helps you stay focussed because you value yourself enough to minimise distractions and not put it off until 'some day' (reducing the impulsivity and delay factors).

The Self-Worth Delusion has the power to stop anyone and everyone in their tracks, no matter what their background or experiences. If you've been brought up in the Western world, you probably started falling under its spell early in life - but this doesn't mean you can't transcend it.

You might be squirming a little or wondering if you can quietly skip this step; but unless you can be 100% confident you won't allow your inner protector to stop you progressing beyond Process 3, I recommend using your Personal Anti-Procrastination Mantra to help you welcome this step with an open heart.

You are wearing your Cape of Possibility. Wouldn't it be wonderful if it was possible for you to exponentially increase your belief that you've been worthy since the day you were born?

To illustrate this, let me share another chapter of my journey with you...

My Story — Looking for Worth in All the Wrong Places

"The most dangerous of our prejudices reign in ourselves against ourselves. To dissolve them is a creative act." — Hugo Von Hoffsmannsthal

It was 1990, and to anyone observing me as a young student nurse, I was respectful, fastidious, compliant, quiet, and shy.

Apart from spending far too long talking to patients, I was easy to train and didn't create any problems. I learned quickly, worked hard, and had common sense. Even though death was something that freaked me out, I learned quickly to hide my reactions and put them somewhere outside myself so I didn't upset Sister.

On the outside I was a model student. Subconsciously, I believed I needed to conform to prove myself worthy. And that if I was regarded as worthy by others in authority, it would mean I actually *was*. A status far outweighing the one I shamefully hid inside, labelled *abject failure who let her parents down, got stoned all the time, and let herself be abused by a man.*

On the inside; however, it was a different story. Inwardly, I was far from the archetypal model student. I was a secret rebel pretending to conform. I remember clearly how soon after taking my leap into 'the promised land', I realised I had made a dreadful mistake. Having overcome so much to get there, this was not a good discovery. (Especially once my ex-boyfriend found me and it felt like it had all been for nothing.)

I had finally put my mistakes behind me, turned the track and started being a respectable adult. I couldn't blow my cover - I had somewhere to live, a clean uniform to wear each day, my own money and regular meals. My proper life had finally started... except it still felt wrong. And for the life of me, I couldn't work out why - after all, hadn't I always wanted to help people? Wasn't that what being a student nurse was all about? How else was I meant to help people when I had no other qualifications?

Yet again, I felt stuck. Except this time, in a web entirely of my own making, and to escape meant risking being judged as a failure. Again. Clearly, I didn't want to add more evidence to back up that fact I had created enough already. Underneath this feeling lay the buried sense I had somehow been cheated. The truth was, being a student nurse appeared to be more about pandering to doctors, cleaning, and doing endless paperwork, than it did about helping people. It also meant doing a LOT of pretending and a lot of smiling. Luckily, I was very good at that.

Back then, student nurses were treated like servants by scary matron-like nurses. We had to mind our manners, do as we were told, and not question the reasons behind anything. We were regularly inspected for clean shoes, clean nails, and having our hair neatly tucked away. This was especially important when doctors did their rounds, or important people appeared - but not so important when handing out drugs to patients. These days I am fairly certain you would call it bullying.

I still remember how cruel some of the nurses were to us when no-one was watching, a bit like a character-building boot camp meant to toughen us up. They probably meant well, after all, how could they know I was already tougher in many ways than most of them could imagine?

I took sneaky opportunities to talk to patients when Sister wasn't looking; because that was the thing I loved doing most. I loved seeing their faces light up when I got them to tell me stories, for a short time they became people again, rather than just powerless patients. I buried my feelings when I got chastised for spending too much time talking to them and hiding my dissent when instructed to do things I fundamentally disagreed with.

I played the game of pretending to be someone else, so I could earn the respect I didn't have inside, from other people who were also putting on an acceptable face. Whether I earned this respect or not, I have no idea. What I do know is it did nothing whatsoever to boost the respect I had for myself. In fact, it totally demotivated me to the point of major depression. Turns out I wasn't such a good actor after all. Pretending is draining and not something you can do long-term.

Inevitably, one day it all became too much, and I started showing weaknesses that ultimately led to me being pensioned off on medical grounds at the grand young age of 20. I lasted 18 months in total. Suffice it to say, failing at my one shot at having a respectable career did nothing to boost my sense of self-worth.

If I'm honest though, as much as I was depressed about everything, there was part of me that was relieved. Not only did someone else make the decision for me—so I didn't have to do anything confrontational—inside I knew nursing was wrong for me and I was squishing myself to fit. At least this meant I could stop bending over backwards to please others. Something I hadn't yet realised was a tricky habit to break.

I now view this as a lucky escape because I was looking for worth in all the wrong places. I thought that by pretending to conform and wearing a respectable facade, I would be deemed worthy and it would make up for my previous failings. At this stage I hadn't realised only I was keeping score. Everyone else was too busy keeping score of themselves.

The Life School has a way of giving us incredible lessons, even if it takes years to realise what they are. In this term of Life School there was an added benefit I haven't mentioned yet: I got free counselling as part of the NHS policy. Of course, I totally refused to attend sessions with anything other than an impenetrable face of strength that gave nothing away; I had 'a thing' about people trying to see inside me. Years later, however, I know these sessions started sowing seeds of self-awareness, for which I will always be grateful.

Maybe you do find your worth on the other side of life's mistakes after all... and maybe our experiences really do teach us valuable lessons.

Head-Led Challenges of Process 2

"Self-worth is not a thing; it is a perception. Just as a gymnast begins a routine with ten points and receives deductions for each mistake, so you began life with a natural, complete sense of worth. (Have you ever met an infant with self-worth issues?) But as you grow, you serve as your own judge, deducting points when you misunderstand the nature of living, and learning—when you forget you are a human-in-training and that making mistakes and having slips of integrity and mediocre moments are a part of life, not unforgivable sins." — Dan Millman

Have you ever wondered where your inner need to keep pushing forwards comes from?

Do you find yourself exhausted some days because despite the fact you're running on empty, you've kept going full-steam anyway?

I bet you've done that thing where you were so busy making sure everyone else was fed, watered, and looked after, you forgot to do the same for yourself.

You probably feel guilty about even considering the possibility that you might want more for yourself and at some level, you berate yourself for not being content to 'just settle'.

Me too.

We all do. We're inherent carers. And it's not entirely our fault. Our DNA carries the energy of survival, nurturing, fear, and the need to prove our worth so that we earn our place. We've been trained to actively avoid being labelled as lazy, so we work hard and avoid play until all the work is done, forgetting that most of the time, the work is never done. Because we will always find more.

We strive to be all things to all people, except ourselves. We settle when we know we shouldn't, because we don't value ourselves enough to say no. We are so busy proving we are worthy by constantly *doing*, we forget how much we benefit from simply *being*. We get so focussed on all the areas in which we lack, we forget to celebrate the things about us that are wonderful.

Like the challenges in Process 1, this is another way our head overrules our heart. And it is endemic in our culture, thanks to the Matrix Myth.

1: The Big But

I have had countless conversations with wise, intelligent, self-aware people who have said things like:

"I love reading, but I feel guilty when I read."

"I feel so much better when I meditate and look after myself, but I just don't do it."

"I feel better when I do things I love, but they always get pushed to the end of the day and then there's no time for them."

Do you notice what each of these quotes have in common?

They start out with a perfectly reasonable positive statement, followed by that innocuous and sneaky word BUT. In each case, the person knows exactly what they want to do *but* something stops them. I bet you can very much relate, I know I can.

You can be fairly certain that whenever the word 'but' sneaks into a sentence, it's about to make an excuse for something you'd like to do; *but* have convinced yourself you cannot do. The reason usually looks logical and entirely reasonable - and perhaps it is - *but* ask yourself why you need to add on the 'but statement' at all.

Subconsciously, you are justifying your unwillingness to prioritise yourself to one part of your brain, using the other part that is stopping you. That part is again the aspect of your brain that wants to keep you safe. This is also where your Self-Worth Delusion lives... which is ultimately what stops you doing things you know are good for you. Your head has got you totally convinced you don't need, want or deserve it. Even if you actually do.

My lovely husband calls this The Big But That Keeps You Stuck.

Is it really surprising that after years of forming the habit of not thinking about your self-care needs until maybe 9pm at night, you now hear a small voice inside whispering: 'What about me?'. That voice is thoroughly fed up with your 'big but' - even if it only whispers to you about it.

The fact is, we are all modern-day warriors in our own way. Fighting everyday battles between what we really *want* to do, and what we feel we *have* to do; even when we're on our knees. Unfortunately, we're rarely taught to recognise the damage we inflict on ourselves, only seeing it when we're physically or mentally breaking.

2: Thinking You Have Failed

The Matrix Myth makes you think you've failed. What makes it worse is you think you're the only one who isn't managing, and this makes you strive even harder to prove your worth. It might not help to know this, but the fact is, you're normal. You're a normal modern-day heroine.

You probably don't fully appreciate this, but the mere fact you're aware enough to know you even HAVE a struggle, never mind want to do something about it, is impressive. Do you have any idea how many people doggedly soldier on, wearing their martyrdom like a badge of honour, and then collapsing as soon as they retire?

You are doing the best you can with the knowledge you have. You balance far more things than your ancestors did on a daily basis. You may not have the same daily struggles your ancestors did. You (hopefully!) have food on the table daily, a washing machine to clean your clothes, a car to drive around in, and the means to get most of the things you truly need, when you need them. In many ways, your life is infinitely easier, but it isn't hard to see why you feel like a failure for not juggling it all *perfectly* and wanting more.

Wanting more or struggling doesn't mean you're unworthy, it means you recognise something isn't working for you.

Unlike your ancestors, you have a gazillion inputs daily. They come at you from all angles and you've been trained since you were small to respond to inputs and filter through them at a faster rate than you know. Your brain is a super-conductor; filtering millions of inputs every single day and if you're getting the crucial stuff done despite that, and still smiling more often than frowning, YOU are pretty amazing.

Your brain hasn't yet evolved at the rate technology has. It's why you have to use your smartphone as your brain storage device! Unfortunately, this doesn't stop your brain trying to make sense of everything that comes at it, and frankly, this is exhausting. No wonder you're too tired to prioritise yourself. Your brain is using up juice every second, just to make sure it keeps track of All The Things.

That's why you have that Superwoman cape. It is the only way you even have a chance of getting through everything, which you have to do, because you need to feel like you matter and you have some control. You also don't really trust anyone else to do it.

It doesn't feel great though does it?

3: You Forget You Are Enough

The Matrix Myth installs an infinite number of misconceptions and misguided beliefs that you're broken and you're not enough (which you're not and yes you are).

You consume more negativity daily than your ancestors were exposed to in a lifetime. You are faced with constant comparisons coming at you from all angles, and our consumer culture thrives on you having self-esteem and self-worth issues. Adverts are always implying you're flawed in some way or you can get better at things; the subtext being that you aren't good enough already. This leads to you subconsciously buying things to make you feel better, more important, and worthy.

It's exceedingly rare to hear the words 'you are enough already, as you are'.

You get so used to filling yourself up with external stuff to shut out the messages saying you're lacking, you leave no time for the inner contemplation that would help you remember your unique magic. You forget to celebrate your wonderful qualities, like love, joy, hope, delight, courage, compassion, empathy, and strength.

Talk to enough people and you'll discover they all believe they are lacking too. I'm pretty sure it underlies the sense of something missing we have in common that drives us all to seek solutions. Maybe what we're actually seeking is a sense of our original self. The self we were born with, the one that gets buried under layers of inherited and acquired myths. Our subconscious drives us to live our life from the belief that we are not enough and that we have to bend to fit in. In my case, my lack of self-worth led to me burning out as a direct result of over-giving from a place of 'lack' and having very few boundaries in place.

We're not truly living when we're in constant productivity, with no boundaries, and it isn't a good example to pass down to new generations.

4: Your Self-Worth Bar

Remember those broken boxes you explored in Part One?

They are responsible for how big your Self-Worth Delusion is, and how high or low your personal Self-Worth Bar is set. This will be set at a level only your subconscious mind knows, if you try to transcend that level without putting your broken boxes down first, you will sabotage yourself without even realising it.

If you are like most people I have met, you are a world-class expert at undermining and criticising yourself. The Self-Worth Bar is responsible for this and any number of self-sabotaging stories you read. It affects many highly successful or famous people; who dive rapidly into free fall and lose everything the minute they have everything they think they want. At some level they feel they are playing a role they don't deserve; not realising what happened is that they exceeded their Self-Worth Bar.

Your mind continuously looks for ways to substantiate its own beliefs, filtering through inputs and throwing out those that aren't relevant. It heightens this activity whenever you look like you might be increasing the level of your Self-Worth Bar. As you already know, it wants to keep you safe so it will seek evidence to back up your lack of belief in your self-worth in the hope that this will stop you. It will look for examples of all the times you failed and present them as proof that you are flawed, so you feel beaten before you begin.

If you desire change because you have low self-esteem, no amount of achievement will feel like enough and it will be hard work because your subconscious knows how you really feel.

How you treat yourself is how you are silently asking the world to treat you...which is why it changes your life when you start treating yourself with love. Choosing to get to know and love myself is how I ended up in a life where I can categorically confirm the truth of this quote:

"Your worst moment in 10 years can be better than your best moment now." — Dan Millman

Heart-Led Solutions for Process 2

"If you think that the key to greater willpower is being harder on yourself, you are not alone. But you are wrong. Study after study shows that self-criticism is consistently associated with less motivation and worse self-control. It is also one of the single biggest predictors of depression, which drains both "I will" power and "I want" power. In contrast, self-compassion—being supportive and kind to yourself, especially in the face of stress and failure—is associated with more motivation and better self-control." — Kelly McGonigal PHD

Well that quote says it all.

We all know willpower is hard to come by and motivation lasts five minutes. If you want to boost them, to stop getting in your own way when you want to make changes, simply be kind to yourself.

This makes sense from a TCM perspective, because willpower (known as Zhi) originates from your Kidney energy. If you've weakened your Kidney energy by pushing yourself and treating yourself badly, your willpower will be lacking and your mind will be easily led astray. If you are kind to yourself and live in a more nurturing way, your Kidney energy gets stronger and your willpower rises. It's all about reducing stress and lowering your adrenaline by being kinder to yourself.

Luckily, you have your set of self-care tools in your Cape of Possibility from Process 1. There is a consistent theme emerging already...

If only it were that simple.

If only I could tell you that you were not born to waste your precious life force on proving your worth and being what you think people want you to be - and as you heard those words, it was enough to change your habitual self-critical patterns into self-compassionate ones. Imagine if from that day forward, you never again told yourself off, apologised when you didn't need to, criticised your own face, swallowed your truth, or put yourself in the dog house for simply being human? If you did, you apologised to yourself for it and then moved on without it impacting your motivation or desire to follow through on what you really want to.

It would be some kind of miracle wouldn't it? A pretty epic one at that, given you're suffering from a normal quirk each of us has to overcome to achieve what we truly want. Instead the conversation happening in your head whenever you're about to do something different, probably looks a little like this:

Day 1 - *'Ooh! A new thing. This sounds great. It's exactly what I was looking for. I bet it's too expensive. Oh no... it isn't - I can afford that. I wonder if I should though. What if it is too hard to fit in?*

10 minutes later - *'I saw it at the perfect time - it was meant to be and will change everything. I can't miss out'* *Clicks shopping cart as buys thing*

Day 2 - *'Ooh! I get to do the new thing today. That's exciting!'* *Smiles as imagines joy of new thing, having not yet thought through logistics of making space in life for it.*

End of day - *'Oops... I forgot about the new thing. Oh well, it's too late now. I'll start tomorrow.'* *Goes to bed disappointed in self, but determined to do thing tomorrow*

Day 3 - *'Today I am going to do the new thing!'* *Actually makes a start on new thing*

Several hours later - *'This new thing is harder than I thought. I'm not sure I can do it. I might need to gather more new things to help me'* *Starts seeking more wisdom to gather from Guru Google*

Day 4 - *'I really ought to do the new thing today'* *does all normal jobs plus several extra ones that are suddenly vital, like emptying out clothes cupboard and cleaning all hard to reach areas*

End of Day - *There's no time to do the new thing now. Why did I do that other stuff? I'm an idiot. I'll never amount to anything. I might as well give up even trying.'* *Spends rest of night beating self-up by dredging up memories to use as evidence of obvious human failings*

Day 5 - *Uses previous 4 days as evidence of inability to achieve anything* *Impetus of new thing gets lost.*

A sorry, but common tale of the everyday battle going on not only in your head, but almost everyone else's. This is because we are all in our heads, thinking about what others think of us, and using various failings as evidence that we are flawed. We then use up our porridge pot of energy, seeking approval in various forms, in order to prove we are worthy, so we can shut up our own heads. Meanwhile our motivation and willpower give up under the weight of such oppression. You can hardly blame them.

In an ironic twist only our clever heads could create, those with the biggest self-worth issues are actually so self-obsessed they fail to notice that on some level they value themselves quite highly. Highly enough to be convinced everyone is watching and judging them and that the entire world has been created to trip them up and mess up their day, because they ARE that important. Those people are unknowingly in the grip of their Ego puppy dog... and he is running around rampant, taking over the show.

When I say 'they', I do of course mean you. And me. We're all in this together - navigating the daily seesaw battle between believing in ourselves and doubting ourselves; which means we get to pool resources and help each other find an easier way through.

Your brain has lured you into fighting with yourself long enough to stay stuck (therefore safe), deplete your energy and forget what it was you wanted to achieve in the first place. After all, if you are as flawed as your head would have you believing, there really isn't much point in trying to change anything. You also haven't got a chance of hearing what your heart wants, because you're so busy dealing with your head.

What you're actually fighting against is two sides of your head. The ongoing battle between your ancient Ego and Inner Critic, with a bit-part played by your evolved, intelligent Inner Champion who barely gets a word in.

Well played, brain. That is one very clever ruse you've got going on. I see what you did there. We're onto you, and we're not playing the game anymore.

The overriding solution to all this madness is just to STOP!

Press pause, get out of your head, stop fighting with yourself, make friends with your ego and inner critic, start living from your heart more consciously and stop believing your thoughts when they tell you lies about your value. You are enough as you are and there is nothing to be gained from denying your own miraculousness.

Every time you engage in battle with your head, you are using your energy destructively against yourself, when you could be using it to focus in a more constructive and positive manner.

So, to interrupt this feedback loop, here is your first solution:

Solution 1: Make Friends with Your Puppy Dog Ego

"Try looking at your mind as a wayward puppy that you are trying to paper train. You don't drop-kick a puppy into the neighbour's yard every time it piddles on the floor. You just keep bringing it back to the newspaper." — Anne Lamott

Imagine what it would be like to stop fighting with yourself all the time, now that you realise how often this happens. How much easier would it feel to make friends with yourself? How much energy would that release? Imagine how much longer your porridge pot of energy would last each day, and what you could do with all that spare energy.

Forget all the definitions and theories you have about the Ego. Put them to one side for now, as I invite you to view your Ego differently. In this case, as a Puppy Dog.

Most puppies just want attention, to be fed and watered, and know they're safe. They are generally soft, loving, and sweet, but also annoying because they cause chaos. They have your back and they want you to have theirs.

Your Ego also just wants to be loved.

It doesn't know the world doesn't revolve around its needs; but luckily you do. Because whether you realise it or not, your Puppy Dog Ego is not the boss of you and it's easier to control than you might think. There is absolutely no point fighting with it, because all that does is make you hate a part of yourself. Hardly a recipe for increasing your sense of self-worth or motivating yourself. Instead, choose to make friends with it and not let it tell you what to do. It can help to name and identify your Puppy Dog Ego. Mine is called Sammy.

He's male, and a labradoodle puppy - intelligent but also quite scatty, bouncy, and wilful!

On the virtual car trip representing your journey through life, you get to take the wheel. You can invite your Puppy Dog Ego to sit in the back and behave nicely, alongside your inner critic (see below!). When it plays up or gets too noisy, you can choose to take it for a walk; something that gets your body moving. This shifts your energy out of your head, which is where the Puppy Dog Ego hangs out.

How would this help you in a real-life scenario?

Imagine you're driving in traffic, Puppy Dog Ego right beside you, when a car driver in a hurry cuts you off. Your immediate reaction is probably to express something we will politely name 'distaste'. Note the use of the word immediate, that's your Puppy Dog Ego rearing up and baring its teeth to protect you. There is no thought, only a reaction.

Now imagine the same scenario, but with your Puppy Dog Ego sitting in the back seat. You feel the same instant rising indignation; but as soon as it starts to rise, you notice your Puppy Dog Ego trying to take over, and rather than let it spoil your day with angry thoughts about the injustice, you choose a different response. You think something like: *that man is in a hurry. Maybe he's rushing to see someone in hospital.* That thought might not be true, but it doesn't really matter; because you have saved your day from getting railroaded by a random incident that the other person dismissed the moment it happened.

It doesn't matter whether it was fair or not, what matters is you *responded* rather than *reacted*. As a result, you didn't let your Puppy Dog Ego dictate your day by keeping your focus on feeling aggrieved. This kind of Ego reframe also helps you stay more positive because you are appreciative that you are not in the same situation as the person in a hurry.

Solution 2: Make Peace with Your Inner Critic

I have already made a case for befriending your Puppy Dog Ego, and everything I shared above can also be applied to your inner critic. We all have one and it *will* have its say because, like your ego, your inner citric wants to protect you; by ensuring you don't go getting ideas above your station and changing too many aspects of your life.

Earlier in this chapter, I wrote that you can transcend this without causing your inner protector and critic to rise up and stop you; the way to do that is to make peace with them. Welcome them into the fold, wrap your arms around them, and thank them for trying to keep you safe. For bonus points, you can treat them lovingly too, even if that takes a while. Once I realised (with the help of a lovely coach called Saskia), that my inner critic was my ally and not my enemy, my whole relationship with this aspect of myself changed.

Rather than get frustrated with myself and beat myself up for failing to follow through on something for the millionth time, I now stop to ask my inner critic what its concerns are. This doesn't mean I have to believe the response or act upon it, it means I no longer expend my energy resisting a voice that will come through anyway, regardless of whether I want it to. Instead, I accept it, and am getting really good at making peace with it. I don't always like what she says, but at least I recognise when the inner voice is her, not *me* and this is life-changing.

My inner critic has a name, it's Tina the Tyrant. No offence to anyone named Tina; it is what popped into my head when

I first started consciously connecting to her energy. You can name your inner critic too, I find it gives mine less power and helps me view her with more compassion and acceptance. She only wants the best for me after all.

This might sound like mind games and nonsense, but aren't you letting your life be derailed by the games your mind plays with you anyway? You might as well become a player, rather than be played. You would be amazed how much it empowers you and stops you from feeling like a failure, held hostage by your own head.

Try to catch your inner critic in the act the next time you hear that voice say 'who do you think you are'. Rather than resisting or pushing the voice away, answer it truthfully with your name and maybe ask your inner critic what his or her name is; it might be the opposite sex to you. In my case, she's definitely female and my Ego is male, make of that what you will! Like anything else I suggest, don't try too hard and don't underestimate your capacity to know exactly how best to change your relationship to this side of your head! Again, it starts with awareness. Trust your instincts.

Solution 3: Play 'The Brain Game'

You may well be wondering why I am advocating these seemingly childish solutions? (Unless you're a bit like me, and never let your child side go; in which case you will love them!) I offer them because no matter what your experience or knowledge of mindset strategies, they are easy concepts to understand; which means as you play with using them, you are less likely to be up in your head and to worry your inner protector.

When I started my student nurse training, I was taught that the brain was fairly fixed, and that different areas had specific roles. This meant we had little flexibility in terms of how we could impact our brains; however, neuroscientists now know that our brains have neuroplasticity, so we can literally shape and rewire our brains with the power of emotion and our attention.

This means, if you learn how to play the brain game, you can exponentially shift your life. It comes with a caveat though: your brain is the same as any other muscle - if you don't introduce new movement or you keep using it in the same old way, you reinforce the old patterns and they become harder to shift. When you start making changes, it can feel unnatural and uncomfortable in the beginning. Once the new pattern becomes more familiar it creates new pathways and neural connections, making your new thought patterns easier and more intuitive. Over time, you can *literally* re-wire your brain and create a more fully expressed version of you. Turns out you have far more power than you might think, and it starts with changing your thoughts and how you talk to yourself.

The first two solutions help you play the brain game, and you can also try this one:

The Victim to Heroine Readjustment:

You know those times when you get caught up in an immovable line of traffic, with nowhere to go and no choices to make? It is almost always because there is an accident. What is your default response to this? Does it vary depending upon the situation, or is it fixed?

It isn't a fun scenario and at times it can be scary and very frustrating. Especially when your bladder starts filling… however, you are here reading this, which means you got through it. So far, you have a 100% success rate in coming out on the other side. Which means you have nothing to lose and perhaps plenty to gain by recognising you do in fact, have a choice.

That choice lies in how you respond— as Viktor Frankl said, no one can take that away from you.

Victim Mode

You can be reactive and tell yourself this always happens to you, you are cursed, you're an idiot for choosing this route, you should have left earlier, and the world will end because you'll be late. You can then choose to let your head run through the entire chain of events that being late will set off. None of which you can do anything about right now - because you of course, are stuck in traffic… even if your head has already gone to live in the future - where your boss/ partner/ friend hates you for being late and you've been fired or dumped.

Heroine Mode

You can be responsive and choose to be thankful for the fact that right now, you're not the one who is caught up in an accident ahead of you, quite possibly fighting for their life, or having a much worse day than you for any number of reasons. You appreciate the fact that even though you're stuck in a traffic jam, you are intact and can choose to look at the view around you. It might be inconvenient and mess up your day, but you know it won't change anything if you focus on that, so instead you surrender to the situation. It's just one of those things, and no one can blame you for being late. If they do, you'll deal with that when it happens.

Which would you rather choose? Which feels easier or harder to you?

What do these two scenarios tell you about your default responses and how can you start changing them to be kinder to yourself and others?

This is a process of gentle self-enquiry and navigation. An adventure into greater awareness and expression, simple step by simple step.

Process 2 — Summary for Your Soul:

You are a small miracle of creation growing and evolving daily alongside other small miracle in a world that is the biggest, wondrous miracle of all.

You started out as I did – egg meets sperm. Two completely separate, minute, cellular entities that when combined, miraculously contained all the information required for you to grow from a single cell into magnificent you.

Can you imagine how much energy it took for that process to occur? How much life force and sheer will from the Universe it took for you to be here? It's truly a miracle. I've worked in Obstetrics, I know the statistics and it is barely conceivable that any of us make it through the first cell division, never mind beyond it!

You are miraculous. You are a wonderful example of human evolution. You earned your place.

Now take it and be proud of who you are.

Process 2 Self Affirmation: I honour the miracle that is me.

Magical Mission — The Self-Worth Booster

"The most important kind of freedom is to be what you really are. You trade in your reality for a role. You trade in your sense for an act. You give up your ability to feel, and in exchange, put on a mask. There can't be any large-scale revolution until there's a personal revolution, on an individual level. It's got to happen inside first." — Jim Morrison

Your magical mission for Process 2 is simple. All the best solutions are. Before I share it, I want to remind you that there are no flaws unless you perceive them with warped eyes. You don't have inabilities, you have skills you have yet to learn. There are no failures, only experiments and lessons.

You're here once. What makes you who you are is what others love about you. By all means strive to be the best version of you, endeavour to learn, grow, and evolve. Honour your ancestors by reaching your potential; but don't let your Puppy Dog Ego hold you to impossible standards, or let your inner critic beat you up because you're not 'there' yet. As you know, the Land of There is an illusion... let it go.

Here is your Magical Mission focus to motivate yourself and boost your self-worth:

Part 1: Grab your journal and a pen for this quick exercise:

Without over thinking or analysing it, I invite you to rate your current level of self-worth out of 10. The immediate number that pops into your head is the one you write down in your journal, along with today's date.

Let go of any judgement about your immediate answer.

Whatever the answer, pause and then ask yourself this question: *'Why didn't I pick a lower number'?*

Give your brain a moment whilst it searches for positive things to tell you, it loves answering questions. Write down anything your instincts tell you to write, again without judgement. *(If your number was zero, ask yourself what you can do to take it to one.)*

Part 2: The action-taking bit:

When you wake up, start each day with a short, positive statement about yourself from the answers your brain gave you. An example could be: *"I am kind to other people"*

Then when you get into the shower or bath each day, write the words: I AM ENOUGH either in the water on the enclosure, or in the steam in the mirror. As you write it, say these words inwardly to yourself and notice how it makes you feel.

Repeat this daily, for as long as you remember and it feels good for you, if you do, over time, you'll rewire this belief into not just your brain, but your whole being.

It seems simple, but I have seen how impactful this has been for me and my clients.

Part 3: The review:

Set a date in your diary for six weeks' time to rate your level of self-worth honestly again. As before, note your answer and ask your brain why the answer wasn't lower.

If you repeat this process every six weeks as you continue to adopt other processes in this book, you will be astonished how the number increases. Not because your Ego is running rampant, but because you know, deep in your gut, that you are a miraculous soul, with an incredible amount to offer the world.

"To be beautiful means to be yourself. You don't need to be accepted by others. You need to accept yourself." — Thich Nhat Hanh

CHAPTER 6
Process 3 — Assess Yourself
Embrace Your Uniqueness

*"The moon does not fight. It attacks no one. It does not
worry. It does not try to crush others. It keeps to its course,
but by its very nature, it gently influences. What other
body could pull an entire ocean from shore to shore? The
moon is faithful to its nature and its power is never
diminished." — Deng Ming-Dao*

Who Am I?

That is great existential question that has confounded
mankind since time immemorial.

As babies we naturally learn through discovery, growth,
and play. As we make sense of our world, we gain better sense
of ourselves. We desire validation, information, connection,
belonging and understanding. We want the safety of
knowledge; to discover our purpose and work out why we
matter and how we fit in. We do psychometric tests, read
astrology, gather data, and draw conclusions, trying our best to
choose the most appropriate path.

And yet, still we change and evolve... making it impossible
to ever pin ourselves down. And so the endless search
continues. That sense of seeking 'something', even though we
have no idea what that something is.

How much inner stillness would you derive from the simple acceptance that you're nuanced, unique, flawless, and divinely expansive? That you will always seek understanding and what you discover and conclude will shift and change with the seasons of your life?

This process aims to help you do exactly that.

You are about to embark on a personal treasure hunt, where you will start unpacking your broken box, forgiving the past and making peace with where you are right now. This helps you continue your journey onward with a clean slate; so that rather than using your life force energy up trying to fill holes that don't exist, or find the perfect place to start, you accept that where you are right now is perfect, as is the person you already are.

Gather your self-care tools and take a few slow luxurious breaths, whilst I assuage your inner protector with a story.

My Story — Honouring My Head and Breaking My Heart

"The great epochs of our life come when we gain the courage to rechristen our evil as what is best in us." —
Friedrich Nietzsche

Confession: my name is Helen and I am a seeker.

I always have been and always will be. You have no idea how hard it is for me to share that, because I used to do anything I could to avoid that label and to be honest, I am still making peace with it to this day.

In my head, the word seeker comes with an invisible boot-load of undesirable attachments. Words with negative connotations; like needy, messed-up, lost, difficult and damaged. Words that make me squirm and want to run away because that was exactly how I used to view myself. I was so ashamed of my past, I wanted nothing more than to distance myself from my old self as fast as possible. Which is why I ended up following my head, in a misguided attempt to negate my previous 'undesirable' self and in the process broke my own heart.

After leaving my non-successful nursing career before I even finished the training, my life went through a somewhat unconventional 'interesting' stage I now call the wilderness years. During that time, I met some great and not so great people, had a lot of fun, toughened up, learned more about love, lost months, lost several people too young, lost myself, and then found myself again.

To some extent anyway.

I remember quite clearly the day I decided to leave behind the wilderness years and change the trajectory of my life. When I say decided, I mean 'nudged'.

I was in my early 20s and worked as an administrative assistant on one of East Anglia's biggest construction sites. I was one of only three women working in a company comprised of tough, burly blokes from Newcastle and one of the few women across the whole site. Initially this was intimidating, but I was used to being around bikers and held my own with no problems. We all looked out for each other, as we worked stupidly long hours and most of the men only got to visit home every few weeks.

I had some great friends there and was treated like an errant daughter by my boss. He was one of those knowing people who could see right through you and every now and then he would try talking to me about my life plans. I worked hard and could do my job with my eyes shut and he knew I was coasting through life. I knew it too, but there was no way I was admitting it out loud; I could barely admit it to myself.

Then the day came when a strange inner voice I had never heard before, totally freaked me out by asking me something I didn't want to hear. Yes - *that* question:

'Would you feel cheated if you died tomorrow?'

Having just lost a young friend to cancer I would be lying if I said I wasn't thinking about my own mortality. I knew there was more to me than I was showing the world and this inconvenient question brought me face to face with that, because I knew immediately the answer was yes.

Once you hear that yes, you can't un-hear it.

To be honest, the main emotion I remember aside from anger, was guilt. I felt guilty that I had been gifted a brain and I wasn't really using it. I felt guilty about the lifestyle I was living and about some of the choices I had made. There was a big part of me looking to make up for having made so many mistakes, and this part of me stepped in to make some sensible, logical decisions.

I didn't know what to do next, but I knew I had to do something before I wasted my life away. The nursing path had failed and I felt like I should get a good degree to make up for messing up at school. That seemed to be the acceptable thing that gave one status in society and I didn't really know what else to do.

The moment I decided this, I knew in my heart I really wanted to do an English degree.

I had always loved reading and writing and it was the one subject I always did well in, even when I thought I had written utter rubbish. One of my English teachers used to take me aside to praise me at school and encourage me to write more, but at the time I was in the self-destructive phase and I thought she was just trying to make me feel better about myself.

My logical head said I needed to do something vocational, as by this time I was 24 and before I could do a degree I would need to do an Access course to make up for my lack of school qualifications. That meant by the time I finished my degree I would be 28; therefore, my head said I needed to do something that would guarantee a job so I could support myself.

I don't remember anyone, including me, backing the idea of me indulging my dreams by choosing the English degree. Why would they? It was selfish and 'apparently' not what people did unless they wanted to become a teacher. I knew I had no desire whatsoever to do that, why would I want to deal with kids who were like me!

This was life before Google and the digital age. The sensible choices available to single 'late starters' were few and far between. So I chose to do something else related to helping people, with a bit more autonomy. The company I worked in used radiography to test structures and somehow the idea of doing a Radiography degree was born.

It was the perfect solution. It would make my parents happy. I was likely to get a job at the end, I got to start again and make up for all the mistakes I had made. Best of all, no one in my new life had to know how much of a mess I had made of my old life. Yet again, I chose the path of reinvention, believing I could disown the previous aspects of myself I was ashamed of and ignore my heart. I didn't know that then that broken hearts only mend when you stop lying to yourself and make peace with your past. Which is why I now sometimes use the word *seeker* instead of my preferred words *curious soul* to describe my insatiable thirst for knowledge and self-actualisation.

Curiosity got me to this place in life and will never leave me, but the seeker in me honoured the curiosity and followed the path.

The question is, where has your seeker led you? Where would it like you to head next? Will you follow it?

Head-Led Challenges of Process 3

"Confront the dark parts of yourself, and work to banish them with illumination and forgiveness. Your willingness to wrestle with your demons will cause your angels to sing." — August Wilson

In Processes 1 and 2 you pre-armed yourself with vital magical mindset tools such as self-kindness, awareness, understanding, patience, and the Self-Worth Booster. These will keep serving you well throughout every step of the MAGICAL process. They are especially useful to have with you for this next step as you take a closer look inside your Broken Box.

Once you have reclaimed the power held by your Broken Box, you can start using it as a force for good, rather than a force that keeps you stuck. Remember, energy flows where your attention goes; once you realise how much of your energy and attention is wasted dealing with these challenges, it empowers you to use it more constructively.

The further along the Bridge you walk, the better equipped you become for the next lot of challenges. Ultimately, they all come down to the same thing: navigating the battle between opposing parts - not only of yourself, but also with the Matrix Myth.

Here is how they might present in relation to the purpose of this step, which is assessing yourself so that you can start embracing your uniqueness:

1. The Shame Illusion

Until now it's highly likely you have subconsciously selected the 'bits' of you that match the story of yourself you want to be true, and you've shown the outside world only that which you felt worthy of showing.

You have pretended that the rest didn't exist, that your shadows weren't there, and that eradicating the bits you didn't like was the best way forward. You may have blotted out bits of your history, hidden your stories of failure, failed to mention aspects of your character and exaggerated your achievements. You have done this because you feel ashamed at some level. Which happens because the Shame Illusion has us believing no one ever messes up and if you show up as you are (warts and all) you will be ostracised from society.

There are very few of us who haven't fallen for this illusion to some degree; even if it is doing something as small as changing dates on your CV to demonstrate you're reliable. The way the Shame Illusion shows up is subtle; so much so, sometimes we barely realise we're doing anything at all. Which is where the Shame Illusion gets all its power. Slowly and stealthily over time, it sucks up your shame and puts it all in a cupboard, that you then have to use up your energy to keep shut.

You might think that selectively papering over the cracks of your life history does no harm - after all, it isn't as though you're deliberately lying – it's more like being inventive with the truth. The trouble is that negative emotions such as shame compress your system, squashing all the joy and expression from you. They eat away at your emotions and have you believing you have things to hide, when in reality, showing up in your real human outfit sets you free and gives others permission to show up fully too.

2. The Broken Box Delusion

You have already started to view your broken boxes differently and may have even stepped away from them already. This delusion is so ingrained; however, that it's well worth reviewing briefly here. Feel free to pause and revisit Chapter 2 if you want a more thorough recap.

The Broken Box Delusion makes you diminish yourself to stay safe and do your best to fit into a certain image of how you 'should' be, so you don't stand out. Your inner safety committee has helped you build walls out of your delusions, so that you can keep them safely wrapped around you to hide the real you. Your broken box keeps you very busy holding onto misguided beliefs, justifying yourself with erroneous society rules and feeling vindicated when your Ego proves you're right about something you think you know to be true.

Whilst all these things make you feel safer, the walls that protect you also hold you back from showing up fully and honouring your buried dreams. This means you struggle to feel deeply content because you cannot feel deep inner fulfilment whilst there are aspects of yourself you disapprove of, hide or disown. You struggle to feel peaceful because you battle with aspects of yourself, trying to hide your inner knowing and escape your busy head.

Without realising it, you've already started unpacking your broken boxes by becoming aware of the delusions and lies your mind uses to keep you occupied.

3. Feeling Like An Outlier

You may think you are the only person who feels the way you do, the only one who can possibly understand all you've been through, and the only one struggling with aspects of your life. This challenge is very different to the Victim Complex, where you feel like the world is out to get you. This is more about feeling as though you're standing on the edge of life looking in, or you were born into the wrong time, place, sex, or family.

In short, you feel misunderstood and isolated.

I hate to break it to you, but this is yet another one of those lies your head has you believing, which effectively keeps you stuck. After all, how can anyone help you shift if no one understands what it is like to live in your head? It serves as a very useful reason to stay as you are, even if you feel unfulfilled.

This challenge can be so effective at convincing us no one else feels like we do, we make the mistake of never telling anyone about it in case we're labelled 'weird'. We'll do anything to avoid getting this label, because when we do, our head starts doing cartwheels in an effort to reboot and act like a normal person who can fit in, rather than be ostracised.

I've felt like this my entire life. It was only when I started showing more vulnerability and having honest conversations that I discovered I was not alone in feeling like this. In fact, the more open and honest I have become with others the more this feeling has dissipated, as I have realised it is a shared experience.

When we come together to share our challenges, we connect heart-to-heart with other souls, shifting us out of our own heads. It is pretty hard to let your head terrorise you when you're busy doing something nourishing. Like all the challenges, we have to accept that this one is made worse when we perpetuate it by thinking about it, because this gives it more power.

In a sense we *are* all alone in terms of what happens in our heads and this can terrify us. Ironically, we fail to recognise that in keeping ourselves so busy we avoid facing this fear; we don't access our intuition that is trying to tell us how imperfectly perfect we are.

Heart-Led Solutions for Process 3

"It takes courage to grow up and become who you really are." — *E. E. Cummings*

What would it be like to release the idea that the things you struggle with show that you're somehow not enough, or you haven't earned the right to fully express yourself?

How would it be to re-establish a peaceful relationship with yourself and with the world around you? To restore your sense of self-worth, show up for yourself and treat yourself like the precious powerful soul you are?

Can you imagine a life where you don't apologise when there's no need to, where you speak when you want to, and where you know deep in your bones that you ARE enough in all your uniqueness? It's a rebellion of sorts, a gentle loving rejection of your Broken Box and a reassessment of who you really are. And it feels liberating!

The following solutions help you to come back home to yourself, to embrace your unique qualities and experiences and set yourself free from the myth that they are weaknesses. They are not weaknesses, they are your strengths, what makes you who you are, and it's time to acknowledge that because therein lies your power.

Solution 1: Remember Who You Really Are

If you were standing in front of me, what I would see is a miraculous fellow human being, full of life and potential, with beautiful hard-earned scars of adversity, incredible lessons learned, tough challenges overcome, interesting stories to tell, unique skills and talents, your own insightful perceptions, and a face full of character, courage, and love.

I would see your uniqueness and vulnerability, how your eyes sparkle when you talk about something you love and deep inner strength you barely know you have. I would see someone with generosity, love, and wisdom at their core. A truly extraordinary, once in a lifetime, wonderful soul, who deserves to feel happy for no reason other than that they are here.

I would want you to see this too. Because all this is true. And I want nothing more than for you to feel the truth of this in your heart, and once you've felt it, never let it go.

Seeing and claiming all that you are, without judgement, shame or censoring, is one of the fast-track routes to feeling deeply happy to your very core. It creates a state of grace and alignment, an inner peace and contentment and a deep knowing that you came here to fulfil a purpose and you deserve to take your space in the world.

My dream for you is that you feel the truth of these statements deeply within your heart and soul, and that you revisit them daily until you begin to believe and embody them in all aspects of your life. Because loving all aspects of yourself is truly the path to liberating your inner peace, potential, and purpose, and there is no better time to start than right now.

Solution 2: Make Peace with All Aspects of Yourself

Generally, what you really mean when you say you want to become a new version of yourself is that you want to feel better about yourself and your life. This usually stems from an underlying sense that you are somehow not enough, and that the only way for you to become whole is to become something 'more' than you are now. Rather than realising you would be better served by stripping layers away to reveal your beautiful core self underneath, you use up your porridge pot of energy trying to build a new shiny exterior instead.

After spending years searching externally for my true self, I finally realised it was sneakily hiding inside me all along. I hadn't registered this before, because I was so focused on trying to hide or improve the parts of myself I disliked and was ashamed of. Based on countless conversations with beautiful souls who could not see themselves as I saw them, I know this is very common.

If you truly want to feel peace in your life, you have to first make peace with yourself. Not just the parts you like and are proud of, but *all* aspects of you. The good, the not so good, the flawed, and the fancy.

This includes making peace with your past, drawing a line under it, letting it go and moving on. The only person you harm by holding onto it is yourself, and how much healthier would it be for you to reclaim that energy and use it to build yourself a brighter today?

Everyone has a story to tell and that's what makes us all interesting and unique. Your story is important to you and it forms who you are, where you've come from, and how you got to where you are now; however, if you become too attached to using it to tell yourself off and hide behind, you have very little chance of moving on in your life.

"I don't regret the painful times; I bare my scars as if they were medals." — Paulo Coelho

All you are now is directly because of all you have been. The person you were got you through it all and brought you to this point. Embrace that truth, welcome all parts of yourself home. Get to know all aspects of you and surround them with love and acceptance. That sense of love will eventually send a wave of peace through all the pains, trauma, and failures, so that they fall away when they are ready, revealing your flawless blueprint inside.

When you have made peace with yourself, your inner critic will struggle to use your own history against you. Can you imagine no longer being triggered or sabotaged by her?

You don't need a new you. You simply need to re-integrate all parts of yourself.

Start doing that today with one small gesture of peace towards something from your past you struggle with and prepare to rewrite your story with a new, positive one you'll want to shout about from the rooftops.

Solution 3: Learn to Love Your Inner Cast of Characters

I mentioned earlier that in TCM theory, all your organs have their own distinct spiritual aspects and characters, which are said to impact your inner and outer world. Psychologists use different words and theories to describe the forces controlling your brain and habits; but essentially both agree that we are at the behest of different characters that rule our world, if we let them.

Have you ever had that experience when your head is so crowded, busy, and noisy that you would do anything to take a pill and go straight to sleep for several hours, just to get some peace?

At times we all feel like there is a party going on in our head, to which we're not invited. **Whether we realise it or not**, when we have these annoying moments, there is a gift in them. That gift is *the realisation that we are not the noise in our head*, we are a separate consciousness that becomes aware of, and irritated by our noisy head. This knowledge is power, because we can use it to better manage the noise-makers.

You have already met the Stress Siren, your Puppy Dog Ego, and your Inner Critic. Accompanying these are your Fear Fairies, Negative Nancy, Comparison Annie, the Worry Whirring Monsters, and the Scenario-Building Police. I doubt any of them need explaining further, and I bet you can introduce some extra ones of your own.

These characters all live in your head and as well as trying to keep you safe by lying to you about yourself and others, they also tie your energy up in knots or scatter it around your body, so you can't use it to make changes. No wonder you get tired and it is so busy in your head. You are using your energy and time trying to manage your disparate characters and corral them into some kind of order.

It isn't going to happen because your inner characters will have their say, and they will whisper things to you that make you think negatively about yourself. They are often referred to as your shadow side and the default response, once you're aware of them, is to try to fight them. As I established earlier, all this does is make you direct negative energy at yourself, and it gives the characters more fuel.

The more empowered approach is to accept that these characters will always be part of you. Without them you wouldn't be you so embrace and accept them. Rather than fight fire with fire, and try to quiet them, criticise or tell yourself off; meet and greet your inner characters. Bring them into the fold and surround them with love.

The simplest way to put this into action is to:

- Train yourself to notice when a negative, critical or fear thought sneaks in.

- When you notice the thought, there is a momentary pause where you can choose whether to react or respond, and this is where you yield your power.

- Rather than reacting by telling yourself off, instead choose an empowered response; such as something along the lines of 'thank you for sharing your insights with me, but I've got this, so feel free to quietly disagree. If you want to stay, please sit at the back of the room.'

The more present you are, the more you'll be able to do this. The more you do this, the more thoughts you'll catch in the act. The more thoughts you catch in the act, the less negatively you'll regard yourself. The less negatively you regard yourself, the more you'll accept all aspects of you.

Solution 4: Dive Deeply into The Mud

"The lotus flower blooms most beautifully from the deepest and thickest mud." — Buddhist proverb

When I started working 1-to-1 with clients as a Shiatsu therapist, I used a lotus as my logo. I kept that symbol through the next two iterations of my business. I chose the lotus because I learned how fundamental the messy muddy parts of our life are for our growth and later blossoming. The very same mud that we have to fight our way through to become who we were born to be, is what gives us strong roots.

We have to learn to love our mud because it's part of us.

If we want to understand who we are underneath the layers, we have to peel them away and dive deeply into the mud to find our roots. That is effectively what I helped others do throughout my years of hands-on bodywork and yoga sessions, and it's one of the things that links together every modality I have learned.

Resist this as much as you like, but there is treasure buried in your roots. That treasure is what inspires and informs you, because it represents your original core self.

When you start diving into the mud you can look for clues into what shaped you, gave you your values and positive qualities and made you who you are. You can dig deeper to work out why you do certain things, what drives you, and what you feel triggered, angered, or excited by.

Play with this right now by thinking of something that makes you feel deep in*dig*nation…

Dig a little deeper…

What lies under that feeling?

Dig deeper again and ask yourself what lies underneath the feeling.

Repeat several times over until you get to the cause; the core truth.

It will be there… keep digging.

Your mud will serve you more when, rather than burying it, you bring it out into the light to see it because then you can make peace with it and thank it for giving you strong, deep roots.

Solution 5: Learn to Dance With Fear

Yes, I am mentioning fear again. I share it again here because it is one of the key sticking points that will repeatedly come up as you assess yourself and embrace all that you are. The thing about fear is when you start to understand and reframe it, you can transform it to use its energy as fuel, which is why it offers you a solution as well as a challenge.

In TCM terms, no emotions are good or bad, they are just different manifestations of energy and are essential for moving the emotion through your system. Each emotion has a different physiological effect on your system, and as they move on, a state of balance momentarily returns. There is a constant flow, yin and yang energies circling in an endless dance to maintain equilibrium.

Our problem with fear is we think of it negatively, so we try to fight it and stop it in its tracks. In modern life; however, fear often sends us a false signal, which is summed up well by the common phrase 'FEAR is False Evidence Appearing Real'.

When we use up our energy trying to stop fear, it's exhausting, because the physiological response takes a while to stop and reverse. It is a myth that you can convince yourself you are calm when you're not. You can tell yourself that, but it won't make the adrenaline disperse any faster.

Instead of trying to fight the rising yang fear on its own terms, meet it with the softer, yin energies of love and acceptance. Instead of fighting the physiological adrenaline response in your system, turn it around in your favour by re-labelling it as excitement. As you do this, breathe mindfully and keep telling yourself you aren't scared, you're excited.

Do this often enough and you will stop labelling your fear response as a negative aspect of your character. When you reframe fear and use it to fuel your excitement, you will see yourself as the courageous soul you really are.

Solution 6: Show up and Share Who You Are

It's incredible what can happen when you get brave and commit to taking small steps toward openness and vulnerability. You allow all the assumptions about who you think you should be to fall away and instead, you step bravely into who and what you are. If you do that from the perspective of sharing it with others, it no longer becomes about you. This can be enough to free up a level of self-assurance you never knew you had.

No matter where you are on your life path, your greatest power lies in starting where you are and showing up as you, whilst you take the next small step forward. If you could find it within you to share your journey honestly with another soul, unencumbered by justification, excuses or apologies, you would soon find that sense of self you've been looking for.

The aim of any self-development journey is not to selectively show the best bits of yourself to the world, but to embrace and harmonise all of you, so that others find the courage to do the same.

Imagine a world where those around you no longer felt they needed to wear masks or be ashamed of the path they have walked. Where no one judged you for the way you look, sound, move, or interact. If they did, you were so grounded in the truth of who you are, it would be irrelevant to you. Not because you feel superior, because you recognise they're a step behind you on the same path.

Everything that makes up who you are is part of the same energy making up this world. It makes no sense to pick and choose and treat some bits differently to others. By all means be selective in what you disclose - but do so in a healthy way - not from shame, but from a place of authenticity, integrity, and a desire to honour yourself and others.

Important Note...

Whichever of these solutions you choose, know they are best taken one small step at a time toward better embracing your true self.

The process of working with these solutions may take a long time, and with some of these steps, you may find you need a helping hand from a therapist, coach, bodyworker or movement-based teacher. If that's your instinct, honour it.

There is no right or wrong.

Your Magical Mission for Process 3 takes you on a deeper dive to assessing your uniqueness. Remember to embrace all your inner characters before you start. Welcome them along for the ride, but make them sit in the back whilst you take the wheel and drive.

Process 3 – Summary for Your Soul:

You were born with your own unique perspective, your own skillset, your inherent constitution and a totally unique blueprint.

Your unique blueprint represents your wonderful soul… as well as containing all the information related to your life purpose.

All your natural gifts, skills, insights, flaws, weaknesses, and strengths stem from your blueprint – and it is utterly beautiful in its rarity.

Your blueprint is as rare as your unique fingerprint and it will only appear in its current manifestation this one time.

Embrace your uniqueness, trust your inner knowing, follow your heart and live the life you want to live. No one else will ever be able to contribute to this world in quite the same way as you. Only you can share your unique gifts, because there will never be another you. You are truly amazing.

Process 3 Self-Affirmation: I truly embrace my uniqueness.

Magical Mission — The Treasure Hunt with a Difference

"And I said to my body. Softly. 'I want to be your friend.' it took a long breath. And replied 'I have been waiting my whole life for this.' " — *Nayyirah Waheed*

Who is it you think you have to be to become the person you think you want to be?

What if you could detach from that for a while and instead, reconnect to who you are right now?

Your Magical Mission for this process, should you accept it, is to embark on a journey to identify which areas of your life are currently calling to you to be realigned or energised. This mission offers an opportunity to simply notice how you feel, rather than think about what you need. Noticing your feelings ensures none of your cast of characters are feeding you erroneous information and takes away any sense of needing to get things right.

A Word of Caution:

Let go of any sense of needing answers, don't worry if you can't feel much at all. This is a fairly brief exercise and you can make it as simple as you like. Be curious and open to discovery. You should read through the whole focus first, and then go through it step by step. ◀

https://www.helenrebello.com/p/MagicBookResources

Your Treasure Hunt with a Difference

You are going to slowly scan your body, starting with your feet and working up toward your head, mentally answering some questions as you go. As before, write down the immediate answers that come to you - otherwise your mind is telling you what it wants you to hear!

Grab your journal and a pen. Before you begin, take a few moments to move your whole body in whatever way you want to - maybe give your limbs a shake, stamp your feet, or jump up and down. *Don't skip the movement! It helps you get back into your body where your feelings like to hang out.*

I invite you now to sit down with your back supported, your feet flat on the floor, and your arms resting wherever they are comfortable. If you struggle to sit, you can lie down, but make sure you won't fall asleep!

Take a couple of breaths in and out and then send your attention into the surface your feet are resting on, sending your energy there. Now slowly scan up through your body following the prompts. You might need to shut your eyes to be able to tune into each area before reading the prompts. Spend at least a couple of minutes in each place before you move to the next area.

If you notice yourself trying too hard, over-thinking, or struggling to find sensations, move your body again and then return to the area you're on. If you still don't feel very much, don't worry about it. You can revisit this at any time, and as many times as you want.

<u>Notice each area in turn and record your feelings and body responses as you consider the prompts below:</u>

1. **Your feet and legs — representing your foundations, security, and grounding. (Muladhara - the Root Chakra)**

   How do your feet and legs feel? Are they warm, cold, comfortable, sore?

   Do your feet feel tight or relaxed? Are they easy to feel?

   Does this area feel grounded or is it hard to tell?

   Does anything change in your feet or your legs when you think about money?

   Give your toes a wriggle and see if you can complete this prompt: 'my feet want me to know that...'

2. **Your lower back and belly — representing your relationships, playfulness, and sexuality. (Swadhistana - Sacral Chakra)**

   Place your hand on your lower belly and gently move your pelvis an inch from side to side to help you feel into this area.

   How does your lower belly feel? How about your lower back and the base of your spine?

   Do they feel comfortable, full, empty, sore? Free or stuck?

   Is it easy or hard to feel sensations here? Is your belly warm or cold? Is that changing as you think about it?

Does this area feel happy when you think about your relationships?

Ask this area if it feels honoured and well nourished... don't second guess or judge the answer.

3. **Your solar plexus — representing your sense of personal power. (Manipura - Solar Plexus)**

   Place your hand on your midline, where your ribs come together and meet. Breathe into your hand to shift your attention to this area.

   Is it easy to breathe into your hand or is it hard to send your breath down this far?

   Can you feel the area behind your hand? How does it feel? Do you notice any sensations there?

   Does it feel calm or buzzy? Solid or relaxed?

   Does anything change in this area when you think about how well you maintain boundaries in your life in terms of saying no or yes to things and to people?

4. **Your heart — representing your ability to give and receive love. (Anahata - Heart Chakra)**

   As you focus on your heart area, it can be good to bring your hands palm to palm and place them against your chest in prayer position, with your thumbs lightly resting on your sternum.

   How is your breathing? Does this area feel warm or cold?

   Can you feel the corresponding area on the back of your body?

   Does anything change when you focus toward the back of your body?

   Does your heart feel happy? Comfortable? Sad or neutral?

   What does your heart want you to know today?

5. **Your throat — representing your expression and communication. (Visshudi - Throat Chakra)**

   This area can be surprisingly difficult to sense. Turning your neck gently from side to side can help you feel into it more.

   How does your throat feel? Is it spacious, hard to feel, sore or tight?

   Does your throat feel like it is part of your body or does it feel separate?

   Does anything change in your awareness of your throat when you think about expressing your needs? Does your throat feel dry? If you were to speak right now, would your voice feel strained or full and rich?

6. **The space between your eyebrows — representing your intuition. (Ajna - Third Eye)**

   You might want to wrinkle your eyebrows to get a sense of this area, or gently rest your fingertips there for a moment before relaxing your arm back down.

   Do you have any sense of this area when you send your attention here?

   How does it feel? Could you put it into words?

   If this area could speak, would it say it feels cloudy or clear?

   Does it feel comfortable to place your attention here, or does it feel heavy? (Shift your attention to your feet if it feels heavy.)

7. **The top of your head — representing your spiritual awareness and connection. (Sahasara — Crown Chakra)**

   Take a couple of deep slow breaths and try to send your attention to a few inches above your head (it can feel compressive to place your hand directly on your head).

Are you aware of any sensations on the crown of your head as you slow your breathing?

Can you sense space above your head?

Does this area feel tingly, soft, heavy, or light?

If this area was a colour, what colour would it be?

Ask this area how connected it feels to you. How connected does it feel to the wider Universe?

Take a couple of deep breaths. Send your attention back down to the surface underneath your feet. Notice the room around you, the view in front of you, your hands and clothes to bring you back to your sense of the wider world.

Wriggle and stretch then do a brief overview using these prompts:

- Write down your responses if you haven't already.
- Which ones stand out to you in some way - maybe because they surprise you or seem especially relevant?
- Pick the three that felt especially lacking, relevant, or like they wanted your attention.
- Which areas of life do these relate to? Were you expecting these areas to show up?
- What does this tell you about those areas of your life that most want to be acknowledged?
- Which of the solutions from this process could you explore to help you do this?
- Notice how much resistance you felt to doing this exercise. Is this really resistance or is something else behind it?

CHAPTER 7
Process 4 – Ground Yourself
Uncover Your Superpowers

"Get yourself grounded and you can navigate even the stormiest roads in peace." — Steve Goodier

Have you ever noticed how different you feel when you go away on holiday, get a change of scenery, and maybe some sunshine as an extra bonus?

You probably think it's because you've slowed down, relaxed, stopped rushing from here to there, and left normal life chores behind, and you'd be right. But that's not the whole picture.

When you go on holiday or take a break, you are naturally getting out of your head and back into your body. You are unconsciously expanding your awareness by noticing more of the world around you, and less of the world in your smartphone. You are breathing more slowly, walking more often, resting, being, enjoying, and connecting.

Going on holiday reconnects you to your Superpowers. And it feels wonderful... until you get back home and normal life intrudes on your new sense of wonder with all things.

Thankfully, reconnecting to your Superpowers is not just for holidays.

When you learn how to get out of your head and into your body, and how to control and direct your inherent energy, rather than keep it locked up in your head, you'll be astonished by your ability to access this state more often.

My Story — How Getting Out of My Head Changed My Life

"Life is short; energy is precious. You don't know it yet but the soul's path unfolds for us, while the ego's story happens to us. You have to be able to tell the difference. Is something unfolding or is it happening?" — William Whitecloud

I was 28 and I'd made my new life happen. I was working as a Radiographer in a busy hospital and shared a house with a friend with whom I had trained.

I was finally a proper grown up.

Despite realising halfway through my degree that I hated the job, I soldiered on because I had no idea what else to do and didn't want to be a failure again. As part of my training I had done ultrasound scanning and I quite liked it because you got to work 1-to-1 with patients. I figured I would do my required 18 months of post-qualification work and then I would be eligible to train in Sonography. If all else failed, at least I would have my degree.

In short, I had a Plan. One I was determined to make work better than the previous ones.

I was single, had no friends outside work, and life consisted of working long hours or going to pubs. I did what I could to make the most of work by remembering every patient was a person with fears, not just 'the broken leg in A&E'. I used humour to connect with them and smiling to calm them when they got angry. I got really good at dealing with trauma and staying calm whilst working under pressure and discovered I actually liked it.

This however, was not going to distract me from my Plan.

One day a lovely colleague told me about a man she knew, who she said would be perfect for me. I had no idea what his name was and knew nothing about him, apart from the fact she was convinced we would be great together. My friend barely had a chance to even try and convince me before my head marched in, with a very determined no. The time was not right, I was doing okay on my own (I wasn't!) and this was not part of the Plan. There was no debate; my head was firmly in charge and not remotely interested in deviation. I forgot about it, burying it in the Box marked 'Things I'm pretending I don't want'.

I got my ultrasound training placement and discovered I had a knack for working 1-to-1 with patients. One day, not long into my training, another colleague told me about a man she knew, who she felt would be perfect for me. It was two years after my previous colleague tried to set me up. This time I remember feeling torn between wanting to know more and wanting life to stay as it was. Again, I had no idea what his name was and knew virtually nothing about him, but unlike last time, my curiosity triumphed over my head and decided it wanted to know more.

I wasn't the happiest I'd ever been at this point but was far happier than when I was a radiographer. I had bought my first flat and lived alone for the first time in my adult life. I was getting to know myself and even beginning to like myself. Not before time, given I was already 30. My friend told me a few details and after battling my head's warnings to say no and back away, my curiosity overruled again and made me say yes to meeting him.

A few days later, she arranged the blind date. My first one ever. As the date loomed closer, my head started talking me out of it. I was mostly a slave to my head, and also scared of getting hurt, so I made an excuse and chickened out. For a few days it felt like a relief. My friend and my curiosity were not so easily outwitted however. For some reason, even though my head was shouting 'NO', I said yes to the blind date. The new date was set and all the details put in place by my friend. I was to stay at her house and, to stop me from backing out, the date was going to be at a pub with her and some other people I didn't know.

On the day of the date, I left work with my friend and got changed at her place. I tried to ignore the butterflies in my belly as we made it to the unknown man's front door, which was on the way to the pub. It was opened by a beautiful girl who turned out to be his sister. She said he wasn't quite ready, so suggested we all go to the pub ahead of him.

I sat in the pub, trying to quell my rising nerves with my default distraction of alcohol. Not only was I about to have my first blind date with a strange man, I was in a strange town, with strange people in a strange pub. As you can imagine, my head was not happy.

After what seemed like an eternity of trying to stay calm, the man I was meeting walked through the door. It wasn't hard to recognize him because he looked a lot like his sister. I am pretty sure that even if I hadn't met his sister, I would still have known him immediately. Mainly because my inner voice spoke to me as soon as he walked in and smiled. It said:

"There you are, thank goodness you're here. I've been waiting for you."

In that moment, without question, I knew I had found the man I would marry.

It was magical, heart-stopping, unexpected, somewhat scary, and totally illogical. My head didn't know what to do with itself.

***

A couple of weeks later, a female friend of my future husband visited him and saw a picture of me on the mantelpiece. Feeling very confused, she asked him why he had a photo of her friend Helen in his lounge. He told her proudly that I was his new girlfriend; at which point, she told him I was the girl she tried to set him up with two years ago! She left the hospital many months before and we had lost touch. I had no idea where she even lived and never met any of her friends... until I met and married the friend I was meant to meet all along.

Thank goodness I finally got out of my head long enough to let serendipity work its magic.

Head-Led Challenges of Process 4

What if instead of dreaming about walking on the moon, or dancing with the stars, we celebrated walking on the earth?

If you're really honest with yourself, how often would you say you're truly present rather than just being in your head?

Do you notice when that happens, or does it generally pass you by?

How does this impact your decision-making ability? Your joy? Your energy?

How does it impact your day? Your weeks? Your months?

Does it frustrate you, or is it so natural you don't even know it's happening?

Unless you're superhuman or an enlightened monk, it's highly likely you're living in your head the majority of the time. This means you're trying to do everything from a less intuitive place and going *against* your natural flow more often than *with* it.

As we become more technologically advanced, more connected and immersed in the online world, it becomes more and more important to stay connected to practices that calm, ground, and restore us.

Grounding is really fundamental. When you are stressed, overwhelmed, or feeling like you can't stay on top of everything, it's generally because on an energetic level, all your energy is up in your head. Many people I've worked with have almost no energy in their body because it is all up in their shoulders and their head, and the energy in their body is tied up in knots. The result is they miss out on what's in front of them, they don't access their full potential, and they're so trapped in their head, they barely even notice whilst their life passes by.

Later in this chapter, I share the simplest practice I know to help you become a ground reconnecting, superpower liberating master.

First, let's explore why this is such an important issue and how it happens, so that you know what to watch out for.

1. The Technology Effect

No matter how old or young you are, you've been impacted both negatively and positively by technology. It saves you time, effort, and sanity, freeing you up to do more things you love, more of the time. Except it doesn't really, does it? Because we are increasingly spending more time looking down at our phones and less time moving our bodies. Technology is amazing in so many ways, but unfortunately, it's become indispensable in our lives and we are so addicted to it that even when we're outside, we barely notice our surroundings.

On the whole, we spend less time outside, less time on our hands and knees gardening, less time walking, and more time sitting straining our necks looking down at our phones. We switch our phones on first thing in the morning and they are the last thing we look at before we go to sleep. We are always switched on, with our attention directed towards our tech. The result is a misaligned, depleted, abandoned body that feels stiff and achy, and a head full up from constant stimulation.

We are structurally designed to counteract the downward force of gravity. It only takes a tiny misalignment in our head position for all the muscles in our body to be deployed to try and maintain equilibrium. The more misaligned you are, the harder your body has to work, which drains your life force energy. No wonder you then struggle to feel grounded and calm; you've no energy left to connect to the ground.

2. Head Honcho

The Matrix Myth culture of using our logic to work out life has got us all over-thinking, worrying and feeling trapped inside a head that won't be quiet. This is so endemic in our culture that we barely even recognise it's happening. You live in your head and you keep feeding its needs before any others, meaning you're only functioning using *half* your available tools.

It isn't your fault that your head is constantly active, or it tells you that you must do everything, otherwise you've failed. It's a simple side effect of being alive and having evolved to avoid tigers and anything dangerous or weird that might mean you're excluded from the pack.

The solution, as always, is awareness. Once you learn how to redirect your energy away from your head, it no longer gets to rule your world.

3. Airy Fairy Syndrome

This is a different manifestation of being out of your body and results from being so disconnected from your day-to-day life that you spend most of your time in the clouds.

When this happens, you are not present and either live in the Land of Past Perusal or the Land of Futures That Haven't Happened Yet. Meanwhile, life happens whilst you're busy ruminating and daydreaming, and then when you want to make anything happen, you struggle to reconnect to the here and now and ground your energy.

It can be lovely to be in the floaty head place, I am somewhat fond of it and I love visiting it when I meditate. However, when you are so disconnected from your body and daily life that you become effectively dis-embodied, you have no chance of directing your life.

You can only truly access your sense of purpose and potential when you are fully grounded and rooted in yourself and your life. If you float around, and chop and change, you are as effectively trapped in the Matrix Myth as when you fight against it - because when you are disembodied, you are disempowered.

Heart-Led Solutions for Process 4

"In my view, the realistic goal to be attained through spiritual practice is not some permanent state of enlightenment that admits no further efforts but a capacity to be free in this moment, in the midst of whatever is happening. If you can do that, you have already solved most of the problems you will encounter in life." — Sam Harris

Grounding is about directing and channelling your energy in such a way that you feel strongly rooted in your whole being; as powerful and unbreakable as an oak tree.

Which sounds great, the question is, how?

When I was a young child I suffered from occasional migraines.

They were all-encompassing and the pain so intense I would have to stop everything I was doing to lie in a dark, quiet room. As a child brought up in a time when suitable painkillers weren't commonplace, the pain turned out to be a gift I didn't realise the significance of until much later. As I said in the previous process, there are gifts to be found in the mud of your past.

Quite by accident, I discovered that if I directed my attention somewhere else when the pain arrived, and resolutely refused to engage with it, it would be much more manageable. It didn't stop the migraine, but whenever the pain got too much, I would send my attention down to my feet, or away behind me somewhere. It then felt as though I was watching the pain from somewhere else and as long as I maintained my attention, I could more or less control it.

No one told me to do this, I didn't verbalise it or know it was 'a thing'. Like any other child who hasn't yet learned to believe they are limited, I intuitively accessed a technique that worked and I didn't give it much thought. It did what I needed it to do. And that was all that mattered.

I now realise I stumbled across a Superpower we all have; the power to direct our own energy out of our head and into our body to change our experience.

Your energy flows where your attention goes.

Think about how your awareness concentrates toward a sore neck until it becomes all you are aware of, almost as though the rest of you had disappeared. This can also be used intentionally to help you get out of your head and ground your energy.

Grounding is like magic; one minute you feel weak and scattered, the next you feel centred, strong, and rooted — able to bend but not break. This helps you manage life and interact with others from a much more stable place. You cannot be knocked over as easily when you're grounded; whereas, when you're in your head you're more scatty and less aware of what is going on around you. This is not the best place to make changes from. You need to access as much of your potential porridge pot of energy as you can and if it has risen to your head (where your attention is) it isn't available to use.

Grounding is the best tool for getting out of your head and out of your own way. It helps you move away from your inner cast of characters and reduce their influence over you. Grounding is also a great way to protect your energy from any external influences, because the lower your energy is, the less it can be sucked up or attached to. We all experience this in life, both from physical environments and people. You can use grounding as a way to help reduce the effects. As people around you sense you starting to change, they will unconsciously be attracted to your energy and can drain you. Grounding is your superpower to use when this happens.

Explore the following solutions to start uncovering your superpowers:

Solution 1: Unlock Your Posture Power

Your posture has a huge effect on the way that the energy in your body flows or stagnates. It influences how fully you breathe, how well your digestion processes, how effectively your nerves transmit signals through your spinal canal, and how well your blood circulates. It's so much easier to breathe when you're not slumped or hunching your shoulders. This is because your lungs have more room when you're upright.

When you are upright, all the vertebrae in your spine stack up like blocks, designed to negate the negative forces of gravity. In the centre of each vertebrae (apart from the very bottom) is an opening for the spinal cord and energy channels to pass through. In an ideal world, your vertebrae align to form a channel in whatever position you are in. You can imagine it being a bit like a pipe, ideally a smooth one with minimal kinks in it. The smoother the pipe, the more easily the signals flow. Not only your nervous system, but also your energy. The more easily your energy flows through your system, the more you have available to use. When your spine is upright, you effectively have an aerial in the centre that can receive and transmit signals. Not only throughout your body, but also from both the ground and the sky.

In effect, your body acts like a bridge between the earth and sky, and when you consciously choose to view it this way, you unlock your capacity to receive energy from above and below. Regularly standing to ground your energy then creates an energetic increase in your system, which helps decompress it, meaning you'll feel lighter and brighter.

Try playing with the intention to create a smoothly flowing energy 'pipe' through your spine whenever you are standing; such as in the shower, brushing your teeth, waiting for a train, or boiling the kettle. You'll find that with more awareness, you start noticing a shift in your energy that becomes exponentially more powerful over time.

Solution 2. Be now here, not nowhere.

If you are never present in real time because your head has gone off exploring options or pondering what it wishes it had done better, you'll struggle to consciously ground your energy. If you're not present, your energy is in your head - and if you want to free up your own potential, you have to be present to do it.

"You have to gather your energy together in the same manner, conserving it and insulating it from dissipation in every direction other than that of your purpose." — Walter Russell

You can only be fully grounded and rooted in life when you bring your whole self to the party. This doesn't mean you have to try and keep your head quiet, because that will never happen, it means you have to stop paying it attention, because you have a greater need for your life force energy than your head does. Your head doesn't really care about your energy or about grounding, it's doing its own thing regardless. Energy doesn't come into it.

When you become aware that your attention has drifted, simply breathe consciously and expand your awareness to what's around you right now. Once you've done this, you can actively choose to think about what you feel underneath your feet - this will ensure you send your energy down in the ground, ready to receive reciprocal energy back up again.

Solution 3. Remember Your Feet Are Your Foundation

Your feet are the interface between you and the ground. They walk you around through life and have more impact on your physical ease and strength than you probably realise.

Like trees and plants, you require strong roots for your whole body to thrive. You have soft tissue and fascial connections running all the way from your feet, up the backs of your legs, and up your back. If you look after your feet and keep them flexible and mobile, your legs and back will feel more supple. (If you have a backache and have no-one to ease it for you, try massaging your feet, it will help!)

When you stand fully and are well balanced, you feel stronger and more confident in your body because your energy flows more easily. The more connected you are to your feet, and the more mobile your feet are, the better your body will function. The quickest way to ground can sometimes be to rub your feet and then place them on the ground, without shoes. Imagine that the undersides of your feet are made of heavy lead and focus your attention on the surface under your feet. It sounds almost too simple to be effective but try it and see how it feels.

Walking barefoot in the grass is also highly recommended.

Process 4 – Summary for Your Soul:

You are an incredible human being, made of the same wondrous elements that form the entire Universe. You have within you the keys to deep expression and unfolding of who you came here to be.

Gift your soul regular periods to connect to the ground to access a deep oasis of nourishing energy. This will return you to your natural state of grace and peace, as you learn to inhabit your entire being, with the support of Mother Earth beneath you.

By gifting yourself small amounts of time daily to ground, you create small ripples of inner peace that will spread outwards, helping you feel centered and still, whilst also nourishing those around you.

Learn to connect to the ground daily and get ready to hear what the ancient sages referred to as 'the unstruck sound', the beautiful, vast, deeply peaceful stillness of the Field of Awareness itself.

Then watch as your life becomes a fuller, richer expression of who you are.

Process 4 Self-Affirmation: I embrace a deeper connection with the earth.

Magical Mission - Mindful Grounding Focus

"What is the binding force that holds the many worlds together and with its intensity also attracts us to each other? Can we call it gravity, energy, Love? To re-establish contact with our body is to be in contact with nature is to be in contact with the Cosmos. Balance is restored, space is around us and that tremendous power arising from the earth in unison with these universal forces, will become part of us." — *Vanda Scaravelli*

This focus empowers you to quite literally get out of your head and connect to an energy far greater than the energy you use keeping up with the worry whirring monsters inside your head. Your head will feel much more spacious, you will feel more embodied and calm, and your feet will feel fully connected to the ground.

Allow yourself anywhere from 5 - 15 minutes to play with this focus.

To begin with, you'll be in your head because it's new to you, but it will become more intuitive the more you do it. It will feel awkward at first and your muscles may ache. Take it slowly, this is not an endurance test.

Over time, you'll be easily able to drop into awareness of this practice whenever you need some head space. The key is to practice and play with the focus. *If you cannot stand for any reason, or fully feel your feet, you can still do this sitting down. Sending your attention to your feet will still send your energy there even if you don't feel it.*

Read through the focus first and then repeat it whilst reading through. Ideally take your shoes off to connect better with the ground. ◁
https://www.helenrebello.com/p/MagicBookResources

191

1. Stand with your feet parallel and hip-width apart to allow your weight to transmit into the earth. *Hip-width is roughly the same distance as two fists placed side by side between your feet.*

2. Feel into the underside of your feet and move them around until you get a really good connection with the ground. Spend time on this - your feet are your foundation; the greater your connection, the more optimally your body aligns.

3. Lift and spread your toes as much as is comfortable for you and then lower them down.

4. Keep a soft bend in your knees and try not to lock your thigh muscles. Breathe and release them.

5. Imagine your pelvis is like a bowl holding fruit - don't tip it too far forwards or too far back. Gently move it millimetres back and forth until it feels just right.

6. Very lightly, draw in your abdomen, and notice as you do so that your upper chest lifts slightly.

7. You may want to gently rotate your shoulders at this point until they feel softer. Feel free to gently move your head from side to side to soften the muscles in your neck.

8. Now, rather than trying to get your upper body perfectly aligned, gently lower your chin until it feels as though you have a large orange under it, and then imagine someone has attached a thread to your crown and is gently elongating it.

9. Notice your breath, notice your feet and soften your jaw and face. Smile.

10. Place the tip of your tongue gently on the roof of your mouth, just behind your top teeth and keep it there as you breathe.

11. Once you feel you are in a stable position, keep tuning into the sensation of someone lifting your crown and keep noticing your feet.

12. Play with shifting your weight from the back of your feet to the front, and from side to side, holding everything else in position as you do. Settle back into stillness with your weight evenly distributed.

13. Keep softening, breathing consciously, and relaxing whenever you notice you are holding tension.

14. Breathe softly in, and as you breathe out, imagine sending roots down your legs and deeply into the ground through a point called The Bubbling Spring (Kidney 1), on the sole of each foot, in the middle, just behind the ball of your foot. *The Kidney meridian controls the direction of chi flow, so this helps you to literally 'sink your chi' and ground your energy.*

15. With each inhalation, play with bringing your energy back up to your belly, and with each exhalation, send it down through this point in each foot.

16. Repeat this as many times as you like but stand for no longer than 10-15 minutes each time.

17. When you are ready to move and let the focus go, notice how you feel; how your breath has changed and how your head feels.

Notes:

- Trust that where your attention and intention goes your energy follows, even if you don't feel it.

- Grounding is not something you 'think' your way in to, it is something you feel as you become more used to it and your head is less involved.

- For some, this is an easy exercise, for others it feels alien at first. Accept that anything new takes time to feel the benefits of. It takes as long as it takes and doesn't reflect on your worth.

- It may feel frustrating, achy, and pointless at first; this is your head trying to talk you out of it. Don't listen!

- The more used to relaxing your body you are, the more you will feel your own chi energy and the sensations in your body.

- The more you practice this, the more your body will feed back to you as its own intelligence system learns to interpret new, subtle sensations.

CHAPTER 8
Process 5 — Ignite Yourself
Honour Your Inner Sparkle

"Have the courage to follow your heart and intuition. They somehow already know what you truly want to become." — *Steve Jobs*

Have you ever reached a crux point where you're faced with two potential paths, both of which seem equally scary, and you've no idea which one to take? Or had one of those experiences where even though your instincts said do one thing, you did something else that made more logical sense, only to regret it later? If you had a better way to make those important decisions and save yourself the heartache of missed opportunities and time-wasting, would you use it?

Recognising you are on the cusp of change and then embarking on a journey towards it, requires trust, courage, and willpower. It requires willingness to be vulnerable, to be open, to learn how to listen to your heart, flow through fear, and know what to do when the resist-dance arises; all possible when you learn how to open and listen to your heart.

This is my favourite MAGICAL process, and the one that has made the biggest difference to my own life. You could say it's the one that truly touches my heart.

Earlier I introduced the three treasures; fundamental aspects of our being in TCM, without which we are 'dispirited'. One of these is Shen, the aspect of our character that lives in the Heart. It can be translated as 'spirit' or 'sparkle' as I prefer it, so this chapter is about opening your heart to rekindle your sparkle.

Once you are able to ground yourself, which shifts your energy and helps you start accessing more of your own potential and power, it's much easier to connect to your heart energy. As you do this, you start to slowly expand your state, and access more intuition, so that everyday life becomes more fulfilling and purposeful.

Let me share with you just how powerful listening to your heart can be. So powerful it ought to come with a *'will definitely change your life'* warning...

My Story — Learning to Listen to My Heart

"Some birds aren't meant to be caged. Their feathers are just too bright." — The Shawshank Redemption

The day I wished I hadn't seen an abnormality on an antenatal ultrasound scan, was the day I finally conceded I had to leave my job.

That day was not a happy day. But by then, not many days were. Not whilst I was at work anyway.

I knew this career wasn't right for me halfway through my degree and I was clutching at straws by creating the alternative plan to try and make it work. I knew even whilst I carried out the plan by studying another two years to specialise in Ultrasound. Yet I carried on regardless, hoping that if I buried my head in studies, somehow it would magically work out.

I was wrong.

I was wrong because this career resulted from a clear decision to ignore my heart and not take a chance on studying what I really wanted to.

I had been brave enough to change everything and take a leap into one of the hardest degrees I could have chosen, but I wasn't brave enough to stand up for what my heart wanted. Instead, I followed my head down a perfectly logical path towards a vocation that enabled me to help people and gave me a guaranteed income to support me. But it wasn't a path that lit me up.

If I'm honest, I was seeking validation and striving to prove myself to my dad. Because I had disappointed him and let him down in so many ways, I wanted to make him proud. I wanted to be the daughter he once thought I was, forgetting this didn't mean I had to build a life based on his standards for success.

Standards that ironically changed for him years later when he escaped the Matrix Myth and changed his life completely too. Turns out I wasn't the only one who followed my head.

By this time, I was married to my lovely soulmate and in a happy, healthy relationship for the first time in my life. The Universe had found me the perfect partner and we were helping each other become better versions of ourselves. This aspect of my life was as perfect as it could be, given how much I still had to learn about vulnerability, self-awareness, and self-expression. We were very happy together apart from dealing with our struggles to have children. A fact made harder by me being surrounded by pregnant women daily. It wasn't all-encompassing, but it wasn't the best place to be working, especially as having insider knowledge meant I knew exactly what the odds were of me managing to get pregnant again. Let's just say you wouldn't bet on them.

I was the consummate professional, no one would ever have known what was going on in my personal life. You can hide a lot behind a smile. I showed up fully; looking after those I had to break bad news to, staying impartial when scanning those considering terminations, and being empathic with those going through fertility treatment. I always remembered that obstetric scans marked an important event for those I was scanning and I hid my resentment when they were disappointed that they got the 'wrong sex' baby.

Slowly but surely; however, as I scanned more women who were ambivalent about their pregnancy, smoked or drank throughout, or worse, lied to their GP about my findings to try and get a termination, the cracks in my composure started to show. I was fine when I dealt with 'normal' situations, but the minute I had to deal with something I found challenging, it became harder to hide how I felt about it. I remember scanning a woman whose baby had an anomaly at her twenty-week scan. The anomaly I saw was one that could have been sorted out early in her baby's life, but despite the specialist team giving her the best advice and support available, she couldn't deal with giving birth to a baby with an operable problem. She chose to have a termination, and it broke something in me.

Hearts are clever that way, they break so we start listening to them. And the more we listen, the more we learn about ourselves.

I didn't want to feel that because of me, a baby never got a chance.

I didn't want to contribute to 'screening-out' imperfections.

I didn't want to work in an increasingly litigious field, where mothers-to-be would lie about things to try and get what they wanted.

I didn't want to pretend any more. I had done it for long enough. My heart had won.

Except I had no idea what to do about it. So I dropped a day a week and started taking antidepressants to stop me from sliding downhill, while my colleagues and my lovely man did their best to support me.

Fast forward to the day my heart finally stamped its desires lovingly but firmly, into my consciousness. That was the day I wanted to lie to a mum-to-be about an anomaly I'd seen, in case she terminated her pregnancy like the other woman did. The day I risked losing my integrity by pretending not to see something; thereby taking away someone else's right to follow their heart.

I had crossed the line. If not in reality, in my head.

And that was enough for my heart to step in and firmly state its case.

I woke up that day to face the fact I was in the wrong career and I had to honour my heart and make a plan to walk away from a job that saw me daily compromising my values. Even though it scared me, and some of my old radiography colleagues thought I was delusional, I knew I had no choice but to trust my instincts, ignore the naysayers and choose the unknown path. Even though it made no logical sense, I finally listened to my heart.

Head-Led Challenges of Process 5

"Why do they always teach us that it is easy and evil to do what we want and that we need discipline to restrain ourselves. It's the hardest thing in the world—to do what we want. And it takes the greatest kind of courage." — Ayn Rand

Many of us reach a point in life where we start to question whether the life we are living is the life we want to live.

This is not solely because we are bored or unsatisfied; it's our inner voice shouting at us to wake up and start living in a way that is aligned with who we are. It can happen anytime, but in my experience, it happens when we acknowledge our self-worth, and start questioning the Matrix Myth.

Reaching this point does not feel comfortable, but we have to dive into the discomfort if we want to stop hearing the inner voice. We cannot bury ourselves in distractions all our lives, and we cannot pretend we will live forever.

Your heart won't ever give up on you and when it starts shouting, the only peaceful way forward is to listen to what it has to say.

Easier said than done because of some very common challenges underlying it:

1. The Fanciful Myth

Do you remember the days when you could go out for hours without having to check in with anyone or have an agenda? Or you could lose yourself in a book or a film without a care in the world.

It doesn't happen often as an adult, mainly because the Matrix Myth told us it was fanciful and somewhere along the line, we started prioritising productivity and responsibility instead. This is not unreasonable. We do all have to contribute to the functioning of our families and the world in some way, but when did we start believing it was an all-or-nothing choice? Since when did indulging in fanciful moments become something only mavericks, rich people, and artists get to do?

Fanciful moments connect us to our heart. Losing ourselves in something we love is the one time we barely notice our head. These times feel nourishing, free from rules, and quite literally heartwarming.

2. The Intuition Fallacy

I've lost count of how many times people have asked me if intuition is something only certain people have. They believe it is either made-up, or only reserved for 'special' people.

It isn't.

The problem is that the voice of intuition is subtle, which means you have to get really quiet to hear it. You have to learn to soften, relax, and let go of the need to try, which isn't something we're taught in school.

Every single person has intuition and every single person knows it. They just think they don't because they've mislabelled it, put it in the wrong box, and have forgotten about it. They then look for it in the wrong places; thinking they need a certain practice to find it, or it needs to make sense, or feel a certain way.

It doesn't.

The voice of your intuition is often a niggle, feeling, instinct, or fleeting sensation you quickly dismiss. It often doesn't make sense. The key to finding your intuition is to follow the breadcrumb trail that isn't logical, because then you know your mind can't have created it.

3. Compartmentalising Yourself

You cannot build your life out of selected 'bits' like a kit. You cannot compartmentalise yourself, and deny yourself what is important to you, and still expect to feel whole and content.

Denying yourself what brings your heart joy creates fragmentation and will leave you feeling scattered, ungrounded, unfulfilled, and weak. Your inherent spirit will feel squashed and will revolt. It will whisper to you in your dreams, quietly nag at you whilst you're working, and eventually manifest as something louder and challenging to stop you in your tracks when you keep ignoring it.

When you live life exclusively from your head and do only what you feel is acceptable and achievable, you effectively shut down part of your being. This makes it harder for you to find inner peace and fulfil your potential. To have the life you want, you have to bring your whole embodied self to the party we call life; leave even a bit behind and it will make itself felt.

4. Head versus Heart

Challenges arise from your head, forming part of the age-old battle between your head and your heart. You often have no idea this is happening, but it's a constant internal dialogue.

One informs the other, and depending upon which part wins, you act accordingly. You might not consciously realise it, but thankfully you've already transcended this loop many times. When the desire for something you really want to do outweighs any fear of doing it, you have unknowingly outwitted your head, so you can act from your heart.

Science documentary filmmaker David Malone interviewed cardiac surgeons and neuro-researchers for his film, *Of Hearts and Minds.* He wanted to understand more about the latest findings on the communication between the head and heart, and whether they correlated with the long-held poetic and Eastern view of the heart as an emotional organ full of love. Scientists used to believe the brain controlled the heart, and it was a one-way communication street. Whilst science is still investigating the full extent of the process, Malone has beautifully summarised their findings so far:

"The heart is a pump that does respond when the brain asks it to, but it is not enslaved to the brain. Its relationship to the brain is more like a marriage ... with each dependent on the other. It seems science is now restoring to the heart something that rightfully belongs to it: Our emotions."

Your Brain — the 'Official' Version.

Your brain is a complex, multilayered machine with many functions. When it comes to change, it wants answers and to know things are safe before it explores them. It likes familiarity and predictability. When something happens to threaten this, the ancient Chimp part of your brain (known as the limbic system), gets agitated and starts creating noise to signal danger, before your more evolved human part even registers what's happened.

Your limbic system is controlling you when you lose yourself down a social media black hole even though you're 'supposed to be' doing something that serves you better. Your neural responses to emotion live in this part of your brain; which is why you often give yourself instant rewards rather than delay your gratification by digging deep and doing something challenging. Whenever you know you'll regret something whilst you are actually doing it, your Chimp brain is running the show. It is too primitive to understand the bigger picture, wanting to have fun and play right now. The more evolved human side of your brain then has to deal with the subsequent guilt and regret.

The evolved human side of your brain lives in your frontal lobe—as the name suggests—at the front of your head. It's the part you frown with when you're thinking too hard, and the part that gets involved with processing your internal struggles. You may have heard about the prefrontal cortex, that's at the front of this lobe. It is highly evolved, more reasoned and rational. Far less emotional than the chimp brain, if it was able to take control more often, it would do things without worrying so much about what others think because it sees the bigger picture.

The trouble is, you have two opposing forces in your head controlling you before you even consider the role of your heart. One is a higher-level, modern day, evolved being. The other is a prehistoric animal addicted to adrenaline. The latter makes so much noise when it's rattled, it creates something we know as 'Brain Fog', which prevents us from seeing and hearing the voice of our evolved human.

Only when we clear the fog can we see the forest AND the trees, and hence see the path ahead.

Your Heart

Your heart is an incredibly intelligent organ in its own right, which you will discover more about in the next section.

Even though your heart is a highly emotional and intuitive centre, which accesses and transmits useful information extremely quickly, in the Western world we are simply not used to hearing it. We are so used to living in our heads, we miss its signals. Or if we sense them, our brain jumps in when we pause; to question and interrupt the instinct in case you are considering upsetting the status quo. Even though your heart tries to guide you, it is hard to trust its unexplainable instincts when your brain gets there first.

This battle will never change; it's part of being human.

What you *can* change; however, is your relationship to the battle and how much impact you let it have on your choices. By changing your awareness and understanding, you can change the outcome, more of the time. Simply knowing about this battle empowers you.

As you become more skilled at using the solutions I am about to share, you create new neural pathways between your limbic system and your frontal lobe, making your ability to get out of your head and into your heart markedly easier.

Courage, as you will discover, comes from your heart; therefore, take heart as you move forwards, because courage is already within you.

Heart-Led Solutions for Process 5

"Your heart is the path of least resistance. If you know your heart, life will always be rich and life will always be easy. That's why you must always ask yourself, is this a path with heart? Is this mood my heart? Is this course of action my heart? Is this outcome my heart? If you ask yourself that in all your affairs, then you're going to go a long way." — William Whitecloud

Learning to open, hear, and trust your heart helps you access your inherent wisdom, so you can identify what is truly important in your life. This becomes your guiding compass; enabling you to do more of what inspires and nourishes you, and less of what doesn't. Opening your heart is like opening the door to more freedom because your senses attune more finely, allowing you to save time and energy by making better, more aligned decisions.

It took me many years to learn how to open and listen to my heart, but once I'd started to live with that awareness it transformed everything for the better.

I know this is possible for you too.

It might sound magical, but the truth is, humans have been navigating through life using their heart for centuries, and many still do. It's only since we became 'domesticated', as my friend and self-development author Faith Canter calls it, that we started pushing our way through life more exclusively from our head. You do run greater risk of getting hurt when your heart is more open but my goodness, it is so worth it.

The first step to opening your heart is to demystify heart energy so your head can stop being quite so scared of it. That way, it is less likely to stop you before you start…

Solution 1. Understand Heart Energetics

When I talk about the heart, I'm not only describing an organ, but also the energetic field around your heart, which extends throughout your upper chest and out around your body and is far greater than that of your brain. Your heart is a physical, emotional, and energetic space, with its own unique vibrations and associations.

We all know that tugging feeling we get in our heart when we are shocked, upset or excited. We instinctively place our hand on our heart when we talk about something we love, or hear about a loss. We can also tell when someone speaks from their heart and when they're up in their head. We don't think about it *consciously*, we feel it *instinctively*. That's because the Heart Chakra (Anahata) is the energetic centre of your body and acts as a bridge between the physical and subtle realms of the body. As a rule of thumb, when you follow *feelings* you are following your heart and when you follow *thoughts* you are following your head.

In TCM theory, the Heart is considered to be the 'supreme controller'; in charge of the body, mind, and spirit. An imbalance of Heart energy creates a feeling of inner panic and a sense that you have no control. Modern science is now confirming what the Eastern world has known for centuries: that our heart really does impact the world around us. It is so much more than just an incredible pump and processing organ; it has its own nervous system. Thanks to extensive research by the Institute of Heart Math, an organization researching the link between emotions and heart-brain communication, we know our heart can produce an electrical field 60 times greater than that of our brain, with a magnetic field 5,000 times greater. It effectively acts like another brain, only an infinitely more powerful one.

The only difference between our heart brain and the brain in our head, is that society hasn't yet evolved to 'speak heart brain' the way it speaks 'head brain'. We are so used to communicating verbally, we tend to forget how much communication happens *energetically* through our bodies. It's how we know someone's mood before they open their mouth. It happens before our head has even registered it.

Whilst both the heart and the brain emit an electromagnetic field, the heart emits a field that is so powerful, it can be detected and measured several feet away from our body. If we tap into our heart the right way, we can bend the brain to our heart's will, because the heart is so much more powerful. The way to do that is to evoke positive emotions because the subconscious doesn't know the difference between real and imagined emotions and; therefore, it responds to both. This is the basis for some of the solutions below.

Solution 2. Befriend Your Shen

In TCM theory, your Shen is the spiritual, wise, knowing aspect of your being that lives in your heart and radiates through you into the world. The Shen is also your emotional intelligence and your connection to the Universe. It helps you see things with discernment, stay calm and balanced, and shapes your personality.

Think of your Shen as being like a little wise man who lives in your heart. He is perfectly happy and content when all is well and he gets to sit comfortably in your heart, and will transmit a sense of inner peace around your system. This manifests as your feeling happier in yourself and better able to cultivate positive, loving, and altruistic emotions.

When you have a shock; however, your poor Shen gets knocked out of your heart home and goes running around your body, trying to find his way home again. Because the Shen represents your mind as well as your spirit, this makes you feel scattered, like you can't focus on anything.

We all know how discombobulated we feel when we have a shock, how hard it is to function, string a sentence together, or make sense of anything. When you ignore your heart's desires and keep pushing them away, it's as though you're constantly making the Shen justify his right to live in your heart, resulting in you feeling like you've lost your spirit or sparkle.

Therefore, the more you honour your heart and stay connected to it, the more you befriend your Shen, rekindle your sparkle, and regain your sense of peace.

Solution 3. Unite Your Head and Heart

If I've done my job well, you'll by now be open to exploring a different approach to living your life. One uniting your head *and* your heart and using both intentionally; enabling you to tap into two incredibly powerful resources.

Your heart will act as your guiding compass and send you quiet messages telling you what the next step is, and your head will find solutions to any problems you give it. Use them both with this intention and you'll unlock the secret to living a fulfilled life: following your heart and taking aligned action from your head.

Your subconscious controls 95% of your behaviour and functioning. Use this to your advantage. When you focus on what you want, you can use the power of your heart to help you move towards this by evoking strong emotions. Emotions work well to support your desires because your subconscious mind responds to them, and it has no idea whether emotions relate to reality or not. This means once you've identified what you want - if you then visualise this whilst imagining how good it would feel - your subconscious gets to work to support you in moving towards your goals.

You will need to take action. You can't just conjure up emotions and expect your brain to do everything else, but your brain will find ways to help you work out what the next best action is.

It works like this:

- Picture your wise Shen leading the way, dressed (of course) like Yoda.

- He says to your inner cast of characters: *'We are going to this place next, so over to you - how do we get there?'*

- Your inner cast of characters, delighted to be acknowledged as the wise beings they are, cannot wait to suggest multiple clever solutions because they have been guided by their leader and told what to focus on.

- Everyone wins and peace reigns as your heart and head form a happy alliance!

Solution 4. Embrace Your Inner Child

"Is your inner child in house arrest by Sister Mary Have-No-Fun?" — Sonia Choquette

The best way I know to get quiet enough to hear your heart, is to get good at moving your body like a child first.

Several of my teachers have taught this, including some very well-known ones, so I have had to get over myself and put this seemingly strange theory into practice many times. Because it works, and it's also great fun.

Moving your body gets you out of your head, opens your heart, and shifts your energy. It expands your system, making it much easier to connect to your heart. If you want to exponentially increase the power of this, add in noise too. Any kind of noise will do, obviously be respectful of your neighbors! Noise helps because it loosens two of your body's diaphragms; the one you know at the base of your lungs and the diaphragm at the top of your lungs and base of your throat. These areas are often tense and tightly held but once they're physically softer, they are energetically softer too... and as your heart is between the two, it helps open your heart.

The last way to embrace your inner child is to honour your inner 4-year-old by doing something that brings her joy. It can be absolutely anything; try asking your child self what she wants. She is still inside you after all. Give yourself permission to do something illogical and fun, that takes your head away from day-to-day worries, and instead expand your energy with totally meaningless play.

You could do a lot worse than decide right now to do something small each day that honours your inner child... bring more joy into your life and you will most definitely access your heart more easily.

Solution 5. Fill Yourself From Within

If you're denying yourself something that is fundamental to you as a being at a heart level, you won't feel full. When you invest in your heart and pay attention to it, you elevate your self-worth, feel happier, and create positive ripples in your whole energy field.

If you feel empty, you have to stop looking to fill yourself up with what is outside and instead fill yourself up from the inside. A great place to start is by asking yourself 'what makes your heart sing?' I have asked this question of my clients more times than I can count and it never fails to connect them to their heart in that moment. A question like that cuts through your noisy head and takes you straight back to a memory of something you love. You'll immediately start remembering sights, sounds, positive emotions, and sensations. Your head doesn't know when emotions are in response to a real thing or an imagined thing, so when you evoke these memories, your head and your heart feel happy and start actively looking for more of this feeling.

This means you will notice more opportunities to do what make your heart smile, which raises your vibration and shifts your state from compressed to expansive; also known as from fear to love.

Actively noticing what brings you joy and makes your heart smile is the simplest act of self-love and care. It rebalances and nourishes you and returns you to the present. From this place, you are better able to tune into your heart and notice when your head is misbehaving!

"Follow your bliss and the universe will open doors for you where there were only walls." — *Joseph Campbell*

Do something every single day that makes your heart sing. It could be smiling at someone, looking at the sky, reading a book or a quote from your favourite author, listening to music, spending a few moments longer in the shower, or indulging in fresh coffee in your favourite mug.

Solution 6. Adopt an Attitude of Gratitude

Your attitude is fundamental to your mental and physical health. Emotions and tension hugely impact your life force energy, and they change according to how you choose to perceive things.

Chronic stress arising from more negative attitudes sends you into flight or fight mode, upsetting your body's hormone balance and switching off the rest and digest hormones required for feelings of happiness and fulfilment. This makes it very hard to connect to your heart. Adopting an attitude of gratitude can *literally* change your life.

Gratitude is an expansive emotion and changes your state from the inside out, opening your heart and helping you see more of the gifts of life. What you focus on creates your reality. This is one of the simplest, most common ways to expand your state, raise your vibration levels, and start living more from your heart than your head.

There are so many gratitude practices you can try out, something as simple as being grateful for your water each day as you shower, appreciating your moisturiser as you gift it to your face, and being thankful for whoever made the bowl holding your breakfast.

One of my favourite gratitude practices is to start each day by saying thank you to the Universe/God/Higher self, for the fact I have woken up to see another morning. Before I've even opened my eyes, I say to myself: *'Thank you for another day, in which I get to live, love, laugh, work, and play'.*

Feel free to steal that for yourself or make up your own and prepare to inhabit a happier body and a more positive life.

Solution 7. Reframe Your Idea of Courage

I have liberally sprinkled the word Courage throughout this book because finding the courage to show up for yourself will change your life. The word courage derives from the French word *coeur* - meaning heart - which makes sense because we know the heart is the seat of our emotions and embodying courage means we 'take heart'.

I've been helping people develop more courage and self-awareness for the last 14 years. You might conclude; therefore, that I've developed a healthy relationship with courage and I know how to transcend it every time it arises. If you did, you'd be wrong because courage is something you dance with, not something you conquer. Sometimes it's an act of courage to simply get up in the morning.

Courage increases massively the more you transcend your limits and comfort zones but this doesn't mean fear won't rise up again. And that's okay. Because part of being human means you're fallible, which is what makes you uniquely wonderful. The fact you're doing what you can to keep showing up is courageous enough. It doesn't mean you've failed if you're having a day where you can't leave the house. It simply means that today your courage looks different to yesterday. No more. No less.

You are not your courage. And your capacity to embrace it doesn't reflect on you as a person or detract from your uniqueness. Like everything else, courage ebbs and flows in the daily dance of yin and yang; learn to accept that and you won't doubt in your courage again.

Process 5 – Summary for Your Soul:

Your inner sparkle is the nugget, the gem inside your heart that sits quietly waiting for the day when you start to listen out for it.

It quietly sings its song, never angry that you can't hear it, always hopeful that its time will come.

The time when you learn to hear that song and start to act upon its words, knowing and trusting their wisdom, is a time of huge significance in your life.

Suddenly your life starts to open up and unfold in front of you, as you start to develop a deep knowing about what is good for you and what is not so good.

Honour your inner sparkle today by making a commitment to yourself to listen out for it, to get quiet, and to never forget the following:

Inside you, there is a unique song of such beauty that, when you express it, the Universe will want to weep for pure joy.

Process 5 Self-Affirmation: I honour my inner sparkle.

Magical Mission — Heart Opening Focus

"Having a heart means you have an essential nature and that, furthermore, you want to express and experience that nature. You want to indulge that nature. That's your passion. You want to live from your own inner spark and connect with and enjoy the spark in others. That's the whole point of the human race. Even if 98 percent of the population doesn't get it." — William Whitecloud

The connection between your head and heart is not something you have to create, it is something you already have that is waiting for you to remember it and use it. You were born knowing what your heart wanted and that capacity has never left you.

Rather than worry about trying to master all the solutions I've shared in this chapter, simply choose the one that resonates most. In trusting that choice, you've already started to revisit your heart-head connection.

You then get to choose how you want to keep honouring this connection, safe in the knowledge that it is the most natural thing on earth for you to do. It may take a while for you to believe that and see the impact it has on your daily life, but that's okay.

For your Magical Mission, you are invited to try this heart-opening focus to explore one thing that makes your heart smile.

You don't need to be an experienced meditator to use or benefit from it. *This is about you acknowledging your lovely heart.*

Grab your journal and a pen for afterwards. Read through first and then play with it. ◀)
https://www.helenrebello.com/p/MagicBookResources

You'll need a few minutes and a quiet, safe space to sit, where you won't be disturbed - either on a chair, or on a cushion on the floor.

- Get comfortable, wriggling out any tension, and having a good stretch and yawn before you settle.

- Make sure your feet connect to the ground, so that you stay present and grounded.

- Place the tip of your tongue on the roof of your mouth to calm your system, shut your eyes, and breathe in deeply.

- Sigh your breath slowly out and repeat this breath twice more.

- Feel your body calm. Feel your breath expand.

- I then invite you to start saying the word 'SO' to yourself as you breathe in, and 'HUM' as you breathe out. Notice how your inhalation sounds like the word 'so' and the exhalation sounds like the word 'hum'. *This translates as "I Am That" and with every breath you are reaffirming your existence on earth.*

- Repeat this focus for a few breaths until you feel your whole system settling and your breath slowing down; *this makes you more receptive.*

- Placing one hand on your heart and one on your belly, ask yourself what truly makes your heart smile. *Don't overthink this, let the answer come from deep inside you, not from your head! If you struggle, take yourself back to what you loved doing as a child.*

- Take a moment to imagine doing the thing you love to do. *Don't judge yourself in any way, let images arise as they please.*

- Feel the positive emotions in your body and your heart as you immerse yourself in memories.

- Notice the warmth in your heart and imagine that flowing around your whole body... you may even feel tingling as you do.

- Allow the corners of your mouth to turn up into a smile and feel your heart area expand as you do.

- Let yourself absorb the feelings for as long as you choose, soaking them up and enjoying them.

- When you feel ready to come back to the room, lightly stamp your feet first to ground you again.

- Lower your gaze, open your eyes, have a wriggle and a stretch, and smile!

- Grab your journal, or paper and a pen, and WRITE this memory down.

- Ask yourself what is the smallest aspect of this that you can commit to re-introducing daily? For example, if it's reading, commit to reading 1 page a day. If it's writing, commit to writing 50 words daily. If it's dancing, commit to finding 5 minutes to dance.

- Break it down, write it down, and put it in your daily schedule whilst the memory is fresh and vibrant, preferably aiming for each morning before the day has a chance to intrude!

Committing to doing something small to nourish your heart daily will keep your connection to your heart open and help you get better at noticing what lights you up.

Follow that more often and you'll be astonished by where it might lead you.

CHAPTER 9
Process 6 — Centre Yourself
Rediscover Your Core Blueprint

"Only by much searching and mining are gold and diamonds obtained, and man can find every truth connected with his being if he will dig deep into the mine of his soul." — James Allen

Have you always had a sense that there is so much more to you than meets the eye, and if you wanted to, you could turn things up a notch?

Or maybe you feel as though others don't see your true magnificence... but you keep that feeling to yourself because heaven forbid anyone should think they are magnificent.

Have you stopped to ask yourself where that sense came from?

What part of you has that deep, unexplainable knowing?

We spend our lives looking for that elusive part of us that has magical inner knowing. It is the part we disconnected from when the Matrix Myth tried to take over our heads. It has always been with us and it's the part that knows we are enough.

Your core blueprint has been with you from the very beginning of your existence. It is your true self; the quiet unsung hero that never wavers from its belief in you, no matter what negative, self-doubt messages you might periodically send out into your system.

Your core blueprint is one of the most powerful aspects of your being. It holds the key to your happiness, your fulfilment, joy, and love. It is your true nature and reconnecting and aligning to it unlocks your core potential. Your blueprint is stamped deeply into your DNA and your energy system. The most primitive aspect of you, it contains a unique and incredible combination of skills and talents that no one will ever see again. When you start uncovering and expressing these, you will feel so centred in yourself, you'll never feel the need to look outside yourself for validation again.

Changing your connection to yourself internally helps you better respond and make changes externally because it reconnects you to this deeper power and presence within. Getting clear on who you are at your core helps you find a way through anything because your core will always be there for you and it will never change, no matter what the world throws at you.

Creating a life that brings you inner peace, a sense of purpose and fulfilment, is really about being deeply in touch with yourself. You're connected to yourself so deeply that you know what you want, who you are, what you're about, and what you're here for. This knowledge helps you transcend fear long enough to show up each day in a way that *truly* honours you. Knowing how to get centred helps you to detach from external inputs and tune into your own guidance. The more centred you become, the more deeply you connect to that essential core part of you, so that you live more from that place.

My Story — Rediscovering The Core Blueprint I Never Lost

"Deep in the soul, below pain, below all the distraction of life, is a silence vast and grand – an infinite ocean of calm, which nothing can disturb; nature's own exceeding peace, which 'passes understanding'. That which we seek with passionate longing, here and there, upward and outward; we find at last within ourselves."
— C.M.C. quoted by R.M. Bucke

I stumbled across Shiatsu quite by accident - at least that's what I thought at the time.

With the help of my lovely husband, after realising I had to make some big changes in my life, I embarked on a very logical search to work out what my next path should be.

I looked at what I was good at, loved doing and knew a lot about. It made sense to me to use those skills and knowledge. I also wrote down what I no longer wanted to compromise on. There were practical considerations, such as how much time did I want to take exploring a new direction and how much money did I want to spend. Once we had that outlined, I surveyed my list and decided I wanted to do something requiring 'proper' training; clearly the Western science mindset still had me firmly in its grip!

Thanks to the wonders of the Internet, we discovered Shiatsu. I had never heard of it before but had always been interested in self-development and wellness practices like yoga, and it sounded intriguing. Shiatsu required three years training and had great reviews, and there just happened to be a training school in my town.

I signed up to do a weekend Basics course, to see whether I liked it or not, and as a result, I was curious and interested enough to sign up for the whole course. Keeping my practical head on, I resigned from my employed Sonography job and became a locum instead. This gave me the money to fund the training, the freedom to work around the course, and the knowledge that if Sonography got too much, I could leave any time I chose.

Over the course of the training, I slowly learned how to get out of my head and into my heart. I started processing years of stuck emotions and began addressing my lack of self-worth. I became more confident, more expressive, wiser, and more grounded. It was the start of a huge, lifelong self-realisation journey that feels as though it was divinely guided. I only embarked on the training to learn a new skill and I ended up discovering a new approach to life!

I felt so transformed and inspired by the unexpected benefits of training in Shiatsu, that after qualifying, I wrote a summary of what I wanted my work to offer others:

The true spirit of my work is to give stressed and unfulfilled women the deep joy, healing, self-acceptance, and contentment that results from being given a calm, non-judgemental and nurturing space in which to truly reconnect to themselves. This rekindles their inner sparkle, liberates their unique potential, and enables them to fully stand in their own magnificent power.

Fast forward a few years, when after studying ever deeper levels of energy-based bodywork, my instincts told me to find a way to do yoga teacher training, alongside my husband. This was definitely heart-led. We wanted to train with the same amazing teacher we were in the Sri Lankan jungle with, because we loved her style of yoga. For me, it also echoed the ethos of the bodywork approaches I had trained in. The very first training course was in Goa - my husband's ancestral home - which seemed like a sign; but we had no idea how to fund it or create the space to go away for six weeks.

Where there is an intuitive will; however, there is a magical way.

I have no idea how we managed it, but somehow the Universe conspired to work with us and we made it happen. It was the most profound and intensive training I had embarked on, and by then, I had done some deep-dive training. During that time, I did a lot of crying, shed more layers of old stuff, opened my heart even more, and made peace with deep issues that had haunted me for years.

In every class, I kept finding myself doodling the same spiral symbol. It wasn't a conscious thing; it just kept happening. It had been years since I allowed myself the indulgence of doodling and it felt like it mirrored the unfolding that was happening on the course. It wasn't a symbol I recognised, and no one else had seen it before either.

When I got home, I searched the Internet for the symbol. I researched images, looked up ancient symbolism, searched social media and tattoo pictures. I never found it, but still I kept doodling it. About two years later, I saw the symbol tattooed on a woman's leg and couldn't believe what I was seeing. She left before I had a chance to ask her what it was, but then I started seeing the symbol on others too. I found out that the symbol is called a unalome, an ancient Buddhist symbol representing the spiraling pathway of life to self-realisation. My version appears on the cover of this book.

Discovering this made me realise that something higher than my own consciousness led me to this work. Even though it has changed and evolved alongside me, at its core, my approach still remains the same as it did when I first qualified in Shiatsu. The words I wrote about the spirit of my work many years ago, still represent what underlies my work today. Those words came through me to express what I most value and want to offer others. I had no idea when I wrote them that they would still be true today. The form my work takes now is very different to when I wrote them, but by taking small steps and trusting in my path, I magically discovered my core blueprint; represented in words.

It was there all along, I just didn't realise it until I was given a sign in the form of an ancient symbol and later uncovered what it meant. It couldn't be a more perfect representation of my own journey and the journey I offer others.

You could almost call it Magic.

I don't know what you came here to do, but I do know your core blueprint lies inside you. Trust in that and hold onto it unapologetically and wholeheartedly.

Create the space and time and it will come to meet you.

Head-Led Challenges of Process 6

"The universe is full of magical things patiently waiting for our wits to grow sharper." —Eden Phillpotts

Have you ever stopped to think about what it means to be centered?

If someone asked you whether you feel centered, what would you say? How would you decide whether you meet the criteria or not when it seems like such an elusive concept?

In the Western world, the human body is viewed and treated in a very fragmented way. Specialists are trained in one aspect of the body, such as orthopedics, urology, obstetrics, or gynecology, with little awareness of the whole system and how different aspects interrelate. This fragmented way of looking at ourselves permeates our collective consciousness. We view ourselves as distinctly separate systems: body and mind - some of us adding spirit. If we have a problem with one area, we visit the appropriate specialist; handing over our care to someone outside ourselves, rather than try changing something inside.

We generally forget about the fact that we are not merely a body and mind, we are also made of energy. Even when we learn to view ourselves more holistically, it still takes a long time to unpick this lifetime habit. Is it any wonder we struggle to be centred when we see ourselves as broken physical entities and forget our true wonder and magic?

You can't find the centre of something that is split into separate parts, which is why we struggle to find a sense of being centered. Hopefully by now; however, you are letting go of that old paradigm as you progress further along the bridge towards the new one.

In order to smooth your journey further, there are a few more challenges to consider:

1. The Yang Default

Modern life causes us to 'live in our heads' and focus forwards, rather than living in the present. We therefore do not function in 'real time' and are very unconnected to ourselves. We like to think our way into solutions and lack belief in anything more esoteric. Our default methodology is to keep pushing until we feel the burn because we think softer approaches don't have results we can see.

We get so busy 'doing' that we have no time to 'be', and as the saying goes, we are human beings not human doings! It is no wonder we struggle to get centred, as we are using up our porridge pot of energy constantly pushing water uphill and living life in the fast lane.

This very Yang way to live our lives is often not balanced by softer, Yin activities which we need in order to access the more subtle aspects of our being.

Becoming centred requires us to be in balance, get quiet enough to tune into our intuition, and be aware enough of our systems to course-correct when we need to. Because it comes less naturally to us, we have to be patient with ourselves, and not push through or rush the process.

2. Getting Lost in Nowhere Land

I didn't understand the concept of getting present until I started training in Shiatsu.

Like anything in life, you don't know what you don't know, which is why I used to spend half my life daydreaming or directing my energy at old grievances, and stories. I was so unaware at one stage, I had no idea that was even happening, and certainly didn't know it could be any different. I was simply living life. Except I wasn't because I was wandering through Nowhere Land, never actually living in the same moment my body was in. This is not unusual, in fact it's our normality. Most people, most of the time, are not present in the present because they're elsewhere in their heads.

When your attention is somewhere different to your body and to the present time, you can't really notice or enjoy what's happening to you in that moment. This can be a valuable tool if you have to do something traumatic but removing yourself mentally massively limits what you can achieve and experience *in that moment.*

When you are distracted and somewhere else in your head, you cannot connect to anything or anyone around you, never mind centre and connect to yourself.

3. Forgetting the Power of The Breath

Learning how to fully breathe is one of the simplest ways to become more present and connect to yourself. It expands and relaxes your system, making it easier for you to access a sense of your core blueprint energy.

If you're not present, you don't fully breathe. If you don't fully breathe, not only are you not oxygenating your system and replenishing your energy, you're making your body and awareness more compressed. Your upper chest, heart and lungs become a bit like a protective cage, making it very hard to take in anything new.

Most people have reduced, shallow breathing, meaning they are not fully connected with their own body. We've also lost our connection with our belly and this area is often regarded negatively: we worry about our 'fat bellies' and constantly try to hold our stomachs in. This causes disconnection between our upper and lower bodies, making it very challenging for us to tune into our own energy, because it ends up so compressed and stuck.

Life is motion; the more movement you have in your system, the more efficiently your body runs. Your body filters out toxins faster, processes food more quickly, and you feel much better *in* yourself. Learning how to breathe fully contributes to this, and when you live in a happier body, you find it easier to ignore the mind chatter and centre yourself, because your attention isn't being dragged off to sore areas all the time.

4. Letting Your Head Lead You

In order to really step into your potential, you have to let your heart lead the way, because your head will only ever lead you back into safety.

We all want to be safe, but the kind of safety your head wants for you is the kind that wraps you in a cotton wool blanket and keeps your real self hidden so you are less vulnerable. This can become a lifelong habit of hiding who you really are from the world, because you believe the myth that this keeps you from getting hurt or failing.

The trouble is, it keeps you from really feeling the good things in life too.

When you let your heart lead the way, you'll access enough courage to transcend the fear messages from your head and come into a deeper sense of your core self.

This doesn't mean you'll spend every moment of every day living in a consciously aware and courageous way, but it means you'll spend a lot less of your lifetime hiding somewhere that keeps you safe, but unfulfilled.

5. Forgetting To Celebrate

As you evolve into future you, how often do you remember to celebrate your journey to date?

One of our biggest failings, is forgetting how far we've come, how much we've learned, how much we've overcome, how loved we are, and how many beautiful moments we've had. We focus on our current limitations and consequently doubt ourselves, not believing we have what it takes to evolve into the greater expression of who we came here to be.

This causes anxiety and frustration as we try to honour the inner call to keep going and try new things. We desperately search for solid ground, a sense of certainty, and to regain forward momentum; in the process, getting trapped in our head and falling back into the safety loop created by our inner cast of characters.

We get so tired of feeling bad about ourselves, fighting with our heads and wishing we could change things we can't, that we stop believing we can change anything. When you forget to celebrate yourself and your journey, you effectively shut down possibility. Without that expansive energy, your chances of getting centred are slim.

The more centred you become, the more you can let those old patterns fall away. The following solutions show you how.

Heart-Led Solutions for Process 6

"Surrender is a bold spiritual stance, the stance of a spiritual warrior, because what we are surrendering to is the next stage of our evolution." — Michael Bernard Beckwith

The modern world is a noisy, busy place and you have had to learn to adapt as you've travelled through life. Some of the adaptations you have made complement you and others don't.

The more you hold onto things that are less natural for you, the more you will struggle as you move further away from your core self. This is because at the deepest level of your being, there is something quite magical and primeval driving you and guiding you, even if you aren't aware of it. That part of you has your original self imprinted firmly upon it; made from a combination of the stars, your ancestral energy, your genetic code and your life force energy. The less you express this, the more your system will revolt.

No one else on earth has had, or ever will have, the same combination of these influences as you. As much as it goes against the grain, this is something to celebrate, not undervalue or hide. The only aspect of you invested in hiding it is your Puppy Dog Ego, and quite frankly, I think he or she has ruled your world for long enough.

There is the aspect of you that feeds your thoughts with lies and the aspect of you that is aware this is happening. It's a bit like having both an inner heroine *and* your inner cast of characters that want to keep you safe. Those characters create a lot of noise and drama if left unattended. Like naughty children they cavort around with the Puppy Dog Ego, gathering evidence like sticks they present to you. This evidence is used to try and convince you that this is your true reality, rather than just a made up story by the part of your head trying to keep you safe.

Centering yourself is a beautiful way to shift your energy and attention away from this noise, back to the quieter, more knowing, much more powerful essence of your true nature. When you get still and quiet and drop deeply into your centre, you'll connect to the truth of who you are, why you are here, and you'll inherently know what to do because you'll connect to your highest self.

When you centre yourself you come back into connection with the deepest strongest part of you, both physically and energetically. This aspect of you lies within your spine, where your original blueprint is stored.

The question, is how?

The simplest and possibly most challenging way is through meditation. It brings the processes together, is free, and is something you can do yourself, which means your head can't use the excuses of needing more money or the right class to stall you. To centre and connect to your core blueprint, all you need to do is dedicate time to embodying a state that heightens your awareness of it. In my experience, this happens when you get quiet, get present, breathe, get out of your head, get to *the back of your body* (I'll explain that shortly), and simply observe and feel what is happening.

The core components of meditation; with an extra sprinkling of a specific, powerful and magical intention.

They are all softer yin practices of being, which paradoxically, require practice to get used to, in other words 'doing'!

Your head will be somewhat confused by this paradox, so to avoid getting it all upset and worried, explore the following solutions:

Solution 1. Get Quiet

"Through listening to the truth of the body it is possible to discover what we can do, who we can be, what we can experience, how we can love." — Marion Rosen

You are an incredible human being made of the same wondrous elements that form the entire Universe. You have within you the keys to deep expression and unfolding of who you came here to be, and the best way to access them is to get quiet.

As you discovered in the previous process, your heart and intuition talk quietly, in whispers. Your core blueprint information comes to you not only through the same intuitive whispers, but also through your *felt* senses. In order to really tune into these, you need to reduce anything that takes your attention outside yourself.

When you gift yourself regular periods of silence, you start uncovering an inner oasis of restorative energy. This returns you to your natural state of peace, as you start to notice the space behind the noise of your inner and outer world.

Within that space lies your true nature, and as you get quiet and calm your system, your brainwaves shift along with you and you can access a sense of your underlying self more easily.

Solution 2. Get Present in the Present

This is a useful way to remember that in order to make any kind of change, access any state, or influence anything at all, you need to be 'now here', not 'nowhere'. When you are, you can tune into yourself and into the gap between stimulation and response. This is an empowering place to hang out, but it's a difficult state to maintain because of the way your brain is wired.

According to social psychologist and author Amy Cuddy, presence is, *"the state of being attuned to and able to comfortably express our true thoughts, feelings, values, and potential."*

Rather than try to attain some impossible state of constant nirvana, give yourself permission to simply bring yourself back, again and again, whenever you notice you have drifted off.

There are various ways you can do this more intentionally when you start to meditate. I like to think of my mind as being on two train tracks. The busy track with your inner cast of characters who are trying to get your attention, and the quiet track, which feels more mellow.

All you have to do is notice which track you're on and when you realise you've inadvertently wandered over to the busy track, return to the quiet one. No need to tell yourself off or try shutting your mind up, simply notice and shift as needed.

Solution 3. Breathe

"Breath is the bridge which connects life to consciousness, which unites your body to your thought. Whenever your mind becomes scattered, use your breath as the means to take hold of your mind again." — Thich Nhat Hanh

Eastern societies have been using breath awareness to heal and invigorate for centuries through practices such as Yoga and Qi Gung. The two characters for Qi Gung translate as 'the breath practice of life'.

Your first breath after birth acts as powerful ignition bringing you to external life. Reconnecting with your breath relaxes and grounds you, calms your nervous system and returns you to the present.

Enhancing your breath gives you more life force, as it reduces impurities and detoxes your system more effectively with improved exhalation, allowing each cell in your body to be more nourished and revitalised by the increased oxygen from each inhalation.

Breathing into your belly (your energy centre or hara) encourages opening of your core energy pathways – the extraordinary meridians – making it easier to connect to your core blueprint and tune into the essence of who you are.

Solution 4. Get Out of Your Head

In the fourth process, you learned how to ground your energy. When it comes to connecting with your own core energy, this is one of your most important tools, because it is only when you're in your body that you can perceive subtle shifts and feelings.

Everything in nature spins and moves in a spiralling motion right through from the planets to the smallest micro-levels of your cells. Learning to ground your energy and get out of your own head helps you to harness the power of your energy by gathering it into your body.

From this place you can direct it in a way that helps you connect to your core strength. This is as true for practices such as meditation as it is for running in a race.

Solution 5. Get to the Back of Your Body

Your Extraordinary Vessels act as the underground reservoirs of your body's energy, sending your chi energy out to your meridians as required. They are your core energies that form first after conception and are regarded as 'the ancestral blueprint'. These vessels are powerful and the more motion and freedom you have in your body, the better these vessels function and the more vitality you have.

One of them, known as the Governing Vessel (GV), is located along the spine, which is also where your central nervous system is located, cerebrospinal fluid circulates, and where sensitive membranes line your spine. The GV has several powerful acupoints located along it, intersecting with your chakras, making the whole area around your spine an extremely important and powerful processing area.

Your spine is incredibly strong and it has to be because it protects so much of what makes you who you are. When you connect to the back of your body, you connect to a deeper sense of yourself and it feels like coming home because, in a way, it is. It is coming home to the part of you that existed first, after conception. Being in this place helps you access resources you cannot access when you're living in your head.

Learning to direct your energy and attention to the back of your body enables you to detach more from the busyness at the front of your body. All the noisy processing happens in the front your body; it's where your stomach gurgles, your head cogitates, your heart pumps, and your belly moves. When you send your attention backwards, you start to let this all go, as you observe it, rather than be part of it.

Used regularly, this powerful shift of perception has the power to change your life, which is why I use it daily.

Solution 6. Feel

"Understanding the blueprint is an experiential process. It's something we have to come into resonance with so that we can actually feel it. It's something that happens between the words and phrases. Something that occurs outside of thought. It comes from perception and attention." — Ray Castellino

We cannot help wanting to understand why and how things work; we are wired that way... however, in terms of knowing how to connect to the deepest part of yourself and hear your own answers, you have to *feel* your way into it.

This is a journey you have to explore yourself, I can't take you there. You need to get a sense of who you are and how your energy feels in darkness. Ask yourself how you know it's you when you get up in the night. What are you sensing? What is it that others sense around you? Get to know how you feel in your body when you can't even see your own hands. This gives you a sense of your 'baseline' - something you have to *feel*, not *think* your way to.

When you get quiet, sit at the back of your body and simply wait with no expectation or effort. You'll start to notice where you feel empty, how your heart feels, how expansive it feels when you breathe. You'll start to tune into your own sense of self so deeply that it becomes a beautiful place to hang out because you've come home to your true nature. Eventually you get so good at connecting to this with your eyes open, you are able to hear your intuition and your inner guidance more clearly, more of the time.

When you centre yourself, it enables you to access a state of being at home in your own skin. We often don't consciously realise it, but at our core, all we really want is to feel comfortable with ourselves and happy with who we are. Once you are clear on who you are and you've embodied a sense of that deep within you, you'll be so much better at letting go of any sense that you are not enough already, as you are.

You have what it takes, just as I do. You've served your apprenticeship and you've been worthy since you were born.

Process 6 – Summary for Your Soul:

Your core blueprint is one of the most powerful aspects of your whole being. It holds the key to your happiness, fulfillment, joy, and love.

It impacts upon your interactions with others, and your ability to follow through with your intentions and reach your desires.

Within your core blueprint awaits your greatest source of intuition.

When you get still and quiet and drop deeply into your centre, you'll connect to the truth of who you are, why you are here, and you'll inherently know what to do because you'll connect to your highest self.

Connect to your centre so that you are able to receive more love, abundance, joy and fulfillment each and every day.

Process 6 Self-Affirmation: I am open to rediscovering my core essence.

Magical Mission — Come Home to Your Centre

"What is it that stands higher than words? Action. What is it that stands higher than action? Silence." — Saint Francis

Now that you have more awareness of how fundamental reconnecting to your core blueprint is, you are ready to gather the tools you have collected to get more centred.

Earlier on your journey, you started identifying how your system feels and you also explored the processes of opening your heart and grounding. I invite you to get to know yourself more deeply, by learning a powerful Taoist focus to reconnect to your core.

After the following practice, there are some additional prompts to help you access your intuition.

The focus below is suitable for anyone, regardless of your experience with meditation. I have taught it to people with no experience whatsoever of any 'energy' practices, and they loved it. You are returning to a natural state of getting quiet, present, breathing, grounding, getting to the back of your body and feeling whatever is there. When you know how you feel, you get better at spotting it when something shifts you from your natural baseline - in a good or bad way.

Come Home To Your Centre Practice

The following is an edited version of a much deeper process, to offer you a glimpse into an alternative approach to connecting to your core self. Read through it first and trust you will retain what you need to for now. Repeated regularly this will change your awareness not only of yourself, but of the world around you. ◀

https://www.helenrebello.com/p/MagicBookResources

- To help you get out of your head, give your body a good all-over shake, wriggle your shoulders, gently rotate your hips, and smile to release your jaw.

- Grab your journal and pen and prepare a space where you'll be comfortable and able to sit upright for a few minutes.

- Sit yourself down with your spinestraight and your feet on the ground.

- Use your tools to ground and quieten yourself, thinking into your feet, consciously breathing, softening, and lengthening your spine by imagining a line attached to your head.

- Give yourself a few moments to do this and settle. Keep breathing with awareness and notice as your breath slows.

- Move your head backwards very slightly until you feel a response at the back of your head and as you connect to this, imagine your skull is like a cave, with your eyes representing the entrance, and the back of your head representing the back of the cave.

- Rest your attention at the very back of the cave of your head and imagine watching the world pass by the entrance, without feeling the need to get involved.

- Keep breathing slowly and relax your chest, imagining as you do so that you are moving your awareness away from it, back towards your spine.

- If you feel your attention shifting forwards, bring it backwards in the cave of your skull.

- Notice the back of your body, the back of your spine and keep shifting your attention to the back of yourself.

- Notice how you feel, how much quieter it feels to rest here. Notice your breath, how much quieter your brain is now.

- Stay with this for as long as you like and when you feel as though you have a sense of quietness, gently let your attention come back to the room, the ground, your hands, and body.

- Breathe and trust that you learned exactly what you needed for now.

- The more you remember to use this focus, the more you will access your core blueprint.

Staying with a sense of how you felt, grab your journal and answer the following prompts with a view to noticing how your body feels as you read them. Trust your first instinctual answer and write as much or little as you like... no rules!

Prompts to help you connect with your core blueprint:

1. If you were to describe the way you feel right now, what would you say?
2. How does that feeling differ from your usual state?
3. Which state do you prefer?
4. What can you do to access that state more often?

5. What are your favourite tastes, smells, sounds? How does it feel to imagine them?

6. What word describes how your favourite place makes you feel?

7. What gives you energy?

8. If you were an ice cream, what flavour would you be?

9. If your favourite human was describing you in three words, what would they say?

10. Who are you when no-one is watching? Did this exercise make you feel more or less like that?

These prompts will give you a true flavour of who you are. Let your answers percolate for a couple of days and see what other insights come your way.

The more you use the practice above and the more time you spend being quiet, the easier it will get to connect to your core blueprint. It may feel challenging sometimes, but that's normal and it will pass.

As you become really practiced at this, you will discover how deeply rooted in yourself you've become, and there is no power quite like it.

CHAPTER 10
Process 7 — Align Yourself
Unravel Your Magical Manifesto

"And the day came when the risk to remain tight in a bud was more painful than the risk it took to blossom." — *Anais Nin*

What would you say if I told you it is perfectly okay to throw out the rule book when it comes to deciding what you want from your life?

Would your shoulders ease if I invited you to let go of any sense that you *must* have money, a partner, an epic career, and a big house to be successful? Would your smile widen as you release your mind from this part of the Matrix Myth, safe in the knowledge your new way will serve you better?

Living with alignment is about congruence; integrating all parts of yourself and being true to who you are. Navigating life according to what you value, what your heart desires, and what is for the greater good of you and those around you. It is about reducing friction in your life as much as possible by honouring your natural energy flow, adjusting to seasonal shifts, and using your strengths to flow more easily through challenges.

In this process, you get to rewrite the rules your way by discovering what is truly important to your heart. You can then assess how well you are currently aligning yourself with that and explore ways to align yourself more.

The Taoist concept of wu-wei is one of the most powerful concepts I've been taught. In Western terms it is a lot like 'going with the flow' only richer and more nuanced. Living with wu-wei is about flowing more peacefully and purposefully through life, by yielding to something bigger than you and doing your best to live in alignment with your core blueprint.

The MAGICAL process is very much about approaching your life from this perspective, although I didn't realise that until after I created it. I could never fully do the concept justice, as it is an ever-evolving, intangible way of living, unique to each person in each moment. It is indefinable in much the same way that describing connecting to your core potential is; you have to feel your way into it and let go of any need to understand it or grasp it.

This of course, makes it almost impossible to explain, but not impossible to embody.

The more I have aligned my life with who I am at my core, alongside letting go of control and yielding to the greater force of the Actual Matrix, the more the magic of wu-wei reveals itself to me.

Normal life will play tricks on you and sway you from time to time, which is why being in flow isn't a permanent state. It becomes a mere blip in the Matrix though, once you've learned to view life through the life lens of wu-wei. You get jolted a bit, but then you remember that a lot of what you think is important, *isn't*, and you let it go. You smile at yourself for accidentally getting pulled back towards the Matrix Myth and lean back into your core strength, ready to resume your journey.

We all know the effortless, delicious sense of losing ourselves in something we love doing. In my experience, living from your heart, aided and abetted by your head, is the perfect recipe for accessing that flow state more often and creating magic in your life.

As I have discovered…

My Story — Learning to Do Life Differently

"The most beautiful experience we can have is the mysterious. It is the fundamental emotion that stands at the cradle of true art and true science." — Albert Einstein

I am not entirely sure when I realised I had started to create my own version of magic in my life.

It certainly wasn't during any of the times I have shared with you; when I met the man I always knew I would meet, when I was in the Sri Lankan jungle, or when I trusted my instincts and signed up for a yoga training course I couldn't afford. It wasn't when I found the house I had visualised in the location I wanted and despite being up against many other bidders, we somehow got it. It wasn't when my Shiatsu assessment went exactly as I had visualised it, or when I got invited to join the Cranio-Sacral Therapy teaching team about two weeks after my heart told me that's what I would do.

On all those occasions, my head made it seem logical in case I started getting ideas.

Magic of course, is something we each define our own way, so you could argue that my head has rewritten my own history to make it fit the story it tells itself. In a way you would be right, but there's more to it than that. I feel it in the depths of my soul and, if you're true to yourself, you can't really argue with that feeling.

Although I managed to argue with it for years.

Thankfully, somewhere along the line, I started to see how the threads of my life had interwoven to create a pathway that made sense. Events I could never have planned created core themes that appeared again and again throughout my life. Like a matrix in its own right, life unfolded in layers, sneakily revealing its magic bit by bit. Further along the line, I started seeing how as I shifted my own state, the state of my life shifted alongside it. Even further along the line, as I got more out of my head and into my heart, I saw how many incredible dreams somehow fell into place, almost without trying. A vision that felt right would appear seemingly from nowhere in my head, and not long afterwards it would happen.

Eventually it got to the point where I was getting so used to acting from my heart and trusting in the power of the Actual Matrix, it became challenging to do anything that went against the grain. Not that this stopped me doing things I knew I'd fallen out of love with. Knowing what is right for you and acting on it don't always happen immediately when you've already committed to something. I told myself it wasn't convenient to make changes and I also had fear to overcome.

Heart-led living doesn't come with a manual… it's a process you discover in little moments, by taking one step forward and two steps back.

The more finely attuned I got to my heart, however, the less I could ignore what didn't resonate or feel good. Life gets more magical the more aligned with yourself you get, but it still asks you to meet it halfway.

I won't lie. To a lifelong avoider of conflict who is also a people-pleaser, this felt scary. My old patterns are deeply ingrained. They run almost as deeply as my core blueprint. You don't get to experience deep levels of fulfilment and inner peace without feeling guilty about it; or like you're being self-indulgent. Not at first anyway.

I had to learn to trust that everything would work out eventually, and it wasn't helpful to feel bad about my decisions. I had to accept the possibility that if I was honest that something no longer felt right to me, it would empower others to be honest with themselves too. I needed to realise that if I did things with inner resentment because I didn't want to let people down, in truth I wasn't honouring anyone.

Sometimes the best way forwards is simply to develop love and compassion for what is, and stop thinking everything is so important. Which is when things get really interesting... especially if you're still living somewhere you don't want to, working in a way that no longer works, and you're still, after a lifetime, suppressing your deepest calling. Which is why, in my case, surrendering enabled my long-suppressed inner writer to rise up like a phoenix with daily intuitive 'downloads'. Once I started trusting in that, the idea for this book dropped into my consciousness.

How magical is that!

Surrendering then led my husband and me to put steps in place to leave behind everything we knew, with no clear plan, other than to hopefully move somewhere we could afford, near water. Our heads' attempt to take over were thwarted by Magic, which had a better plan and sent us an alternative breadcrumb trail to follow.

We now live in a town we've never visited- nowhere near water - with many like-minded people, incredible hills we adore and the same breathtaking view from our bed I've envisaged in my mind for years.

We did not see that coming!

When you align with your core self, surrender to magic and start to Do Life Differently, anything can happen.

Doing life differently doesn't mean changing everything in your life. It means changing your *relationship* to everything and everyone, by changing your relationship to yourself. It means surrendering to something bigger and letting go of what your mind can conceive. Doing life differently can simply mean bringing more of yourself to what you already do; embracing the opportunity to touch someone's heart with a smile or look them in the eyes with kindness. It can mean falling back in love with something because you realise in the busyness of life you've forgotten that it truly makes your heart smile.

If it means something bigger, you can trust it will unfold at a pace you can handle, when you have the relevant resources in place, even if it doesn't feel like that at the time. Which is why in my case, even though it led to me relocating and becoming a writer at long last, it was a process that unfolded organically over many years.

That is the thing about magic: it won't be rushed. You can't control it, and it won't happen unless it knows your heart and soul are aligned with the greater good.

Head-Led Challenges of Process 7

"In many shamanic societies, if you came to a shaman or medicine person complaining of being disheartened, dispirited, or depressed, they would ask one of four questions: 'When did you stop dancing? When did you stop singing? When did you stop being enchanted by stories? When did you stop finding comfort in the sweet territory of silence? Where we have stopped dancing, singing, being enchanted by stories, or finding comfort in silence is where we have experienced the loss of soul.'" — Angeles Arrien

Why on earth am I starting off a section about the challenges of alignment with a quote about the loss of your soul?

Possibly because, in my experience, the most common reason people get out of alignment with who they came here to be, is because they become so trapped in the Matrix Myth they end up living someone else's version of life. Their bodies are so busy keeping up with the hamster wheel of life, they forget they even have a soul to nourish; never mind indulge in the luxury of honouring themselves.

I think we can both agree there's no fun in that.

I am no sociologist or psychologist, but when you live the wrong way for long enough, then find your way out of the broken mess you end up in, you get pretty good at seeing the pattern in others. This doesn't make me an expert on all the contributory factors - and I couldn't begin to unravel the ancestral patterns behind it - but what I can say is there are some very common challenges we face that lead us there.

You are wise now to the sneaky Matrix Myth and the whispers of your inner safety committee, but this doesn't mean these challenges will no longer affect you.

Take a breath, get to the quiet at the back of your body, and as you read, send yourself love and compassion. If you suffer from any of these, you haven't done anything wrong. Thankfully, however, there is a great deal you can do differently as you mindfully move forwards.

1. Having No Vision

It's crazy that we're asked to make decisions potentially affecting our entire lives when we have only just become teenagers. We realize in later life that we can chop and change, but do you remember that feeling of pressure you had at the thought that your choices then could impact your whole life?

If you got really lucky, you made excellent choices, didn't find it stressful, and set yourself on the right course. I suspect that as you're reading this book, you are more likely to have journeyed down a path that no longer feels right. Which can make you feel like a failure, even though you're not.

No wonder so many of us later fail to create a vision for our lives; we don't want to tie ourselves into a path we might later regret. There are those who are the complete opposite of course; so utterly convinced that the only way through life is to set a very clear plan, that when the plan fails, they have no fallback and are unable to function.

The answer is to find a middle way, which represents one of the indefinable aspects of wu-wei.

Without a vision, we've nothing to align with, or aim for. Whilst I very much endorse presence, I also believe that without a vision we wither and lose our hope. We have to find a balance between the two - identifying what it is we want and making small steps towards it - keeping one eye lightly focussed on the end goal and the rest of your attention on enjoying your day-to-day processes.

2. *Having No Compelling Reason to Change Your Paradigm*

Otherwise known as not identifying or being fully invested in your big Why. This is a crucial component for you aligning with what you want. It's also crucial for your sense of inner peace, purpose, and your ability to fulfil your potential.

Without a clear Why, it's very hard for you to find the motivation to stay healthy, focused, energized, and create boundaries; all of which are important if you want to stay in alignment and achieve what you want in life. Lacking a sense of your Why is also the reason you stay in a state of inertia, settling for something that is 'sort of' nice but not exciting enough to shout about, or painful enough to move away from.

Until I found my Why, I used to bend over backwards to look after everybody, not tread on toes, avoid confrontation by never stating what I wanted, and say yes to things I didn't want to. I prioritized others over doing what I wanted, like going to the gym or staying on track with my eating, and in the process, got further out of integrity and closer to the Land of Regrets and Resentment.

I filled up my life with a gazillion things – many of which were great – but the majority of which did absolutely nothing to nourish my heart. Instead, they simply took me away from what *did*, and because my heart wasn't in it, I was doing others a disservice.

Your Why is your personal guiding light, and your life is worthy of honouring it.

3. Trying Too Hard

"To offer no resistance to life is to be in a state of grace, ease and lightness" — Eckhart Tolle

What fuel do you generally use to move towards or achieve your best intentions? Do you use the fire in your belly and the love in your heart? Or does your head and sheer effort lead the way?

If you often feel as though you're swimming upstream, having to put in loads of extra effort just to stay afloat, it's highly likely that you are going against your natural flow, and focusing on the wrong things. If that's the case, and you are out of alignment with your natural rhythm, you'll use up far more energy than you need to get things done.

There is a tendency in the Western world to think so far ahead that we almost fall over ourselves in an effort to race to the next natural stopping point. When we reach it, we barely pause to celebrate, before we head off chasing the next thing. We have punctuated our year with 90-day assessment periods, paying no attention to the natural ebb and flow of our own energy or the time of year.

We also make the mistake of using our heads to move us forwards, driving ourselves towards goals from a subconscious desire to feed our narcissistic Puppy Dog Ego, rather than yielding to the greater force we can access from a more altruistic desire that originates in our heart.

If you struggle with setbacks, constant obstacles, and problems, it may well be because you're going against the flow—doing something that doesn't align with you. Remember that there is more to you and the Universe than you can possibly conceive. When life feels ridiculously hard, maybe a higher power is trying to tell you something.

4. Falling into The Time-Monster Trap

"One of the very worst uses of time is to do something very well that need not be done at all." — Brian Tracy

Do you struggle to find time to do what you love or is that an utterly stupid question?

Your world is busy, you're balancing a lot, people want things from you and you're doing your best. You dream of what you would do if you were magically granted another 12 hours each day. Places you would explore, amazing food you would prepare, and hours you'd spend blissfully reading or doing that meditation practice you always promised yourself.

You tell yourself that it can come later, when you'll somehow magically have all the time in the world. After all, you're going to live forever. So it doesn't matter if later keeps getting put off, does it?

However, when you tell yourself you don't have time to do 'insert thing', or you need to win the lottery to free your time to 'insert thing', is that the whole picture? Is there more to it? Is there an underlying drive you haven't identified? A desire to please, serve, stay safe, earn money, feed a family, buy handbags, or feed your learning habit?

Dig deeper... what's the reason behind it? What does it tell you about what you've decided is important to you? Is there really so little time, or do you have a tendency to get distracted by shiny things, try and do everything yourself, or get so lost in your busy head you aren't present enough to make the most aligned choices?

There's always a choice, unconscious or conscious. Bring it into the light to see it more clearly so you can either make peace with it or make a step-by-step plan to change it.

Few of the things we fill our time with are truly so important that we cannot shave some time off, do them less often, delegate, or shift how we perceive them. The question is, what is it you're so busy doing, does it fill you up, and why are you doing it, if it doesn't?

5. Underestimating Your Power

"You are one thing only. You are a Divine Being. An all-powerful Creator. You are a Deity in jeans and a t-shirt, and within you dwells the infinite wisdom of the ages and the sacred creative force of All that is, will be and ever was." — Anthon St. Maarten

We come back to that pesky, insidious Matrix Myth. Even though you are more aware now of who you really are, it can take a long time to fully believe in something you've subconsciously denied for most of your life. It's all very well understanding something conceptually, but to deeply believe it, you have to give it time to slowly seep into your bones.

We live in a society that advocates hustle, and the energy used to do this comes from our head and our adrenals. Because this is not where our true power lies, we'll run out of steam and our logical head will conclude we have limited power. This serves our inner cast of characters well because, if we believe we have finite inner resources, we are less likely to go off fighting tigers.

When you do what isn't aligned with you, it will feel hard and you'll resist it, which makes you feel less powerful. That is because your heart literally isn't in it, so all the power you have in your heart remains dormant and your life force has to work that much harder to get you through the task.

The reality is, you know when you feel off-kilter or out of sorts. You know when something isn't quiet right. You feel it in your system, even if you can't fully articulate it. You get through it when life throws you curve balls, digging deep and finding strength you never knew you had. The phrase "I didn't know I had it me" says it all.

It is not that you're not powerful, it's that you underestimate your own power. Life is too short to live in a way that squashes who you came here to be; which includes you thinking you don't have what it takes.

6. Unknowingly Adopting Other People's Beliefs as Your Own

> "Never ever go by the book. They will want you to, but you mustn't. If the lust is too strong, tear one page from a hundred books and make your own way. There is no formula for life, no equation on how to be a human being."
> — Christopher Poindexter

I used to do a lot of things I felt I 'should' in relation to my work and my life because we are led to believe that the best way to do anything is learn from someone who has gone before us. Whilst this is true to a large extent, the person who went before you also had their own values, desires, and strengths. They lived in their own body and knew when they got tired or excited by what they were doing. Follow their path word for word, and unless you're a carbon copy of them, you are unlikely to get the same results.

Many of us create a life on someone else's terms; living out someone else's idea of success because we think that's what we're supposed to do. This stems from the Matrix Myth, and if you're not aligned with the path you choose, you'll look back at some point and realise how much time you wasted chasing a dream that was never yours in the first place.

It's the classic cause of a Midlife Crisis, which I prefer to call a Midlife Awakening.

The only way you can access the deeply sustainable energy you need to create your life your way, is to get so well acquainted and aligned with your heart's desires, you ignite your own internal fire. By all means, learn from others and study what they did, but make sure you are using your time to move towards *your* right thing.

You may never get to where you want to head, but if it's aligned with your heart, you'll have a lot more fun and fulfilment along the way.

7. Being Incongruent

How many hours in each day would you say you are totally congruent in terms of aligning your actions with your intentions?

Do you stay focused on what you promised yourself you would? Or do you find yourself getting lost in distractions and superficial tasks that you then add to a tick list so you can feel better about wasting time?

The more this happens in any given day, the more pain you'll experience from being incongruent. Your heart and soul will nag at you inwardly and your inner critic will use it as evidence that you are flawed and unworthy.

It would be wonderful to think that once we know who we are at our core, we don't deviate from that anymore. It would be so much easier if we knew that by following our heart and managing our heads, we always showed up in life the way we really want to. It is painful when we fall short of our own expectations and lose traction on something important.

Let me reassure you that it's normal. It isn't ideal, but we all fall off the wheel of good intentions at times because we don't live in a bubble, and we aren't robots. We all give up on diets because we ate one bar of chocolate, and we all sometimes act in ways that don't align with who we really are.

If you beat yourself up every time this happens, you'll be in constant trouble with yourself.

The more you get to know yourself and practice processes that are aligned with who you came here to be, the easier it gets to install them as daily habits. The payoff is that because you're developing your self-awareness, your conscience nags you more when you have a 'bad day' and fall short of your own expectations.

There's always a gap between how you want to show up in the world and how you perceive your ability to do that, because the more you evolve, the more you will expect from yourself. It's part of your brain wiring installed by the Matrix Myth and I don't believe anyone ever fully frees themselves from it.

What happens instead is you learn to accept the gap, you make peace with your process, and you accept that life is a journey with peaks and valleys. You get honest with yourself and others, stop letting your Puppy Dog Ego justify actions you know aren't serving anyone and do your best each day to navigate your path from your heart.

This is true alignment, as well as part of the secret to inner peace.

Heart-Led Solutions for Process 7

*"To be great, be whole; exclude nothing, exaggerate nothing that is not you. Be whole in everything. Put all you are into the smallest thing you do. The whole moon gleams in every pool." —
Fernando Pessoa*

The more you get to know, value, and like yourself, the more vital it will feel for you to move towards living and working in a way that feeds your soul.

Even if that currently feels like a pipe dream...

Sometimes living with more alignment is simply about taking ownership of what you want, getting better at expressing your needs, and bringing more of yourself to the things you do already. Sometimes it is about seeing less of people who deplete your energy, having better boundaries in place, and treating yourself with more kindness and patience. Sometimes it means stepping up to a new level by taking back your power from your inner cast of characters.

It's different for each person; which is why the starting point is to build your sense of self-worth, get wise to your head's whispers, and get better connected to your core self.

Tapping into your feelings allows you to take full responsibility for your life because you will be acting from the guidance of your heart. Only you know how you feel and what your instincts are and knowing this protects you from the opinions of others. They may want the best for you and mean well but they don't know what it feels like to live in your body, and they come with their own agenda, core blueprint, and perspective.

As Oscar Wilde said: *"Be yourself, everyone else is taken."*

You have every right to dance to your own tune and honour yourself by creating healthy boundaries and an aligned structure to your life. This not only nourishes your heart, but also protects your energy levels, maintains your self-esteem and self-respect, and creates healthy relationships with others.

As scary as this sounds, you don't have to overhaul your entire life. You'll often find that as you make small shifts in each of these areas, you develop greater love and appreciation for the life you have.

The following solutions all offer pathways towards greater alignment in your life. Once you have explored them and assessed how relevant they are to you, the Magical Mission will help you gather your conclusions together to create your unique Magical Manifesto.

Play with them and trust your inner wisdom to help you choose what to keep and what to throw out with your redundant rule books. You are now connected to your core blueprint and your heart, so you have all you need to decide.

Solution 1. Align Your Body

"It is through the alignment of the body that I discovered the alignment of my mind, self, and intelligence." — B.K.S Iyengar

Your posture tells a story, it reflects how you see yourself, your beliefs, and your ability to stand up and be seen.

We can all picture someone who is downtrodden, their posture reflects it immediately. We know when others are confident, sad, focussed, or loving life. We read other people's posture and stance without even consciously registering it, so it makes sense that aligning your own posture will change how people respond to you too. Adopting optimal posture helps you to feel more confident and assured, and this transmits itself to the outer world.

We are more drawn to people with good posture as they appear more attractive. This is because they are allowing their life force to flow, giving them more glow!

When you are in alignment physically, you feel more mentally aligned, more able to adapt and change direction, and your life force energy flows unimpeded. You think more clearly, you feel more enthusiastic about life, and you are better able to stand your ground in the face of challenges.

Optimal posture for your body does not mean rigidity, it means having an open, grounded, strong, and fluid structure. Life equals motion; the more motion there is in your entire system, and the more freedom your entire spine has, the better your energy flows.

There are many approaches you can take to explore body alignment. Ones I know and love are hatha yoga, somatics, chi gung, and Alexander technique. The grounding focus from Process 4 is a wonderful way to create a better sense of your own internal energy and alignment. Used daily, it will really help you not only ground, but also realign your body and increase your energy flow.

Once your body is more aligned structurally, you experience greater freedom of movement too. It may be that the best way for you to feel aligned and embodied is actually to move your body more, free from any rules. Examples could be hula-hooping, skipping, joining a five rhythms class, or turning up the music and strutting your stuff in the comfort of your home.

Your body is not rigid or fixed, and postural habits can be changed over time with focus and consistency. That is the miracle of your body; it always tries to return to homeostasis and is incredibly forgiving. If this is an area you know you could improve, consider these prompts:

- If my body could talk, it would want me to...
- One way I could get more movement would be to...
- Times I could use the grounding focus without it adding more time are...
- The type of movements I resist the most are...

Solution 2. Optimise Your Porridge Pot

How often do you check in and assess whether you need an upgrade of some kind? Or is that something you reserve only for your phone?

We all get stuck in a rut sometimes, doing the same things the same way for so long, we forget to question why we're still doing them. Sometimes we do tasks that are far better suited to someone else, but we hold onto them simply because it's a habit we don't realise we've outgrown. We can also get stuck in someone else's idea of a perfect day or year and without realising it, work against our natural flow.

Developing more awareness of where your energy goes helps you to consider what life choices serve you best. Those choices that are aligned with your core blueprint will light you up, whereas those that go against your natural flow will deplete you.

If you use your porridge pot of energy up really quickly each day, it's very likely that you're doing something that isn't quite right for you. Ideally, you want to spend at least half of your day doing something that feels more energising than depleting. Even if this takes a long time to establish, starting now means you incorporate it sooner, so don't underestimate the power of starting small. It has taken me decades to build my life and work around creating and writing but I am so grateful to be where I am in life now.

Optimising your porridge pot of energy is about learning what serves you best in terms of lifestyle choices, food choices, personal practices and habits, and how you structure your days. These are all aspects of your day-to-life requiring more in-depth assessment than I can cover here, but you are wise enough to know which areas could use tweaking and which are working perfectly.

Many of the processes you've explored already are intertwined with how you use your porridge pot each day, so you have already begun to optimise it and question where you direct your attention. To enhance your own awareness, get to the back of your body as you consider these prompts and notice what feelings arise:

- I feel excited when I…
- When I focus on my strengths I feel…
- When I focus on my weaker areas I feel…
- Things in my life that light me up are…
- I feel grateful for….
- Something that feels like a burden is…
- I could create more flexibility in my life by….
- The season I feel most energised and inspired is…

Solution 3. Know Your Values

> "It's not hard to make decisions when you know what your values are." — Roy Disney

I didn't know about values until about four years ago. Whether you know what they are or not, you have your own core values, which are part of your core blueprint. They determine what makes your heart smile or your blood boil. They are another aspect of your true nature and the more you live in alignment with them, the more inner peace and purpose you'll feel. If you live or act in a way that is misaligned with your values, you'll feel discord and later, regret.

Values are our principles, standards of behavior, and judgement of what is important in life. They are an unspoken language we use to determine who we want in our inner circle and who we don't. People with similar values tend to come together to form communities, even if they have no idea this is what attracted them to each other. If you find that someone's opinions or behaviour really irritates you, it's likely they have stomped all over your values. Your values also dictate how you want to spend your time, where you choose to spend money, what you eat, and how you interact with others.

Your values represent your inner guiding compass. They are an intrinsic motivator; meaning that they are deeply important to you and if you disregard them, it doesn't feel good.

Your values can shift and change slightly as life shifts and changes, but essentially, they stay much the same. Once you know them, you can use them to inform your decisions and choices and also work out why something feels wrong to you. It becomes easier to pivot if something no longer feels good or right to you because you understand why.

Knowing your values helps you stay aligned and gives you the self-awareness to trust your instincts. When your actions are in alignment with your values and your vision, you unlock huge motivation towards your goals.

There are many ways to find out what your values are if you don't already know them. A popular approach is to look at lists of values and select those that feel most aligned to you, but this can be overwhelming. There is also the danger that if you are really good at lying to yourself, you will pick the ones you like most, think are most appropriate for your profession, or you wish were true.

I have developed the following self-enquiry process to help you discover your values. If you don't find this useful, or it doesn't resonate, ask a friend or a coach to work through a values exercise with you.

Digging for Your Values:

Take a breath, ground your energy and still your soul for a moment. Take your attention to the back of your body and then read the following:

Imagine you have reached the other side of the Bridge, where you meet lots of lovely like-minded people. You then learn that you get to build your own community of positive people who light up your heart. You're feeling really excited about creating the perfect community for you; on your terms. You plan what you want, the number of people, how often you get together and what you'll do or how you'll be.

Then, right before you get started, your biggest nemesis appears and starts taunting you; criticising you, telling your 'perfect people' convincing lies about you and chasing them away. This stops your plans.

- What behaviours would annoy or anger you most?
- What would you be most upset about?
- What lie could they spread that would make you want to run away and hide?
- How does this make you feel?
- What dreams did they squash that were important to you?
- What excited you about building your ideal community of like-minded souls?
- What were you feeling as you imagined this community?

Take a few minutes to free-write about this, embodying all those feelings and emotions.

- See if you can identify five factors that annoyed you to your core.

- Now flip those feelings around to the opposite, positive aspect of them. What values were being stamped on? Why do they matter so much to you?

- What felt so important about building your perfect community? Why did it matter so much when it was threatened? What promise was taken away and what values underlie that?

- Explore this more deeply to see if you can identify the values that resonate most in your heart. Keep digging until you have got to the core of what is non-negotiable to you, that you know you would defend if it was threatened.

Don't worry if this takes some time to feel your way into, you have a lifetime after all. I have done many values exercises, and my core values have stayed the same throughout, but it took a bit of digging! They are love, freedom, spirituality, peace, and integrity and they lie behind everything I do.

Solution 4. Honour Your Boundaries

How are your boundaries? If you're anything like me, they're fluid; sometimes lacking, sometimes strong; although mine are 50% better than they used to be!

An especially common trait amongst women is that they want to hug and care for the world... to soothe and support other souls. This means at times it feels too hard to let people down, so you say yes when you mean no. You then quietly burnout in a depleted heap later...knowing full well it was coming, because you didn't really want to say yes in the first place.

You are here to serve yourself as well as others; to help others effectively, look after your boundaries first.

You get to choose how you set, use, and transcend your boundaries. Whether you like it or not, the power is in your hands. If you have specific desires for your life, you have to choose what you are willing to let go of in order to fit them in. Otherwise, you may as well park your dreams in Nowhere

Land where they will stay until you better align yourself with them.

As psychologist and author Mihaly Csikszentmihalyi says: *"After creative energy is awakened, it is necessary to protect it. We must erect barriers against distractions, dig channels so that energy can flow more freely, find ways to escape outside temptations and interruptions."*

I call this wearing horsey blinkers… a technique that helps you stay mono-focussed so that you can prioritise what is truly important to your heart and soul. You must first work out *what* you want. Once you know that, and know *why* you want it, having boundaries will help you achieve it.

Consider the following prompts to help you establish better boundaries:

- What are you willing to give up to create space to let in what you want?

- Why does this matter?

- What needs to happen first to change this?

- Can anyone help, for example, by taking over a task?

- What has historically helped you achieve things in the past you thought you couldn't fit in?

- Do you need more regular sleeping patterns, better exercise or food? Do you need to find a way to get rest periods?

- How can you take one tiny micro step towards making this happen?

- When will you do this by? Commit to that now… your heart is watching!

Solution 5. Redefine Success

I get so fed up with the presumption made by so many online coaches and productivity experts that if you don't earn six figures, or you don't have a massive social media following, you haven't achieved success. I know for a fact I'm not the only one *(this relates to my values!)*.

What if you overhauled the conventional idea of success and instead defined it as being comfortable in your skin, showing up as yourself, being compassionate, caring and genuine?

What if success was simply being grateful for each day, having health, food, and water, doing what you love at least some of the time, and living where you want to?

You haven't failed if you're not where others say you 'should' be. Your life isn't lost because you've fallen down a million times or you're still dealing with your weight issues. You're a success in my eyes every day you get up, and show up, and every day that you do the right thing for yourself and others.

Whether you earn six figures or not, you're a success simply by being a beautiful soul because that is what others truly love about you.

How would you define success?

- What does a life that lights you up really mean to you?
- How do you want to show up in the world and contribute?

Once you are aware of this, you can catch yourself every time you veer off-course towards someone else's idea of success. Checking in with your heart and your values will help.

Here are some of my definitions of what success is to inspire some of your own:

- How many days, hours, and minutes you spend being true to yourself, honouring your heart and soul, whilst respecting the needs of others in your life.

- Whether you are truly present and awake today.

- Helping others bring joy to their lives too, in whatever way that is for you.

- Honouring your boundaries, staying grounded, and connected with what is important to you.

- Being who you are, unapologetically, and having people in your life that resonate with you and love you for who you truly are.

- Being awake, aware, making choices from your heart, and not sleepwalking through a life designed by others.

Solution 6. Uncover Your Big Why

"He who has a strong enough why can bear almost any how." — *Friedrich Nietzsche*

Our days can be like Groundhog Day; beating ourselves up for what we lack or what we don't get done, feeling empty and wondering when we get to start living. This stops once you uncover your Big Why because it grounds you in a bigger picture sense of purpose, and even if you get distracted, reconnecting to your Big Why gets you fired up again.

If something really is important enough to you, you will find a way to do what needs to be done, regardless of the timeframe or your circumstances. Your Big Why gives you measurable reasons for making decisions and acts like your anchor, alongside your values. It's your underlying fuel and your reason for getting up in the morning.

Your Big Why drives you. Identify with it strongly enough and it becomes Magical.

Once you're fuelled by the Magic of your Big Why, you can become downright fearless in pursuit of your goal, because you only see what's relevant and disregard the rest.

Identifying my Big Why helped me transcend my lifelong fear of speaking. My Big Why was so intertwined with my being and my heart that I found the courage, inclination, time, and energy to do what I needed to do...even though it scared me and I had very little free time. I used the hashtag #missionbiggerthanfear and reminded my heart of it daily.

It's the classic case of love over fear, which is essentially what doing anything you want to do is about. And the age-old battle between your heart and your head, which luckily you now have many tools to transcend. You can do anything you set your mind to. All you have to do is identify a compelling, underlying reason Why.

To help with this, consider the following prompts and to tune into your heart, let yourself feel the feelings that come up as you do:

- What deeply moves you to the point of choking back tears?

- What really challenging things have you had to transcend in your life that you would do anything to help someone else avoid?

- What would it break your heart to NOT bring to the world?

- How do you want to be remembered?

- If you could only use one sentence to summarise what you believe in, what would it be?

- What would you do if time and money were no object? Why?

Let yourself daydream, journal, and imagine future you, looking back at your now and smiling because you found your Big Why. Immerse yourself in these feelings and don't worry if you get emotional. My Big Why makes me want to cry every time I revisit it. If you get a lump in your throat when you think about it, you've found the fuel to light your inner flame of desire.

Your heart is so happy for you because your Big Why is your personal guiding light and your life is worthy of honouring it.

Solution 7. Identify the Feeling Underlying Your Desires

I know how frustrating it can be to feel like you aren't getting anywhere in terms of reaching your seemingly elusive desires. I also know how easy it is to get caught up in a sense of loss because you don't yet have what you *think* you need in your life.

When this happens, it ties your life force energy up in knots, as you get locked into your head and disconnected from your heart. This drags you further away from what you're actually most aligned with, and stops you noticing opportunities that would serve you better.

One wonderful way to circumvent this pattern and attract what is most aligned with you into your life, is to discover and embody the feeling underlying your desires. Feelings are the messengers your heart sends you, so tuning into this feeling activates your incredible heart brain energy. The energy your heart sends out is powerful and far-reaching; it acts a bit like a homing device, attracting anything into your orbit that matches the energy you send out. Positive energies are more expansive than negative ones, which is why embodying the feeling you seek can act as a powerful magnet.

Your underlying feeling is what drives you subconsciously towards your dreams. Stemming from your core blueprint, it is related to your purpose, passions and values. It is something you are drawn to and inherently seek, which makes you feel grounded and at home in yourself. It can also be discovered by identifying what feeling you are most triggered by or avoid, because this is usually the opposite feeling to the one you unconsciously move towards.

The following focus is based on a wonderful Taoist practice I was taught by the Barefoot Doctor, Stephen Russell. Play with it, enjoy it and see what comes up for you. ◀ https://www.helenrebello.com/p/MagicBookResources

- Use the tools you have gathered to get out of your head, into your heart, and your core. Don't overthink this, all you need to do is breathe, focus on your feet, smile, and then move to the back of your body when you are ready to do so.

- From the vantage point of the back of your body, give yourself permission to daydream about what you want in your life. Don't censor this, your dreams are yours and yours alone.

- Observe yourself as though you were looking at a screen of future you. See your face, notice the colours, hear the sounds, feel the wind in your hair, and the sun, or snow on your skin.

- Let yourself drift off as you picture the scene: smiling as you visualise yourself behind the wheel of your perfect car, walking outside your perfect villa, or perhaps paddling at the edge of the sea somewhere stunning.

- Really tune into your senses. Notice how it feels to finally have all these things you have dreamed of for so long.

- Soak up all these feelings and ask yourself what feeling lies behind these things as you picture them. Don't let yourself go into your head; you don't need to 'work this out' with your brain.

- Simply feel... feel into what lies underneath the first feeling you sense and the next underneath that. Explore this as though you were peeling an onion - stopping only when you can't go any further.

- Slowly bring your senses back to the here and now, to your skin, the floor, and the room around you.

- Wriggle, stretch, yawn, and smile as you continue to feel the feelings.

- There will usually be one common feeling underlying each thing. Notice how invigorating this feels. If it doesn't feel quite right, explore some more or commit to exploring this again tomorrow.

For example, my dreams used to be driving a blue Porsche around French villages, abundant financial wealth and a glass-fronted Huf Haus by the sea. I would also see myself doing yoga on the beach, eating fresh tropical fruit for breakfast, teaching classes, and writing by a big window, overlooking the sea. Using this focus helped me realise that the feeling underlying these visions is freedom.

This makes sense. I have always hated feeling hemmed in, having rules to abide by, having too many possessions or not being able to move at a moment's notice. I love travelling and am drawn towards having a laptop lifestyle. This is not truly for the lifestyle itself, which is actually quite hard work; but because I love the sense of freedom it gives me.

I have always worked hard, identifying freedom as my underlying feeling helps me see that my work is driven by empowering others to set themselves free too. From hustle, the Matrix Myth, stress, busyness, self-denial etc., so they reach their potential and unfold into a peaceful, purposeful life in their own way.

Once you have identified your underlying feeling, it gives you another piece of your alignment jigsaw. It will usually represent common themes in your past, although you may not see this initially. When a new opportunity comes up, use your feeling to test whether it feels right. Use it to fuel you to keep going through challenging work. Start acting as though you already embody this feeling, and you will be amazed by how many opportunities come your way.

Process 7 – Summary for Your Soul:

The Magical Unfolding invites you to trust in the pathway of your life so that you can more fully become who you came here to be.

The mad spiraling journey of your life is perfectly designed to take you on an adventure that brings you right back home to yourself. It offers the possibility that life can be truly magical, when you follow your heart rather than your head.

Everything that happens to you is a magical gift to help you to slowly re-inhabit yourself. It returns you to the self you lost along the way. It teaches you lessons, uncovers your strengths, gets rid of baggage, releases fear, and gives you greater courage.

Always trust the magically unfolding path of life. It will at times be confusing, chaotic, circuitous, and challenging but it will ultimately lead you to something utterly, perfectly wonderful.

Process 7 Self-Affirmation: I align myself with magic.

Magical Mission — Unravel Your Magical Manifesto

"The greatest achievement was at first, and for a time, a dream. The oak sleeps in the acorn; the bird waits in the egg; and in the highest vision of the soul a waking angel stirs. Dreams are the seedlings of realities." — James Allen

Congratulations lovely soul, you have successfully navigated a very intense and lengthy process.

Process 7 is a movable feast that takes an entire lifetime, so don't worry if you feel as though you're skirting the edges or you don't have answers yet. They will come and meet you when the time is right. I would be surprised if you haven't had any insights at all, so don't undervalue even the smallest ones.

You've already done a lot of digging, so this is the exciting stage where you start to lay down what you really want and where you want to head, by creating your unique Magical Manifesto based on the conclusions you have gathered so far.

This is an opportunity to play, let yourself be creative and daydream, with no rights or wrongs in sight.

You will need your journal, pens, scissors, and a few separate pieces of paper. Read through the mission first and then work through it with a sense of curiosity and play; you can always crumble your pieces of paper and start again later.

Unravelling Your Magical Manifesto

- Get comfy and look at all the conclusions you made in the solutions section. It doesn't matter which solutions you explored or how many responses you have.

- See what words or phrases jump out at you. Did you write sentences you were particularly surprised by, delighted with or proud of?

- Did anything you discovered deeply move or inspire you?

- What non-negotiable things about yourself did you discover if any?

- Using a different colour pen or pencil, circle any words that resonate or feel important. Trust this and don't question it; it's your intuition communicating with you.

Now, with these discoveries in mind, free-write some responses to the following headings, putting each response on a new line:

I Believe....

I want to live in a world where...

Quotes I love that guide my life are....

Having now gathered some beautiful insights from your heart, use your scissors to separate each response, and then choose the ones you love the most. Lose any you're not sure about, or that say the same thing in a different way. Keep editing until you are left with as many core statements as feels right to you.

Arrange these until they form a manifesto or set of mantras. Trust your gut and don't be too attached to perfection! This manifesto represents what is true for you now and can act as a useful set of guiding principles to offset fear or your inner cast of characters.

When you have a manifesto you love, feel free to put it on your phone, in your journal, or on your wall. This is for you, so honour your instincts if you instead feel like keeping it safe and hidden.

I played with this for ages on different pieces of paper before I created a final PDF to put on my wall. I have made a note to revisit it every six months because it will evolve as I do.

My current one is in the resources section of the website if you want inspiration.

CHAPTER 11
Process 8 — Liberate Yourself
Claim Your Personal Power

"The earth is the mother of all people, and all people should have equal rights upon it. You might as well expect the rivers to run backward as that any man who was born a free man should be contented when penned up and denied liberty to go where he pleases." — *Chief Joseph - Nez Percé tribe chief*

Lovely soul, you have made it this far.

You are a true peaceful warrior because you are driven by something that kept you reading and exploring to this stage. You believe in yourself and that is something to truly celebrate. Not many people reach this point... those who do are truly ready to liberate their lives by living in a more peaceful, powerful, purposeful way.

Now you get to start putting all the processes together to make an aligned plan that frees you from constant busyness and hustle and lights you up instead.

On this journey, with each process, you have accumulated tools and insights almost without realising it. It may still not make sense to your head of course, which is possibly tying itself in knots trying to understand the big picture. If that's the case, let it do its thing; get to the back of your body and simply breathe.

Living a life that is more peaceful and purposeful is about making daily small decisions to either move a step forwards in the direction you want, or backwards into safety. It is about accepting the journey wherever it may take you as you take those steps, safe in the knowledge that one day it all works out.

As the saying goes, if you keep doing things the same way you always did, you will keep getting the same result. If you want a different result, you have to Do Life Differently. This doesn't look or feel as dramatic as it seems; however, it still requires the ingredients of belief, courage, presence, intention, trust, and awareness. These ingredients combined create a subtle alchemy, one only heart-led heroines perform. In case you wondered, yes this does mean you... (and if you're male, substitute the word heroine for hero; you can't wriggle out of it that easily!).

You have already been open enough to read this book and hopefully you have also embraced some of the processes. You are now more empowered to create life on your terms because you know more about what you can control in both your internal world *and* your external one. You have already started creating new neural pathways, tuning more into your body, and uncovering your own wisdom. Your subconscious mind has squirreled away all it needs. You have already changed internally; and as change on the inside creates external change, half your work is already done.

All you need now is to further clarify your intentions and desires, learn better ways to support your mind and explore a magical way to construct your day. Keep that lovely Cape of Possibility around you, it will serve you well.

Before you do, I have one last story to share with you...

My Story — Taking Back My Power

"Every decision brings with it some good, some bad, some lessons, and some luck. The only thing that's for sure is that indecision steals many years from many people who wind up wishing they'd just had the courage to leap." — Doe Zantamata

Once upon a time, I truly believed I was a shy, quiet, and inexpressive soul, destined to stay that way my entire life. I was the kind of person who would never express opinions, speak up, say what I really thought, or make decisions. I certainly wasn't the kind who would express themselves by writing a book!

Preferring the seemingly easier path of acquiescing, I gave up my right to have a voice by staying silent. Rather than rock the boat, I preferred to sit on the fence. The trouble with fences; however, is that whilst they seem safe, if you sit on them too long they give you splinters. And if you have to walk around with splinters in places you can't fully reach, you definitely can't walk peacefully, powerfully, or purposefully.

You still get by in life, but you tend not to enjoy it much.

One of the reasons I decided to write this book is because I spent over 40 years suppressing my voice and not fully honouring who I was at my core. When I found out how much better life got after I reclaimed my power, there was no way that I *couldn't* share it with you. What stopped me writing for years was fear in the form of 'what will people think' - supported by its close friends 'who am I to do this' and 'if I raise my head above the parapet, I'll get shot'. For a long time they had their way because I believed the best way forward was to keep my head down and stay quiet.

I realise now that Tina the Tyrant was running the show. She kept me safe by spending time diligently sowing seeds that I was not worthy and nothing I had to say was useful or served anyone. She had me convinced it was far better to stay quiet rather than risk being ridiculed. As a result, I put writing in a big scary box with a danger sign on the front. Speaking in front of groups of people lived in the box already, having gone to live there many years earlier.

I thought that to be a 'proper' writer, you had to do certain things in a certain order; such as get an English degree, be published in magazines, or get paid to write. I thought you needed a big dramatic story or to be totally 'sorted'. It was something other, more confident, successful people did, and my dreams were exactly that; silly delusions I was better off burying.

The day I was gifted the opportunity to share my story to give other people hope, everything shifted.

I was invited by my lovely friend Lesley Pyne to share my insights from being 'childless by circumstance' on her blog dedicated to the same subject. This suggestion resonated deeply in my heart and made me say yes before I talked myself out of it. I thought about how wonderful it would be if my words helped just one person who was where I used to be, and when I sat down to write, the words poured out of me. There may have been a few tears too.

I was still trepidatious because it felt like not only was I 'coming out', I was also risking being trapped in a new box marked 'childless, not by choice'. I'd done years of self-development work by then, but never shared that part of my story publicly. I didn't want to be the person others felt sorry for, so I kept this chapter of my life closer to my chest than a sports bra. Turns out that withholding such a huge chapter of my life was holding me back more than I thought. It took sharing my experiences and learnings to realise I had something very powerful to offer.

Our experiences happen and eventually teach us what we need to learn. When we hold onto them and protect them, it depletes our power. When we stop focusing on what they mean to us, and instead think of how others could be helped by sharing them, this not only sets us free and gives us our power back, it also does the same for others. Being honest and open with others creates deep connections that are infinitely transformative and meaningful. When you open your heart and share from it honestly, in whatever way is appropriate for you, you spark that same flame in others.

If you want to free up your own power so that you can direct it towards what you want in life, you have to find the courage to express and share your truth. Step-by-step, as you do so, you liberate your trapped life force energy and almost imperceptible shifts occur. As you take back your power, your confidence increases. The more your confidence increases, the more you express yourself. The more you express yourself, the more your original self reveals itself. The more your original self reveals itself, the stronger you become as your new self lovingly wraps itself around your core self.

It is a privilege that not everyone lives long enough to have, and when it happens, who you find yourself becoming will astound you.

As Marianne Williamson says: *"Our childlike self is the deepest level of our being. It is who we really are and what is real doesn't go away. The truth doesn't stop being the truth just because we're not looking at it."*

Sharing your unique gifts is not only your gift to the world, but a gift to yourself too. It's not always easy or fun, and it might take a while to work out the finer details, but it is so very worth it.

You are the panacea you seek. When you learn how to master yourself, you can master your entire world.

Head-Led Challenges of Process 8

"It takes great courage to perceive that letting go of an old dream isn't a connection to failure but a brave act of giving birth to a new self." — Alberto Villoldo

Do you remember asking yourself an important question at the start of your journey through the MAGICAL process?

It's worth returning to that question before you discover your last set of challenges, to see if it has changed or stayed the same. The question was:

"If anything were possible, how would you love the next six months to unfold for you?"

Do you remember your answer? How would you respond to it now? Would you revise your original answer, or would it stay the same?

Tune into your response to this, remembering there is no right or wrong. It's always useful to return to a question that fuels you, no matter where you are on your journey. As you get back in touch with your answer to this question, it helps you drop back into your heart. This is a great place to hang out whilst you learn more about the challenges you might face as you step over the threshold of the Bridge into your new paradigm.

Your head might use this opportunity to try and derail you, which is why it's good to drop into your heart. Stay connected to your vision as you read, safe in the knowledge you have already moved on from merely going through the motions. From here onwards you are going to savour your moments whenever you can.

These are the challenges you can face on this stage of your journey:

1. Looking in the Wrong Boxes for Purpose, Power, and Potential

*"You wander from room to room hunting for the diamond
necklace that is already around your neck." — Rumi*

Those pesky boxes really mess things up, don't they? Not only do you start out carrying around a load of broken boxes, you also put things in the wrong ones then wonder why you struggle so much to find them. There is a great deal of pressure placed on the importance of finding our purpose. You might be forgiven for thinking I've contributed to this by writing this book. Like so many other myths I shared in part one though, my aim is to debunk the myth that it is a 'thing' or a 'definition' we must find, otherwise we are doomed.

We think it is a 'do or die' situation, which creates so much fear it can cripple us. I do stand for you finding your purpose but let me remind you again that in my opinion, your purpose is to show up and shine as YOU. Unapologetically.

These boxes are all about perspective and labelling. The same applies to our personal power and to the concept of finding your potential. Your ability to find them depends upon the conditions you have placed upon them and what you have told yourself they mean. Take the pressure off. Put down the boxes. Walk away from those who tell you the only way to find your purpose is to go and meditate on a mountain for months. Don't listen if they tell you that in order to be truly powerful you must be strong and forceful. It isn't true. It can be this way for some, but it doesn't have to be that way for everyone. You included.

Do you really think you would come into this world with all your talents, unique gifts, quirky style, and that gorgeous grin you don't know you have, without also being equipped to share that with the world in your own way? Do you honestly believe that the only people who get to reach their potential are those who are somehow more special than you? Whatever core desires form part of your DNA, you can choose at any moment to embody them in your interactions. *You* get to choose whether you bring them into your work, your world, your being. It might be making people smile, it might be nurturing them, it might be creating things. No matter what work you do, or how your life looks now, you can bring this awareness and intention into each day. You can choose to bring your unique vibe to the party. It's that simple.

That is how you claim your personal power, by living in a way that is not at odds with who you came here to be. You claim your purpose by identifying the thing that makes your heart smile; that you know how to do without even realising it's 'a thing'.

In my case it's helping others open and listen to their heart by helping them get out of their heads. I realised that with help from an insightful coach, but to be honest, I knew it already. I just thought it was a lot more complicated…

It's merely an awareness shift, one that doesn't require effort.

2. Your Days are Not Intentional

Be honest with yourself, what happens the minute you wake up each day?

Watch out for the uprising of your Puppy Dog Ego as you answer this question… you will recognise it by the immediate desire to justify your response.

You are probably still quite sleepy, so it is possible you groggily reach for your phone to turn off your alarm after several snoozes, before quickly checking for texts, emails, looking at the weather, the news, and maybe even social media. Before you know it, you've been dragged into an Internet wormhole, and now you're running late. You skip breakfast or grab something sugary and run out of the door in a panic to start the day.

You totally forget that the day started when you woke up and you've scuppered yourself before you got going. Even if you're more disciplined and discerning, if you're anything like me, you probably still fall into bad habits occasionally. The lure of that shiny, blinking smartphone is like a siren, pulling us in before we've even registered it.

If this is how you begin your day, you've reached a level of stimulation far surpassing any your ancestors had, before you've even got out of bed. Your porridge pot gets depleted pretty quickly by the energy from technology so it's no wonder by the time you reach 3pm you feel done for the day.

Your personal power doesn't stand a chance…

I know how easy it is to feel like you've been sucked into a vortex from the moment you wake up - and then spat out at the other end of the day wondering what happened, how it got to be 8pm, and why you've still got your coat on even though you've been home for an hour. The world is loud and shouty. Things and people constantly call for your attention and expect immediate responses. It can result in you feeling so disempowered, you simply switch off, and your day whizzes by in a blur.

We are not taught in school how to manage daily life, our energy and priorities. In fact, we aren't taught how to prioritise. Instead, we micromanage; dealing with what grabs our attention, what needs to be done to survive, what needs to be done to maintain our environment, or what is easy and ticks something off a long list. Our tasks are drawn at random, our days are busy, and we never make a dent in our to-BE list.

The question is, how much of the stuff you scramble to fit in contributes to your sense of fulfilment? How much of it is done intentionally, with awareness of how it fits into the big picture of what you *really* want in your life?

How often do the things that matters to your heart most, get left to mope around in the background, waiting for their turn? Again.

3. You Lose Sight of Your Big Why

This ties into the challenge above because busy days are one of the reasons you can start to forget your Big Why.

You can get so overwhelmed by trying to ignore pings and pulls by other things and stay grounded and balanced, that you have no energy left to think about bigger picture things. When that happens, you forget to create those positive habits that will help you reach your desires, and instead you let the easier, less helpful habits form themselves.

This is understandable. It's easier for your brain to stick to Operation Normal; however, if you do that for too long, it gets harder to reconnect to your sense of why you do what you do.

The more things you do without really knowing why you're doing them, the more dissatisfaction you will feel. For most of us, that is when we start looking for distractions because we aren't feeling fulfilled.

It becomes a habit that is hard to transcend. Hard but not impossible, not when you know it's happening. What helps you get back on track once you realise, is reconnecting to your Big Why.

Over and Over again.

4. You Rely on Willpower Alone

How often have you bemoaned the fact that you don't have any willpower when you fail to follow through on a new practice you promised yourself you would do?

You are not alone! It is the most common reason for 'falling off the intention wagon' cited by those I've worked with over the years and I struggle with willpower issues too. It's yet another facet of being human and we need to stop beating ourselves up about it and instead, learn how to work with it.

There is a big myth about willpower, which is that those of us who get things done have it, and those who fail don't. The truth is our brains are not wired in a way that always supports willpower; it starts out well, and then declines fairly rapidly. It also uses up a lot of our energy and life force to maintain and is affected by how we eat, move, and focus.

There is a lot we can do to boost it, but until we know how, we can really struggle and push to get things done and honour ourselves. This creates a vicious cycle of depleting our energy and adrenaline reserves, thereby depleting our willpower.

The answer lies in learning how to calm your brain, install positive habits, and create habit 'triggers' and structures. These take the workload off our brains, releasing more energy for exercising our will.

5. Placing Value on the Wrong Things

That sounds like a very judgemental heading I know. I will put it into context quickly before your head gets cross with me.

When it comes to liberating your life and claiming your personal power, the things you are best advised to let go are:

- The desire for instant gratification.

- Valuing results rather than the process it takes to move towards them.

- Valuing extrinsic goals over intrinsic goals.

If you have placed your value on these things, please don't beat yourself up about it. They are all aspects of the Matrix Myth programming, so even if you're wise to them, you probably still have to remind yourself from time to time. I certainly do.

Wanting quick results is an aspect of the human character that has always existed. Ancient philosophers such as Aristotle referred to it and it also appears in old Chinese Medicine texts. However, it feels more prevalent now because in the Western world we can now access almost anything at the touch of a button, to the point that our collective attention span is reducing.

The quickest way to demoralise yourself and fail at anything is to expect it to happen quickly. It places pressure on you before you've started and it simply isn't realistic.

If you want to liberate yourself from a lifestyle you've outgrown, you have to be in it for the long game. You have to do it for future you, whilst also embracing the process that takes you from where you are, towards where you want to get to... otherwise what's the point? It's like going on a hiking trip to a breathtakingly beautiful waterfall and failing to notice the incredible places you pass through to get there.

What helps is being motivated by the right type of goal, because this gives you more staying power and enthusiasm. You can have all the riches in the world and look incredible, but still feel empty inside. These types of goals offer false promises, you reach them and immediately look to the next shiny thing. People who place higher value on extrinsic goals rather than intrinsic ones inevitably end up depleting their resources very quickly. Mainly because their head and Puppy Dog Ego is in charge the whole time.

Those who value intrinsic things such as service to others, genuine connections, and meaningful relationships tend to be very heart-led. As you already know, your heart brain is infinitely more powerful than your head brain, so leading from this place gives you much more energy and motivation. Directing your focus outside yourself towards others also leaves you feeling more fulfilled and happy than chasing shiny things ever will.

There is nothing wrong with material things, being well known or looking great, but if that is what you are driven by, you will always want more. Ironically, you are far more likely to attract them as a by-product of living with integrity. The difference is you won't judge your worth on them and you'll truly appreciate them.

6. You Give Up Just Before The Magic Happens

"I know this transformation is painful;, but you're not falling apart, you're just falling into something different, with a new capacity to be beautiful." — William C. Hannan

There are many reasons why you might give up and turn back, not realising you're about to see the view you've been moving towards.

The most common reasons I have encountered are trying to do things the wrong way, which makes it impossible to get anywhere, giving up too soon because you can't see progress, or thinking it will be an easy road with no obstacles.

The fact is your life is not generally changed in big bold dramatic moments, except those sent by fate. Big epiphanies and magical occurrences do happen sometimes but they tend to be the exception rather than the rule.

The quiet unsung heroes and heroines of our world are those working diligently with focus towards an outcome they know will add something to the world. They are not the winners of reality shows who become stars overnight; although in fairness, many of those actually have been striving and trying for years, we just don't see that.

Life changes by a series of small daily decisions, that one day stack up to make a big change. To stick with this and not give up, you need Toddler Tenacity.

Toddlers spend their time having fun, finding out about boundaries and relationships, and learning new things. They get tired quickly and throw tantrums, but they are tenacious. Toddlers don't question the art of learning to talk. They fall and they keep getting up. They persist because it never occurs to them that they could choose not to. It's only as we get older that we give up because we think if we take longer over something it means we are stupid.

Change is always hard before it's easy, and when it comes to personal development and self-actualisation practices, it's no different. It can actually be a lot harder because sometimes things feel worse before they feel better, even when those things are good for you.

Heart-Led Solutions for Process 8

"Look closely at the present you are constructing, it should look like the future you are dreaming." — Alice Walker

Many of the solutions for this process have been scattered throughout the book, hiding in plain sight, so that as I introduce them here, your brain will view them as familiar friends. They might be wearing slightly different outfits but essentially they're the same.

The idea of liberating yourself and claiming your personal power may well seem elusive to you, but really, it is about taking ownership of what you want, knowing why you want it, then tuning into that vision so well that it becomes easier to take daily micro steps towards it.

It sounds relatively simple, doesn't it?

And yet moving towards what we want and honouring our intentions is one of our biggest struggles. It can be so challenging that we put it off to sort out in the future, when we have more time. Time has no idea it has been invited though, so alas, it never arrives. Suddenly it's December, you're writing the same intentions down as you did the last few years and you feel like you've failed and let yourself down. Again.

Living your ideal version of life does not happen only by magic!

I am not going to pretend to be an expert at goal-setting; my brain is not wired that way. I am pretty good at knowing how to get things done that matter to my heart however, without my head getting too much in the way. I also know how to navigate this on a day-to-day basis and stay flexible rather than fixed, so that if I need to pivot and change direction I can do it without drama.

That is really what this section is about. It is a soulful approach to goal-setting, productivity and life-hacking. It's purpose is to help you approach each day more mindfully, so that you reach your potential without stressing and striving.

Otherwise known as living intentionally.

This section shares the approaches I use to live more from my heart and use my head to build my days intentionally. They are not fixed in stone and you can pick and choose from them. I have spent many years learning about mindfulness, productivity, goal-setting, and mind-hacking. I hope what I share will save you time having to do the same.

Everything you have discovered up to this point will serve you well if you incorporate it into your life. Once you have a daily practice of getting grounded, dropping into your heart and getting centred at the start of each day, you'll feel very different. It is in living each day more purposefully however, that you harness the power of these practices.

This is something you evolve and feel your way into, so as you read, bear in mind that you don't have to do them all at once. This is a marathon, not a sprint, there's no need to launch yourself at it full pelt and then burn out a few days later. Self-kindness and compassion, tempered by self-responsibility, rule.

Once you have explored the solutions, your magical mission will invite you to further clarify your intentions and desires, so that you can create a plan to move towards them.

Solution 1: Identify Your SoulGoals

Your SoulGoals are those goals that arise from the depths of your heart when you really connect to yourself and get quiet. The ones you barely admit to yourself unless you get brave... which now that you're here, you've already become.

These are your intrinsic goals; the ones that light you up, fill your soul and arise from a desire to contribute and make your life matter. They are about *being* who you came here to be rather than *doing* what you think you should do. These goals are the ones you quietly dream about, or see yourself doing when you meditate. They may feel almost unreachable but part of you senses they are possible, even though you have no idea how to attain them.

SoulGoals are related to your Big Why, to your values and your core blueprint. They come from the core feeling you identified earlier and they fuel and sustain you, giving future you hope.

Once identified, these goals give you the courage to claim back your personal power, put your stake in the ground and declare your intentions to follow your heart. The more that you tune into a sense of how it would feel to realize them, the more empowered you become to transcend fear and start.

SoulGoals can be as simple as wanting to start a meditation practice because you know in your heart it will help you to reach another SoulGoal. It could be related to anything, big or small, that helps you reach your potential.

The more you tune into your heart, the more these goals appear in your head as ideas and seeds. The secret to uncovering them is getting out of your head, dropping into your heart, getting to the back of your body and allowing your inner voice to come through.

Done regularly, this happens more easily than you could ever imagine. I highly recommend making time for a weekly check-in with yourself, to tune in and plan your week according to what your senses and heart tell you. One of the best ways to deepen this connection is by making space and time for regular practices such as meditation and journaling.

Speaking of which...

Solution 2: Create Space

If you want to create change in your life, you have to create space for it.

You cannot truly incorporate anything new until you have got rid of something else, because you only have a certain bandwidth capacity. You have 24 hours each day, a porridge pot of energy and pre-existing commitments. Unless you are a single mum with young children, you also have pockets of time you can control and use either proactively or reactively.

Those pockets of time are often found by looking at the time you fritter away doing something on autopilot when you are bored or at a loose end. The biggest culprit is usually your smartphone.

According to Manoush Zomorodi, who wrote a book called *Bored and Brilliant*, most of us waste 25 minutes a day doing random things on our phone or computer such as checking emails constantly, refreshing social media feeds, and playing games. The things we know we wouldn't do if someone were monitoring us and making notes on what we do all day. We think it means nothing, but those 25 minutes a day add up to TWO years of your life, not to mention the fact that every time you switch your focus, it takes another twenty minutes for your brain to readjust.

What would reclaiming that time and using it consciously and proactively enable you to do?

Creating space for change can sound scary, but it can be done slowly and in small steps, and you can use some intelligent self-enquiry to help you. I'm not suggesting you should fill all your time - far from it - but the reality is that most people's perception is that they have no time left for anything. If that's true for you, the following analogy may help; bear it in mind as you select your tasks each day:

The Bus Shelter Analogy

There are only so many people that can fit under a bus shelter at any one time, which doesn't matter on a sunny, warm day. When it is raining and cold however, suddenly more people want to stand underneath the shelter.

As more people come underneath, no matter how much people shuffle towards each other, someone at the end will always be pushed out into the rain. The most intelligent and aware approach would be to ensure that those with greater priority stay under shelter, whilst those who are more resilient or have umbrellas, step outside.

You have 24 hours each day and only so many tasks fit into that time. What non-meaningful tasks can you lose that eat up your precious time so you can replace them with what is more important to you?

Try this process to work it out:

- Start tracking your time using either tech or your journal, to notice what you currently spend your time on. Be honest with yourself.

- As you gather data, rate what you do on a positivity scale of 1-10, where 1 means a time-sucking soul-sapping activity that adds nothing to your day and 10 means an activity you would do all day if you could because it lights you up. *Remember your self-care tools and do this without judgement.*

- Take small steps towards stopping as many tasks at levels 1-4 as you can. Most common examples are tech-driven, such as turning off phone notifications, limiting time spent scrolling through social media, switching your TV off earlier or only watching programmes that make you feel good.

- As you start to see areas of your life you can reduce or stop, you can start to block out dedicated blocks of time for more positive activities. This could be as small as using five minutes in the morning focusing on your breath instead of checking the news and depressing yourself.

What has been hanging out under your bus shelter for too long, not earning its keep?

What nourishing activity can come into the bus shelter in its place?

What are you willing to give up to help you move towards living in a way that feeds your soul?

Solution 3: Set Up your Soulful Success Scaffolding

Soulful Success Scaffolding is built up from simple supportive daily practices that help you start the day right, stay aligned and on track, so you make the most of the time you are gifted. They are easy to remember, take little time, and make a big difference.

Read through the practices I use and either borrow and adapt these as your own or use them to spark your own practices. I installed my scaffolding over the period of a few years, building it up bit by bit.

This isn't an all or nothing approach, even making a small daily gesture towards yourself represents a big step in a positive direction. It will boost your self-esteem, sense of worth, energy and focus, helping you stay more grounded no matter what the day brings you.

The four core components of my scaffolding are the 4 Ms:

1. **Morning pages** — a conscious writing practice I set up after attending a workshop with Julia Cameron in 2016, where you free write three pages on paper, without censorship, aim or editing. I started out with one page and then progressed to three very quickly. This

practice has helped me make friends with my inner critic, empty my busy head each morning, re-ignite my creativity, download intuitive insights, create social media posts, blogs and videos, and write this book! Morning pages are nothing short of magical. You can do them in bed and it's free, apart from your initial investment into a journal *(or several)* and a pen *(same)*.

2. **Movement** — I'll be honest, this is a moveable feast! Sometimes I am 'on it' and move my body daily for 20 minutes for weeks at a time without self-negotiation and other times it might fall by the wayside. When I do move my body first thing in the morning, it releases dopamine (feel good chemical), shifts and boosts my energy, helps me think more clearly, makes me feel fitter and more flexible, and gets me back into my body; which makes the next M easier! I live in a Georgian apartment now, so I can't jump around; instead, I combine yoga, self-shiatsu, chi gung and somatics, depending upon what my body needs. All I need is my yoga mat. Having tried many types of movement, at different times and places, I know myself well enough to do my movement at the start of the day. Otherwise it generally doesn't happen.

3. **Meditation** — I wanted to set up a meditation practice for years because I knew how much it was supposed to benefit you and I'd done enough of it to know how great it felt. I set up my daily practice over the period of a couple of years; starting small with just three minutes and then building up from there. Meditation keeps me grounded, present, clear-headed, calm, and focussed. It boosts my willpower because I'm less reactive and more responsive; therefore, I make better

decisions. It has also increased my sensitivity to subtle energies and sounds we don't usually see or hear and helps me stay expansive and connected to Universal energy. Also, it is free and magical! The resources section contains some helpful apps you can use.

4. **Mantras** — without fail, as I wake up I say my morning mantra in my head: *'thank you for another day in which I get to live, love, laugh, work, and play.'* I also have three additional mantras I use after my meditation practice, which mean something personal to me. The first morning mantra ensures I start my day with genuine gratitude because I really am delighted that I get to wake up for another day. This is a far healthier way to start your day than the scenario I outlined in the challenges section. The other mantras reinforce the new positive self-beliefs I have been installing over the last few years, and by saying them after meditation, my system is open and expansive enough to absorb their positive vibes. These are free too!

I also add on my Anti-Procrastination Mantra as needed and use the Self-Worth declaration in the shower whenever I need a self-worth boost. It was used almost daily whilst writing this book.

Combining these core practices ensures I nourish my mind, body, soul, and spirit. I don't always use all four; it depends how much time I have available, what else is going on, where I am and how early I have to leave the house.

The one that is completely non-negotiable is meditation, it is like food for the soul and you can do it anywhere. If you really struggle with meditation, any existing activities like walking and swimming can be like meditation practices. It simply requires a reframe.

On days when I don't move in the morning, if I can, I go out for a walk. I love leaving the apartment with just my keys and a bottle of water and seeing where my feet take me. This keeps me grounded, present, and better able to notice my surroundings. It also helps the neural pathways in my brain, because I am using them to map out new routes and work out where I am in relation to home.

Disclaimer: I don't recommend this if you have no sense of direction or live somewhere where you would want your phone with you in case you get lost!

Solution 4: Set Up Non-Negotiable Daily Habits

"The glorious benefit of a habit is that it converts something that requires a lot of willpower and focus into something that becomes automatic and often outside of our conscious thought." — Tynan

The trick to integrating and implementing any practices you want to incorporate into your daily life, is to set them up as non-negotiable daily habits, one new habit at a time. This applies to your soulful success scaffolding, goal-setting and how you structure your days.

Your brain loves to try and keep track of everything for you. Your conscious mind wants to control everything and run the show, but it can only store two or three items at a time. Meanwhile, your subconscious elephant that never forgets *anything*, niggles at your conscious mind about tasks you haven't addressed yet. This blocks your energy; keeping you from being present and engaged in your life.

The more you can use the autopilot part of your brain (your basal ganglia) to run habit programmes for you, the easier it becomes to integrate them into your life, and the more energy you free up for other things. This is the whole basis of habits; you don't even think about brushing your teeth for example, you simply do it because your basal ganglia loves running repeated patterns.

Introducing new positive habits one at a time makes it more likely you'll stick with them. Associating them with an action you already do, makes it easier still because it won't feel as though you're trying to fit another activity in.

Your brain generally cannot install more than one new habit at a time, so pick one you are most drawn to, let yourself feel into how it would benefit you and then make a start, keeping it small.

How I established my daily meditation practice:

- I started out trying to find 30 minutes a day and as a result, I wouldn't follow through. It was too big a chunk of time for a new thing, especially one I hadn't yet felt the benefit of.

- I realised I had to let go of the 'perfect' scenario, throw out the rules about what meditation 'should' look like and do things my way.

- I then started with only three minutes, first thing in the morning, before I even got out of bed.

- Three minutes was pretty easy and it wasn't long before I started realising how good it felt to do this daily. I also felt proud of myself and started believing I really could install this habit.

- Over time I slowly increased my time to five minutes and then 10 minutes.

- As I started feeling the benefits, I got more and more committed to the practice until it felt so nourishing and calming, it became non-negotiable.

- Now I meditate daily for at least 10 minutes, sometimes much longer. I don't adhere to 'rules', other than ensuring my spine is upright and I'm grounded, because when you impose too many conditions, they provide excuses you use to talk yourself out of your intentions. Life is too short for rules... a short, 'imperfect' practice that might happen during your commute, is more beneficial than no practice at all because you think it has to look a certain way.

Extra strategies:

Research on how long it takes to install new habits keeps changing. As a rule of thumb, I've found that if you want to keep something in your life, repeat it for as many days as you can - at least 21 days - and then make sure you don't break the chain of doing it for longer than two days in a row.

Your brain loves tracking things, use this to your advantage: print out a whole calendar month on an A4 piece of paper, then with a bright highlighter, cross through each day as you carry out your new habit. You will strongly resist missing a day and breaking up your lovely row of crosses. Before you know it, you'll have crossed out 21 days, and installed your new habit without stressing about it.

Habits are also easier to install and keep when you create triggers for them. You can eventually install a series of triggers so that you create an ideal morning power ritual. Your brain nudges you after each thing to do the next thing in the pattern... it makes honouring your intentions so much easier.

This is how I have set up my first hour of the day. It has had endless tweaks and evolutions, and took a while to install, but when I'm able to fit all my 4 Ms in, I feel energised, grounded, centred and ready for anything!

Solution 5: Make Your Days Magical

"Don't think you can attain total awareness and whole enlightenment without proper discipline and practice. This is egomania. Appropriate rituals channel your emotions and life energy toward the light. Without the discipline to practice them, you will tumble constantly backward into darkness." — Lao-tzu

I love this quote because it sums up something fundamental: you don't get to live the life you want without creating structures and habits to support it. The pull towards what is easy and safe is constant; developing the ability to resist distraction and shiny things requires horsey-blinkers, and discipline.

This is where the power that is unleashed by uniting your head and heart comes into its own, forming a supportive structure that enables you to take your place powerfully in the middle. I very much live from my heart; however, without help from my head, I would spend my days drifting along on a blissed out cloud, and this book would not be in your hands.

Your head is the workhorse that offers you solutions and carries out actions. Your heart is the visionary, the dreamer who can see beyond what you currently believe is possible. Combining the two forces consistently and intentionally creates momentum and a series of small wins that help you believe anything is possible. This is a magical combination:

Faith (Heart) + Action (Head) = Momentum & Mindset Shift

Once you know what you want and why you want it, your success depends upon the quality of your daily actions and routines, your ability to trust in what will unfold, and how focussed you are.

The simplest way to optimise these is to embrace the following:

- Keep your Big Why in your mind, alongside your number one priority.

- Start your day the right way and do what matters most in the morning.

- Forget multitasking and instead focus on one thing at a time.

- Embrace the leverage power of small things.

- Take inspired action daily in the form of small steps.

- Commit to your intentions and goals like you commit to turning up when your ticket is booked.

- Leave behind 'I Should'. Act from a place of 'I Must'.

Why Mornings Matter

For almost all of us, the morning is when you have most control over your day; before the rest of the world intrudes with its agendas. It's also when your energy and motivation is higher. When you choose to prioritise what matters to you most each morning, you generate greater self-belief, more confidence, and more fulfilment. Your days feel more purposeful and as you reclaim your personal power, you start stepping into your full potential.

I know this isn't always possible. I don't get up at 5am, so I am not going to tell you to do that either. What I have done instead is realign my life over time to get up earlier, sleep better, get rid of as many tasks that aren't in my flow as I can, and do more of the tasks that are.

Essentially, I use my porridge pot of energy wisely, spending as much of it as I can on activities that move me forwards each day towards my number one priority. Those that don't contribute or are not important to the expression of my core blueprint come last, when I have less energy. This might sound selfish but if you want to feel more fulfilled than you do now, this is a choice you have to make. Like anything else, you find the middle ground, not being an extreme hermit and not being so giving that you don't leave any porridge for yourself.

If you could see your porridge pot of energy being depleted as it happens, would it change the choices you make?

Imagine each activity you do has a porridge pot depletion rating.

Some activities, such as breathing consciously, hugging your loved ones, or taking a moment to rest, hardly use up anything and may even add to your porridge pot. Those that are most important to your heart and your intentions, use up some energy; but you can stretch your porridge pot further. The activities that aren't in your flow or you hate doing, deplete your porridge pot most.

If you want to use your energy wisely, you do the most important, needle-moving tasks first whilst your porridge pot is still full. It doesn't matter so much if your porridge runs out before you get to do the less important ones.

Everyone's day is different and we all have different body clocks, so use your wise inner guidance to help you tailor this to your circumstances:

- If you are a night owl, how could you fit more of what matters into the time of day that works best for you.

- If you are a commuter, consider how you could use your commute to serve you more. On my old commute, whilst everyone around me slept, I was meditating and studying.

If you are a morning person and your mornings are busy, start small by getting up just five minutes earlier and adding another five minutes every couple of weeks.

Why Make Things Small

There is incredible power in focusing on one thing at a time, taking small steps and leveraging the power of small things. This is especially important if you have small children, a lot to juggle, or you are particularly sensitive in terms of being drained when you are overstimulated.

Taking small steps towards your most aligned life works because it doesn't arouse the suspicions of your inner Fear Fairies; instead, it helps you make change 'by stealth'.

Most of us get stuck when it comes to goal-setting, because we make it too big and have no idea where to start. Some of us assess all the areas of our life on life wheels, which are wonderful tools, but then we try to address each area at the same time, which can be overwhelming. We also only value the big wins, forgetting to celebrate the small ones.

It doesn't work for most of us, it's too much.

It's better to break it down into teeny steps, give ourselves permission to address one goal at a time and celebrate baby steps along the way.

I started making the biggest shifts in my life when I decided to simplify everything. I have never liked having too much 'stuff', it makes my head feel crowded. For some reason, however, it took me a while to realise this applied to my approach to intention setting too.

I highly recommend stripping right back when it comes to addressing your life goals. It takes our brains at least twenty minutes to switch focus, so whilst multitasking and addressing multiple steps might feel satisfying, it drains your brain and reduces your focus. It's false economy and empty promises. Given that we're all short on time, it makes no sense to lose time whilst your brain resets itself. It might look impressive having lots of chores done on your tick list, but is it the stuff that matters to you most?

When I decided to make life simpler, I asked myself what three areas of my life would act as the biggest levers for all the others. In reality, everything is intertwined, but you have to make a decision to start somewhere. Those are the areas I currently use the bulk of my porridge pot of energy on.

Anything that truly doesn't contribute gets parked until later. For example, when I am focussed on a project, I set up my email auto-response to explain that I won't reply immediately, so that my brain doesn't have to use energy worrying about my inbox. I set my boundaries up in such a way that it protects the seedlings of whatever it is I am trying to grow.

I know tomorrow is not guaranteed and therefore I might never get to address outstanding tasks or aims, but to be honest, that makes it even more pointless to worry about them. None of us can actually do all the activities we think we should be doing, so it is far better to give ourselves less to do!

As long as you are spending your days intentionally and capturing outstanding tasks (so your conscious brain isn't trying to keep track of them), you can let them go. If they don't move the needle, they are not a priority. You can address them at a later time when it suits you; at which point you will realise they actually don't matter anymore.

Another way to approach your area of focus is to ask yourself which area of your body is calling out to be addressed, and then look at what aspects of life this represents in energetic terms.

This is the focus you visited in Process 3. If you struggled to sense your feet for example, it might be that your priority is to focus most on what would give you more stability in your life. This makes sense. It's hard to think about self-realisation when you don't know how you'll pay the rent next month, or you feel unstable in your relationship. Once you know which life areas correlate to those areas of your body, you can do some honest self-reflection and enquiry around it, before creating your goals to address them.

Goals are reached by setting your course towards your chosen target, identifying each big stepping stone that leads you there, and then taking small, intentional steps forwards each day with trust. You know the route may change as you walk but having full awareness of your target makes it easier to notice when you're moving further away or are completely out of alignment. You therefore spend less time spinning in circles and more time achieving your intentions.

Giving yourself permission to value the small steps takes the pressure off.

This increases your productivity and sense of purpose as you consistently achieve small wins. When you know the role each small win plays in relation to your bigger picture - even if you don't know how the path will unfold - every day feels deeply fulfilling. You enjoy the process, let go of perfection, and stop focussing only on the end result.

If you consistently dedicate small pockets of time to something you value, one day you will realise you're living the version of life you used to dream about.

It all starts with one small step in the right direction. You then rinse and repeat again and again and again.

You cannot get this wrong because there is no right or wrong. The only person you have to please is yourself. This is your journey. Your life. Time is not going to slow down for you, but it's up to you what you do with the time you have right now.

Your Magical Mission will help you to break this down further...

Process 8 – Summary for Your Soul:

You are a remarkable soul on a wonderful journey. Everything that you have been, everything you are now, and everything you will become are all perfect.

Have faith in your journey. Embrace it and trust that every aspect will teach you something you need to learn in order to keep evolving and unfolding.

Always believe in the flow of your life and don't push too hard. There is no point trying to push water uphill – sometimes you just have to let go, with joy in your heart, and throw yourself into the direction the river of life wants to take you.

Let your entire system relax and enjoy the ride. Take in the views, notice the passing world. Enjoy the interactions you have, the food you eat, the small details that make up the miracle of everything in life.

Don't be in a hurry. Trust that the seed of your soul will grow and unfurl into the light to take its place in the world, as and when it needs to.

Now sit back and let your soul thrill in the glorious journey of your life.

Process 8 Self-Affirmation: I relax into the flow of life.

Magical Mission — Unfold Your Peace, Potential, and Purpose

"Listen to the mustn'ts, child. Listen to the don'ts. Listen to the shouldn'ts, the impossibles, the won'ts. Listen to the never haves, then listen close to me... Anything can happen, child. Anything can be." — Shel Silverstein

Your mission, should you choose to accept it, is to wrap your Cape of Possibility around you, step into your power, and set your course towards unfolding your peace, potential, and purpose... each and every day, in any number of small ways.

Forget big lofty scary goals, start thinking about how you would like to feel each day and build from there. You already know you don't want hustle and stress, so this mission will help you further clarify what it is you do want and then make a plan to help you take action.

You have everything you need inside you, so trust in that and let your intuition guide you because you are amazing and the world cannot wait to see the gifts you have brought to the party we call life.

This Mission has three simple steps to help you really claim your personal power. You'll need your journal, or several pieces of paper, a pen, and a space where you won't be disturbed for a little while. 📢
https://www.helenrebello.com/p/MagicBookResources

Step 1 - Unfold Your Peace

Before you can tune into your body and create a plan, you need to get out of your head. It's very challenging to tune into what you want when your head is full up, so to create a sense of space and serenity, in this step, you are going to do a brain dump:

- Grab your journal, or several sheets of blank paper, and a pen.

- Give yourself 5-10 minutes to write down everything that is swirling around in your head right now: the lists, the jobs, to-do's, ideas, etc. Don't hold back, don't judge, don't worry about what or how you write just get it out of your head.

- When your time is up, put the piece of paper aside and take a deep, slow breath. Notice how it feels to empty your head of all that clutter.

- Let yourself simply sit with no agenda for a moment and then fold the piece of paper up and tuck it away in your journal. You can decide whether you want to do anything further with it once you've worked through the next two processes.

Step 2 - Unfold Your Potential

Now that your head is relatively empty and you feel more peaceful, this step will help you reconnect to your unique potential. This increases self-awareness, motivates you, and helps you see you already have what it takes to create your life on your terms.

Start a new page in your journal or a fresh sheet of paper and take a moment to let your attention drift towards the back of your body, before asking yourself the following questions, with love. Use your responses to fuel you:

- What personal achievements are you most proud of in the last three years?

- What qualities do you most admire about yourself that helped you to achieve these?

- Think of people that inspire you, people who have made their dreams come true. List three of them.

- What do you have in common with each of these people? (This will help you see that you have exactly what it takes to bring your dreams to life!)

- What is your BIG WHY; the thing that sustains you and moves you towards a desire to honour your dreams, no matter what? (It's okay if you don't know yet.)

- What makes you feel fully alive when you do it/ experience it?

- What dreams do you have for yourself in the next 3-18 months? Those scary ones no one knows…

- What excites you about bringing your dreams to life?

- Do you have any beliefs that are keeping you from embracing your dreams?

- What beliefs and strengths are truly supporting you and helping you to embrace your dreams?

- Think of a time when you overcame a huge obstacle… what strengths helped you to achieve this? What lessons have you learned from this?

- On a scale of 1-10, (1 being "not at all", 5 being "somewhat" and 10 being "Yes!") How willing and committed are you to clarifying and embracing your dream life and stepping into it?

Step 3 - Unfold Your Purpose

"Everyone has a gift, one of our callings is to uncover it and then inhabit it." — Mark Nepo

Your purpose is to embody yourself, identify your unique gifts, and then find a way to use and share them in your daily life.

Your stance on this is unique to you. What usually lights you up are your gifts, and what you have transcended shows you how you could use them in service to yourself and others.

I have found the easiest way to embody your unique gifts is to base your three most important daily steps on the three areas of your life that are lacking in some way. These are the areas you identified in Your Treasure Hunt with a Difference in Process 3. *This approach led to me reclaiming my inner writer, shifting the focus of my work, and writing this book. Keeping it simple is powerful.*

Trust what you felt and found, remembering that your heart communicates through feeling and your heart is stronger than you brain. By focusing on these areas first, you clear the blocks that are showing up to be addressed, which frees up your energy, so it can flow more freely through all the areas of your life:

- Remind yourself which three areas came up for you and take a moment to revisit what each of these areas means by visiting the Magical Mission for Process 3.

- Take a breath and ground your energy. Keeping your eyes open, bring your attention to the area between your eyebrows, then move it backwards towards the back of your head so it feels as though your awareness is in the middle of your brain. This area corresponds to an area of your brain known as the 'Seat of the Soul', which helps you focus.

- Let go of any sense of needing to get anything right and breathe.

- Think about each area in turn and what it relates to and ask yourself these questions: *what is causing you the most frustration right now in relation to this area of your life? Why would you want to improve in this area of your life? What would it mean to you to change this and how would it impact you? How does this relate to your values and your Big Why? What is it that wants to be expressed through you? Why is this important?*

- Now bearing these answers in mind, for each area, complete these prompts without thinking about it too much: *Creating my perfect idea of balance in this area would look like… This would make me feel… If I was at my best in this area I would be/do/have…The #1 thing I could work towards to achieve this is…Something small I could commit to daily to help me feel this way is…*

- As you tune into your sense of each area and how it would feel to achieve these desires, see that future version of you standing just ahead of you, smiling back at you for taking the time to connect to her.

- Write down the small thing you could commit to daily for now relating to each area. You're aiming for a list of three small, actionable items – one for each life area. If this feels hard, walk around, shift your energy and get out of your head, then ask yourself the same questions later, until you have something smaller.

- Write these down on a Post-It Note or in your phone as your three core daily intentions for right now.

- Imagine if all that really mattered each day was that you did these three things? Imagine if anything else you get to do afterwards is a bonus. Would that be a successful day?

Choose your three most important intentions each day that you prioritise over everything else and you will soon be looking for the next three at the next level.

If you set aside a few minutes each week or month to repeat each of these steps and keep choosing your most important intentions based on the answers you get, you will find that your life shifts exponentially.

Small intentional steps taken daily in the most crucial areas have a compound effect. Whilst this might at first leave you wondering how you'll get anything else done, in my experience you'll intuitively know what your most aligned actions are each week, as you clear blocks and tune more into your intuition.

In part three, you will find more resources to help you build upon this to continue the Magical Momentum...

For now, take a break, celebrate reaching the end of the MAGICAL process and know that each of these steps can be revisited over and over again to help you unfold your magic.

You are a wonderful soul and I love that you're here. Never doubt your significance. You matter more than you know.

INTERLUDE TWO
A Love Letter for Your Journey

"What one can be, one must be." — *Abraham Maslow*

You are here in the world, at this time, and this place, because you are vitally important to it. I don't want you to ever forget that. Truly... it's important.

You have earned your right to be here, to breathe, to live, to love, to laugh, to cry, to scream, to sigh, to be, to do, to take up space, to hide, to thrive, and to not merely survive.

It has always been my hope that everyone I meet or connect with, will someday, in some way, find inside them their unique gift for the world. And then go out and share it in their own inimitable way, drop by small drop... leaving beautiful, almost imperceptible imprints on other people's hearts.

Whether it is that you have a way of looking at people that makes them feel seen, or you're great at offering support, or you write amazing words that touch others, or you're the kindest person around, or you're first to help others in a crisis, or you have any one of an infinite number of other overlooked gifts...

I want you to know that you can never underestimate the power of your presence, or the power of your natural gift, and you have no idea how many people you've helped simply by being who you are...

I know this, because I've been lucky enough to be on the receiving end of an infinite amount of kind, genuine, openhearted souls. If you're reading this book, you definitely fit that description too.

So thank you. I am so grateful for your presence in this world, and I am truly thankful you are here. And I love that in this crazy, busy, bonkers, beautiful, funny old world, somehow, I got to connect with you, so that maybe I could reach your heart.

Your life is happening RIGHT NOW. And you owe it to yourself to live it with full expression and awareness of the incredible person you already are, without apology.

That is your birthright.

And my dream for us all.

Part Three — Maintaining the Magic

"Happiness cannot be traveled to, owned, earned, or worn. It is the spiritual experience of living every minute with love, grace & gratitude." — Denis Waitley

Welcome to the other side of the Bridge, the place where magic happens.

You are probably feeling a curious mixture of excitement, anxiety, and maybe impatience right now. You've taken the long journey across the Bridge and you're happy to be here... however, if you're honest, you're not sure you belong here.

Even if you are wearing your Cape of Possibility like the others here.

You don't feel like much has changed or maybe you should feel more different somehow. You've learned a lot and have helpful tools and feel more empowered and excited, but you also don't quite know what to do next.

These feelings are all normal.

It is easy to worry about what you'll do when life encroaches again once you've left the safety of a defined 'exploratory space', knowing that something has shifted. You know you have to return to normal life, all fired up and enthused, and even though you're on the other side of the Bridge, you worry that before long, life will burst the Zen bubble you have built.

That is what Part Three is here for.

This is your virtual support section to help you maintain your magical momentum, before life intrudes and you start doubting yourself. It is a bit like added insurance for your heart.

It is divided into three short sections, all containing quick, simple tips.

- Celebrate Your Journey and Four Ways to Incorporate New Practices and Habits
- How to Protect Your Cape of Possibility
- What to Do When

You will also find additional resources at the end to support your continuing magical unfolding.

CHAPTER 12
Celebrate Your Journey

"A kind of light spread out from her. And everything changed colour. And the world opened out. And a day was good to awaken to. And there were no limits to anything. And the people of the world were good and handsome. And I was not afraid any more."
— John Steinbeck

Lovely soul, it is time to celebrate!

You have learned so much, explored so openly and been so present… I hope you are high-fiving yourself for getting to this stage. You've earned your right to celebrate. Don't underestimate how much courage, tenacity, faith, and strength it takes to even think about new things. As you've made it to the end, I can safely say, you've got this!

You now have many tools to help you stay grounded, centred, present, energised, focused, peaceful, and purposeful. They are tools for life, as is this process, so play with them and make a promise to yourself today to continue exploring those that most spoke to your heart.

Imagine how you'll feel a year from now when you look back and see how much you've shifted and how much better life feels. You'll be so thankful you started this process, and you won't even have to think about each of these steps by then, because they'll be ingrained as habits.

I started this book by stating that this world needs more peaceful warriors; people who have become who they came here to be. It really does, and since you've reached this stage, that includes you. You *are* a peaceful warrior and I am grateful you're here. Celebrate your magical unfolding today in whatever way you choose.

You might want to review your journal, make a collage from all your discoveries about yourself, make a list of ideas you've had whilst reading, give yourself permission to explore some of the poets, authors and teachers I have quoted. Or head out for coffee and cake, blog about your discoveries, paint something, give someone close to you a hug, or simply head outside to play.

You've earned the right. Do something that makes your heart smile today!

If anything you have read in this book has helped you to unveil gifts you didn't know you had, or have the courage to show the world before, it has done its work.

Mark this day in your calendar as the day you stepped into your power and mark the same date in a year's time, to look back and review the year that is about to unfold for you.

So much energy and time was lovingly poured into the miracle of creation that is you. Never forget how incredible you are. All your ancestors applaud you daily. As do I.

4 Ways to Incorporate New Practices and Habits

"No great thing is created suddenly, any more than a bunch of grapes or a fig. If you tell me that you desire a fig, I answer you that there must be time. Let it first blossom, then bear fruit, then ripen." — Epictetus

During the course of the MAGICAL process you have discovered many tools, solutions and techniques.

The more of these you can incorporate into daily life as practices and habits, the easier it will be for you to embrace life on the side of the bridge where magic happens. Living purposefully happens moment to moment and the MAGICAL processes help you do this. This doesn't mean you have to be ever vigilant, tracking everything, and never relaxing. It simply means you are more aware of what you're doing and why; which means you will feel less guilt about saying yes to unexpected opportunities to kick back and relax.

Below are four simple reminders of the best ways to save your future self from regret by incorporating the tools you've discovered. This helps you use them proactively, rather than reactively because you ended up back on the Bridge.

1. Keep It Simple

Well that sounds simple enough!

It is, and yet our brains consistently try to trip us by making things seem complicated and harder than they are. Do not let yourself be dragged into this illusion. Do yourself a favour and keep everything you do as simple as possible.

Forget trying to master everything at once. Forget multitasking. Choose one area to focus on in terms of incorporating the processes from this book and install that as a foundational habit first. Then choose the next and the next. In one year's time, if you install one new habit every month, you will have 12 new supportive practices to use.

2. Your Path, Your Way

I recognise the irony that I am giving you suggestions and recommendations on what to do and best practices to do it.

I am basing this on years of experience, having worked with hundreds of lovely souls like you. However, this does not make me the Oracle. The practices are designed to help you tap into your own inherent wisdom and answers, so you can create your best path.

You are unique and have your own skills, insights, patterns, and energy flow. Walk your path your way, there are no rights or wrongs. Let the idea that there's a right way go... it was invented by your head and your heart needs no convincing.

I would hate you to think that I would judge you for tweaking things. I wouldn't. I would applaud you for trying them and not making excuses for yourself, and then celebrate with you as you adapt these practices to suit yourself.

When you start doing that, you know you're truly incorporating new practices, because you have to understand them to adapt them. That is the sign of a true magical master.

3. Aim, Monitor, Review, Celebrate

If you don't know where you're going, you won't know when you've got there. If you stall halfway, but forgot to track your journey, you won't know you've already come halfway.

The biggest secret to keeping your brain occupied whilst your heart is busy making plans, is to set yourself a measurable aim or goal, monitor your progress each day, review and make tweaks every week and celebrate the highlights of the journey so far.

on track. Our brains absolutely love keeping track and there is
something very satisfying about looking back at the end of a
week and feeling proud because we have incorporated our
one simple aim into each day.

This is about celebrating yourself and your wins. Taking a
positive stance and making tweaks where necessary when you
fall by the wayside; which you will sometimes, because you're
human and life happens. Rather than let that trip you up
though, if you know how far you've come, you will be more
motivated to continue.

- Set an aim each week to use one focus/practice/habit daily
  for five minutes.

- Monitor it daily with a cross in your calendar to say you
  did it.

- Review your line of crosses at the end of the week. How
  well did you do? How focused and disciplined were you?
  What can you do to tweak and improve?

- Celebrate what you did well.

4. Keep Taking Small Steps

Have you ever watched the London Marathon? There are
always people who walk the entire 26 miles and just keep
going, one step at a time. They may finish several hours later,
but they are driven by something bigger than their pain and
sense of how far they have to go... slowly but surely, they
reach their destination.

The destination doesn't care how long it took them and it doesn't look any different because they reached it small step by small step.

What is important is that they achieved a dream by trusting each step, focussing on a bigger goal and having Toddler Tenacity.

You can do this too, you simply have to believe it and create a daily nourishing, non-negotiable practice bit-by-bit. This is manageable, achievable, measurable, easier to do and maintain, and eventually leads to a big shift.

Taking small steps towards integrating a new practice or habit, has a compound effect, so that every day builds upon the next and the next, becoming easier to do. This is not only the simplest and best way to move towards any new goals, but also the one that builds the most self-confidence and self-belief.

If you ever doubt the power of small steps and find yourself getting tripped up when you try to take a big leap, ask yourself who was in charge of that decision... I am willing to bet it wasn't your heart!

Ode to A Peaceful Warrior

A peaceful warrior represents someone so fundamentally
grounded in their own core truth,
that they have no need to rally, railroad, shout or fight.

Someone who isn't lured into dramas,
because they've identified what's truly important to them.

Someone on a mission, with a quietly powerful, understated,
peaceful presence.

A wise, old soul who plays with Universal energy
and has a compassionate, courageous heart of fire.

Someone who loves deeply,
doesn't compromise on their values
and has a healthy respect for the fragility of life.

Most importantly, someone who has accepted that they have
a choice,
they have a voice
and they are more powerful when they honour their truth.

They *will* fight if backed into a corner;
but really, they're more of a lover than a fighter!

CHAPTER 13
How to Protect Your Cape of Possibility

"You must learn one thing. The world was made to be free in.
Give up all the other worlds. Except the one in which you
belong."— David Whyte

At the start of your journey, you learned about the Matrix
Myth, which empowered you to escape. However, because
you were probably in its grip for a long time, you still have
old beliefs floating around that will pop up and try to derail
you from time to time. Usually this is a great sign that you are
stripping away layers and becoming more fully yourself. This
is because those outdated beliefs need those layers to survive,
so they cling onto them for dear life by trying to convince you
that you don't have what it takes...

Which, as you know in your heart, you do.

This section gives you fuel to fight these old beliefs with
love, as well as give you a few tips for your journey.

First, I thought your heart and head might appreciate my
view on what living a magical life really means:

I'm hoping this will make the concept of a magical life less
elusive and more tangible for you.

A magical life means many things and can change on a
day to day basis. Here are eight things that are true for me
today:

1. Waking up daily feeling grateful, even on a bad day.

2. Seeing the beauty and the gifts in everyday things because you're aware enough to truly notice them.

3. Living a more intentional life from your heart, moment to moment.

4. Spending your precious energy wisely on what truly matters, not on what doesn't.

5. Living with a healthy awareness that you're not here forever, so you make each day count.

6. Developing compassion, empathy, and understanding of yourself and others.

7. Making peace with your past and not fretting over your previous mistakes.

8. Setting your sights on what your heart wants, taking action to get it, then trusting it will unfold if it is in your greatest interests.

You can also throw in as much love as you can imagine, mix it with a dose of healthy curiosity, a pinch of belief, a teaspoon of hope and a cup of playfulness for extra magic.

Learn How To Bend Time Like A Ninja

"If you truly love life, don't waste time because time is what life is made of." — Bruce Lee

I know how hard it can be sometimes to feel as though you're a victim of the time monsters.

Those pesky little blighters mess with the best of us, and I've spent over 10 years working out how to defeat them and become the master of my own time domain. I'm still working on it; clearly, I live in this world too.

Mostly however, I'm 90% there...which, considering my inherent inability to judge time, is something of a miracle!

Here's what I've realised...

The time monsters aren't actually to blame for you having no time. It just seems more like this as you've acquired more roles and responsibilities, and the tasks calling out to you have not only multiplied but starting shouting louder for your attention.

What you forget, is this:

YOU are not a victim of the time monsters, or of time. You effectively ARE your time.

The time you have available emanates from you and your choices. It drags when you do stuff you hate, with every minute feeling like an hour, but somehow flies without you noticing when you're immersed in doing what you love.

It's the exact same 'time' in each case. All that's shifted is the Three 'Ps': your Perception, how Present you are, and your Perspective.

When you get really **Present,** you stop being in Nowhere Land and instead you are Now Here. From this place, you can get more connected to yourself and your core wisdom so your **Perspective** on what really matters to you changes.

Your subsequent ability to alter your **Perception** of time improves, as your awareness of this most precious resource deepens, and you develop ninja-like awareness of those time-sucking activities...

How to Start Shifting Your Three Ps:

- Begin each day by taking time to be quiet for a few moments, just focussing on your breathing. (Yes, that old chestnut again! But trust me, it will change your life. I do not exaggerate!)

- Shift your awareness gently to the place between your eyebrows, at the bridge of your nose and then imagine moving it backwards by a few centimetres to rest lightly behind your eyes.

- Stay here, gently breathing, and see if you can develop a sense of resting quietly in this sacred space known as the Seat of the Soul.

- Stay here for as long as you feel comfortable, just a few minutes is great. And then softly shift your attention back to the outer world as you return to your day.

- From this more present place, get perspective on what matters to you today; remembering that small things count, your day is made up of minutes, and you can be intentional about how you spend those minutes.

If you develop this positive habit daily, for just a few minutes, I guarantee you'll start making more discerning choices that come from a deeper, less hurried place, and you'll become a much better master of your own destiny, as you change your Three Ps.

And then you will make friends with the time monsters. After all, they mean you no harm.

Embrace the Power of Dominoes

Have you ever lined up a row of dominoes and then experienced the simple pleasure of knocking the first one into the second one, and seeing the rest topple in quick succession? If you line up dominoes in the right way, the initial one has the power and momentum to knock over a domino next to it that is 50% larger. You can imagine how powerful this could be if each sequential domino was 50% larger in turn...

Apparently powerful enough to eventually knock over something as tall as the Eiffel Tower, according to physicist Lorne Whitehead. If you ask Guru Google about this, you will even find a video demonstration he set up to prove the principle (it's worth checking out!). You can then use this knowledge to your advantage because your brain loves having a visual image to inspire it, as does your heart.

Imagine if you could line up a series of small steps in such a way that in a measurable time period, you actually achieve something tangible you want to create. If you were able to create a strong visual image of this in your mind, and trust in the final result, it frees your energy up to focus purely on the next step in front of you.

If you trust that the next step you take will be effective, you know that it boosts your motivation thanks to the motivation equation. That means with every successive step, your motivation keeps exponentially growing; until you become so tuned into your intentions to continue your journey, it becomes an inevitable conclusion.

All because you believe in the power of dominoes. It's like magic!

Embrace The Three Soulful Success Secrets

These secrets are a good way to remember the core tenets of heart-based living. Success is not about shiny things, it's about how much joy you extract from life.

These secrets are a philosophy to live by to prevent you from veering back into living from your head and falling back into the path of the Matrix Myth.

1. Do all things with love.

The most fundamental step you'll ever learn is to do all things with love. This applies in your life, business, thoughts, interactions, plans, and your transactions.

If you're doing things with love, there's no room for fear. You're tapping into your heart, not your head: ensuring that your decisions arise from an aligned place of service, rather than a place of 'what will others think'.

To tune into this, think of someone or something that makes you smile and feel how that changes your body. You'll feel lighter and brighter. Use this feeling as a measure in future to test whether you're acting from your heart rather than your head.

2. Trust and protect your dreams.

Trust in your dreams, because only you know what it is that you've dreamed of doing since you were a small child and only you can bring life to that; it is yours and yours alone.

You have something unique to contribute to this world, and when that unique gift is expressed, the world around you benefits. Protect your dreams and surround yourself with encouraging people, this will help your dreams become reality.

To tune into this, think about what you dreamed of as a child. What did you write, draw, or tell stories about? Use these memories as fuel to inspire you and always trust what you remember, this is your soul speaking. Do it the honour of listening and smiling as you feel those lovely feelings in your heart.

3. Live with intention and awareness.

Heart and soul-led goals are reached by setting your course, identifying each small step that leads you towards them, and then taking small daily steps with that intention in mind to keep you on track.

Having awareness of your steps makes it easier to notice when you're doing something that moves you further away or out of alignment, so you spend less time spinning in circles and more time moving forwards.

Identify a small goal you want to reach soon. Imagine how you'll feel when you reach it. Keeping this feeling in mind, brainstorm the steps that will lead you to the goal. Refine and revisit the steps daily to help you take intentional actions with awareness.

Choose the Path of Love Not Fear

The MAGICAL process represents a journey from the old paradigm to the new and from your head to your heart.

You can also regard this as a journey away from living in a more compressed adrenalin-fuelled 'fear' state, to living in a more peaceful, expansive 'love' state. Every day you get to choose whether to welcome the new paradigm with open arms and honour your heart, or whether to allow fear to rise and derail you.

On a day when this feels challenging, know that tomorrow it may all be different... in the meantime, this reminder may help. Feel free to copy it out for yourself.

Choose love, choose yourself.

Choose to choose. Decide and act.

This is your life, right now.

Choose for you. Forget the opinions of others.

They are all worrying about what others think anyway. They're not thinking about you.

Do what is right for you. You are the one who has dominion over your inner world.

You only have to decide which inner voice to listen to and honour.

Choose love. Let the other parts of you be overruled by love.

Do not hate them.

Do not hate your previous decisions. Do not berate the past. Do not give time to regrets.

Start now.

Decide to live differently.

You can do this. It is your perfect time.

Choose you. Choose the path of love and magic.

You've got this. I believe in you.

Create a WOW Wall

Before I had my hysterectomy, I asked my clients, friends and family to send me anything they thought might help my recovery. I knew I could potentially get low, and I wouldn't be able to work for several weeks so this was my proactive strategy to help boost my spirits when it all got a bit too much.

I ended up receiving all kinds of magical things, and I have kept them to this day because I was completely wowed by the wonderful messages and cards I received. People went to so much trouble and took the time to create cards, write poems, send photos, and share their thoughts with me. This boosted my heart rather than my ego and since then, I have adapted it as a heart-nourishing focus for my clients. I call it the WOW Wall.

We can never fully see ourselves as others see us and we consistently under-estimate our effect on others and our own abilities. When we see evidence that shows us how we have touched another soul's heart, it opens our hearts and this helps us trust our path, and our right to hold ourselves in esteem.

The WOW wall is a Wall Of Wonder, a physical or virtual space of place whatever makes your heart smile. Ideally you would have it at your desk or on your screensaver, so that you see it regularly. It may feature photos with loved ones, cards containing words of love, testimonials from clients, thank-you messages, quotes, or anything that lights you up and brings back happy memories.

To boost your journey, I invite you to create your own WOW Wall. If you're feeling really inspired, share it with me on social media, to celebrate your life journey so far.

CHAPTER 14
What to Do When...

This section contains short, simple soul nudges to set you back on track or simply let yourself be, on days when life is going a little less magically.

Dip into them as and when you need them, and feel free to share them with your loved ones, in case they are in need of a boost too.

When You Have Self-Doubt

Have you ever stopped to think about how unbelievably different the sky is each and every morning when you wake up?

No matter how beautifully painted or nuanced it was the day before, overnight it disappears into darkness and it's all undone before it begins again as a fresh new version the next day.

Each day we're given a whole new 24 hours, a clean slate, and a brand new opportunity to start afresh and show up in a different way. Even if we totally mess up the day before, we're only ever a few hours away from a new beginning. The world still turns. The sun still comes out and the sky doesn't fall on your head.

Don't be afraid of starting afresh. Don't label it as failure or going backwards. It's merely a new iteration and an evolution; an ongoing life experiment you get to learn and grow from daily.

Each day you get to wake up and venture on a continuing exploration of what it is to be human and to show up unapologetically as you are, like the sun.

Sometimes you'll show up as a glorious riot of colour and take the world by storm.

Sometimes you'll feel more like hiding behind your friends The Clouds.

It's all good. Because you can begin again and again and again. With each fresh start you'll be better equipped with valuable data from your daily exploration into becoming real.

How would you like today to unfold?

(If it doesn't happen that way you can start afresh tomorrow!)

When You Need Motivation

I wrote and shared this post in a joyful moment, after completing my crowdfunding campaign for this book and getting publisher offers from three publishers I had in my 'ideal wish list'.

To my surprise, the comments kept coming. Seems it spoke to people's hearts, so I thought it was worth sharing here... please use it as a boost, if your motivation temporarily flags.

Once upon a time there was a smiley, sensitive, shy girl called Helen who quietly nurtured Big Bold Dreams. For a few years she believed in the Big Bold Dreams. Until life got mean and taught her that Big Bold Dreams were silly things for girls like her to have. So she stopped believing in the Big Bold Dreams and in herself. She got quieter and quieter and less and less smiley.

Then slowly, like a less Bold dream coming true, she found some magical people who believed in her. And very slowly, the sensitive shy girl started believing in herself again. She even started smiling... not too much, in case the world went wrong again.

One day, many years later, the sensitive shy girl unfolded the Big Bold Dreams and dared to start believing in them again. She stopped caring about whether she was smiley, shy or sensitive, and started believing the Big Bold Dreams were hers for the taking.

The magical people stuck around, which made the girl braver and bolder.

Soon, with their love and support, she got brave enough to share her Big Bold Dreams with more and more people. The people rather liked the Big Bold Dreams because they reminded them of their Big Bold Dreams. And this made them smiley.

Because the people all had beautiful kind hearts, they supported the girl and helped her Big Bold Dreams to start coming true. Which is why today, the previously sad, shy girl is raising a glass to you from her new pad, with gratitude in her heart, publisher offers for her book *The Magical Unfolding* in her inbox, an incredible soulmate by her side, and a life full of magical people who believe in her.

Thank you all.

Not The End*

*Universe willing

How lucky I am to have you all in my life...you know who you are.

When You're Trying Too Hard

Forget the hustle, pushing, strategies, formulas and pretending you've got it all sorted.

You don't need to look or behave a certain way, tick the 'right' boxes, do All The Training, or break yourself. If there's something you really want to do in your life or work, the best way to get there is by getting to know yourself and learning what inherent gifts you have. You do this by giving yourself permission for stillness and self-enquiry. Asking yourself questions to uncover that which is hidden.

Create space and time to simply pause and be and do that consistently. Then you'll learn who you are, what holds you back from full expression of that, and how you can go about releasing the things that stop you showing up fully as you, without masks or made-up stories.

The old rule book no longer applies.

You can collect accolades and show up dressed like a grown-up and still feel totally empty inside.

You can apply successful strategies, earn 'six figures' and still have no clue who you are or what fulfils you.

Or you can show up fully and unapologetically as yourself, representing what 'adulting' really looks like; which is gloriously messy, confusing, blissful, moving, enlightening, and frightening. A kaleidoscope of colour amongst the dark suits.

And a relief to all those you connect with that are exhausted from wearing a facade.

When You Feel Like Being Quiet or Resting

As you go through the MAGICAL process and continue the journey, you will find yourself having days when you simply need to process and be quiet.

And that's okay.

You don't see animals rushing around when they're tired, they rest without judging themselves in any way.

Some days I am very introspective. I have very little to say so I stay quiet. As an introvert this is simply how it is. It's a comfortable place, a familiar space and it's restoration for my being. As a writer it provides percolation time. It allows ideas to slowly form and emerge. Percolation time is a crucial aspect of self-exploration and development. And indeed, of life.

It is yin and yang.

You cannot continue to fly if you never take time to stop and refuel.

What if today, both you and I simply tuned into the quiet truth of the words: I Am Enough.

And what if that truly was enough?

When You've Lost Your Way

If you lose sight of what you're aiming for, or why you're doing this, these eight fabulous focuses will help you get back on track:

1. Ensure you're building the right pathway.
2. Set your intentions for the right reasons.
3. Know yourself well.
4. Follow your heart and stay in your own lane.
5. Take intentional and aligned actions daily.

6. Be kind to yourself but don't make excuses for yourself when you get in your own way.
7. Ask for help.
8. Trust and be patient. There's no time limit for achieving magic in your life.

When It Isn't Happening

Some days we beat ourselves up for what we lack, or for what we don't get done, feeling empty and wondering when we get to start living.

Some days it just isn't happening... even before you get to 7:30am.

You know those days where you start wrong, because *insert thing* happened.

Before you know it, the shower won't work, you spill your breakfast, you rip your shirt and the car won't start. Your head gets all caught up in little whirling circles of ever-increasing annoyance and negative vibes and you just feel like giving up and going back to bed.

So what I do on days like that?

1. I pause, breathe, and catch myself in the act of mentally shouting and growling.

2. I recognise that it's not external circumstances that dictate my mindset. It's what I tell myself those things mean.

3. I remember life is short, and I can either miss out on the good stuff that's happening whilst stuck in my mind loop, or I can choose to stop taking myself so seriously and lighten up.

4. I shift my energy away from my silly head and depending where I am, either listen to music, dance, do yoga, or I take my mind out for a walk.

5. I notice the sun is still shining behind the clouds, I smile, and I move forwards, feeling lighter, into my day. Or I stay grumpy. But definitely a lot less grumpy.

When You Stumble

If at first you don't succeed try, try again... no one said you'd end up where you want to be first time.

In fact, the things you appreciate most are often those that delight you when they unfold just as you'd given up on them.

Never give up on your innermost dreams. The ones you quietly visit when alone at night...They might not seem like they're happening, but one day they'll be just around the corner.

Trust in them and keep moving forwards with faith. That way they'll trust in you and meet you when you least expect it.

All you have to do is Trust, Believe, and be Patient.

And keep taking daily small steps forward until you can see more clearly.

Not always easy I know, but an extremely effective and simple combination... one that always gets you to where you want to go in the end. Even if the view looks a little different from the one you expected when you get there.

Never give up. You've got this.

When You Forget Your Magic

Did you know that you are one of the most incredible living things on this entire planet?

Imagine that! There are a multiple gazillion trillion billion* living things on earth, and YOU blow the proverbial socks off all of them. (*This 'may or may not' be the actual number of living things.)

You are beautiful in a multitude of ways you cannot possibly imagine. There's beauty in your intricate movements, your ability to sense things, your smile, your strength, your courage, and your compassion.

When you're crying you're beautiful in your vulnerability and when you're happy, it makes the world around you happy too.

Don't make the mistake of thinking beauty exists only in the way you look and the symmetry of your face. Even if you're blessed with stunning features, those who TRULY see you only notice the beauty and magic in all the subtle aspects of you that you never see.

If you're struggling to believe this, ask your subconscious the following question: *'why is it that I'm beautiful?'*

Pause and see what answer you get. I bet it will surprise you.

From my heart to yours with love.

Helen xx

Resources

Magical Resources:

The following resources are those that I recommend to inspire you and help your journey run more smoothly. They are resources I use myself, or books that have helped me on my journey. You can find additional resources on my website at www.helenrebello.com

Access the accompanying free course, download audios, and PDF playsheets at
https://www.helenrebello.com/p/MagicBookResources

Books to Open Your Heart, Liberate Your Soul and Inspire Your Mind

Challenge Your Paradigm:

Way of the Peaceful Warrior, Dan Millman (H J Kramer, 2006)

The Alchemist, Paulo Coelho (HarperCollins ,2012)

The Magician's Way, William Whitecloud (New World Library, 2009)

The Monk Who Sold His Ferrari, Robin Sharma (Harper Thorsons, 2014)

Channel Your Creativity:

Big Magic: Creative Living Beyond Fear, Elizabeth Gilbert (Riverhead Books, 2015)

The Artist's Way: A Course in Discovering and Recovering Your Creative Self, Julia Cameron (Pan Books, 1993)

Conscious Writing: Discover Your True Voice Through Mindfulness and More, Julia McCutchen (Hay House UK, 2015)

Challenge Your Mindset:

Loving What Is: Four Questions That Can Change Your Life, Byron Katie (Rider, 2002)

Rising Strong, Brene Brown (Vermilion, 2015)

The Big Leap, Gay Hendricks (HarperOne, 2010)

Playing Big: Find Your Voice, Your Vision and Make Things Happen, Tara Mohr (Hutchinson, 2014)

Learn Mind and Body Insights:

Into The Magic Shop: A neurosurgeon's true story of the life-changing magic of compassion and mindfulness, James Doty (Yellow Kite, 2016)

Mindsight, Daniel Siegel (Oneworld Publications, 2016)

The Biology of Belief, Bruce H Lipton (Hay House UK 2015)

Anatomy of the Spirit: The Seven Stages of Power and Healing, Caroline Myss (Bantam, 1997)

Take Action:

The 5 Second Rule: Transform Your Life, Work and Confidence with Everyday Courage, Mel Robbins (Post Hill Press, 2017)

Turning Pro, Steven Pressfield (Black Irish Entertainment LLC, 2012)

Getting Things Done, David Allen (Piatkus, 2015)

Coming Alive: 4 Tools to Defeat Your Inner Enemy, Ignite Creative Expression & Unleash Your Soul's Potential, Barry Michels and Phil Stutz (Random House, 2017)

Learn About Energetics and Intuitive Movement:

The Tao of Pooh and The Te Of Piglet, Benjamin Hoff (Egmont, 2015)

The Yellow Emperor's Classic of Medicine, Maoshing Ni (Shambhala Publications Inc, 1995)

Breath: The Essence of Yoga, Sandra Sabatini (Pinter & Martin Ltd, 2006)

Awakening The Spine, Vanda Scaravelli (Pinter & Martin Ltd, 2011)

Relax and Renew: Restful Yoga for Stressful Times, Judith Hanson Lasater (Rodmell Press, 2011)

Somatics: Reawakening the Mind's Control of Movement, Flexibility and Health, Thomas Hanna (Da Capo Press, 2004)

Make Friends With Your Body and Mind:

I Love You, Me! My Journey to Overcoming Depression and Finding Real Self-Love Within, Andrea Pennington (Make Your Mark Global Publishing, 2017)

Cleanse: The Holistic Detox Programme for Mind, Body & Soul, Faith Canter (Empowered Books, 2016)

Finding Joy Beyond Childlessness: Inspiring Stories to Guide You to a Fulfilling Life, Lesley Pyne (Make Your Mark Global Publishing, 2018)

Wonderful Apps and Websites To Support Your Journey:

Mindvalley – Global online School
http://www.mindvalley.com/

Optimize – Dedicated to helping you optimize your life
http://bit.ly/optbrianjohnson

Calm app - Helping you establish a daily meditation practice
https://www.calm.com/

Brain.fm – music to improve focus, calm and sleep
https://www1.brain.fm/

VIA Strengths Finder – Discover your strengths
https://www.viacharacter.org/www/

Institute of HeartMath – resources for stress and happiness
https://www.heartmath.org/

Jen Louden - author & guide for creative women
https://jenniferlouden.com

Linda Anderson – EFT magician - clear your blocks
http://www.tapintoyoursuccess.co.uk

Kyle Gray - Beautiful angel cards
https://www.kylegray.co.uk/card-decks

Bullet Journal – set up your journal your way
https://bulletjournal.com/

Acknowledgements

The Magical Unfolding and the journey that led to it were long in the making. Like any living entity, in order to grow, the book needed seeds sown, foundations laid, strong support structures, training, nourishment, love, and a sprinkling of magic. None of us are solo entities – we are shaped and touched by everyone we encounter. I am endlessly grateful to have benefitted from the magic of so many incredible people.

To my Shiatsu teachers, especially Gill Hattersley, Saul Goodman, and Dan Stretton - thank you for opening my eyes to a whole new way of seeing the world and opening my body up so I could help others see the world that way too.

To the teachers at CCST, particularly Thomas Attlee, Richard Kramer, Andrew Stones, Elissa Dell, and Lois Duquesnoy – thank you for seeing something in me I couldn't see myself and for teaching me how much I could offer others simply by being present.

To the juiciest yogi I know, Helen Noakes – thank you for introducing me to the most soulful yoga I've encountered and showing me what it means to be embodied. Thank you to Ru Jahn, Steve Bracken, Faye Riches, and Judith Hanson Lassater for teaching, restoring, and expanding my body and mind. You are wise way beyond your years.

Special mention to Hiro Boga, Jen Louden, and Dale Darley, without whom I wouldn't have had a title, the courage, techniques, or tenacity to own and share this body of work.

To all those I've been lucky enough to work with and teach, thank you. You've taught me so much about the human capacity for humility, openness, courage, growth, and joy. I'm honoured you chose me as your catalyst and that you're still here, supporting this evolution of my work.

Endless thanks to my circle of soul-sisters, magic-makers, and exceptional friends. You know who you are; but I'm especially grateful for the unconditional support, laughter, and love from Ali Hopkins, Fiona Singh, Rachel Crooks, Anna and Jane Harvey-Lloyd, The Jonners, Meg Lyon, Jan Holden, Kate Powell, Linda Anderson, Lesley Pyne, Melanie Mackie, Pat Duckworth, Jools Sampson, Jenny Kovaks, Lisa Pascoe, Faith Canter, Sarah Stevens, and Alexandra and Anthony Thornton-Hopwood.

Huge thanks to my dear friend, mentor, and publisher, Andrea Pennington, MD, without whom I wouldn't be doing what I am now. You are a precious gift to the world and I am honoured to walk alongside you.

Thank you to the rest of the team at Make Your Mark Global, especially Carol Taylor for enhancing my words with her deft and delicate edits.

To Lee Constantine and Guy Vincent at Publishizer, thank you for your belief and support during my successful crowdfunding campaign. You are helping writers make their book dreams come true without needing to tick the right boxes first and I couldn't be more appreciative.

To the magical souls who supported and shared that campaign and in doing so, not only showed me this work matters, but also enabled me to share this book more widely. You have been patient, supportive, and enthusiastic, and I'm incredibly humbled by your generosity.

Those not previously mentioned are:

VIP powerhouse supporter, Imran Hakim, who brought us to Malvern with his magic and is an incredibly inspiring human. I'm honoured you believe in my work and trust me enough to contribute to your tribe.

My generous benefactor, who believes in my mission enough to have donated 50 books for me to distribute amongst women's empowerment organisations in the UK.

An extra special thank you for your huge generosity and belief in the power of purpose: Andrea Pennington, Deb Bannigan, and Sharon Noronha.

A special thank you for your generosity and awesomeness: Amanda Johnson, Amanda Green, Andy Butterfield, Aspasia Holley, Deri Llewellyn-Davies, Francesca Green, Kate Burford, Tamsyn Hawkins, and Tracy Footitt.

Thank you family and friends for your generosity and belief in possibility: Alex King, Alexandra Jones, Alison McDonald, Angela Dellar, Ann Guiheen, Ann Brown, Anna Cook, Cheryl Fernandes, Xandie Fernandes, Chrisoula Sirigou, David King, Dhiren Patel, Elinor Whitehead, Emma Lonsdale, Emma Woodhouse, Esther Nagle, Gitte Winter, Jill Stocker, Jo De Rosa, Jo McLaughlin, Josie Wood, Karen Solloway, Katherine Biggs, Kerry Blaker, Kiri Self, Lara L'Esperance, Laura Wellington, Liz Fleming, Mandy Collins, Melina Abbott, Mieke Tye, Nikki Creber, Nikoletta Malamoglou, Nisha Patel, Rachel White, Rosie Slosek, Stella Tomlinson, Steph Smith, Sue Sims, Tamlin Watson, Trevor Hahn, Vanessa Williams, and Zoe King

Thank you for your support and belief in magic: Alison Willard, Anne Wilkes, Cathryn Whittow-Williams, Colleen Lanchester-Raynie, Deb Rampton, Donna Luxton, Helle Mai Nielsen,

Holly Worton, Liz and Ian Tustin, Jen Marshall, Jo Taylor, Julie Budd, Karen Knott, Kathy Roll, Kindy Kaur, Lara Kynvin, Laura Casini, Lisa Nelson, Lynsey Pitcher, Marc Frankum, Marilyn Healey, Michelle Beach, Michelle Jones, Nadine Millin, Penny Goddard, Rachel King, Radha Upadhyaya, Rebecca Hope, Richard Kramer, Sarah Brandis, Susie Edwards, Tina Achille, Zoe Power

To my extended family, especially Suzanne, Felix, Yvette, and Luke - thank you for your love, for adopting me as one of your own, and for showing me how wonderful it is to be part of a big, worldwide, loving family.

To my darling dad David, inspirational mum Zoe, talented sis Rachel and phenomenal brother Niall, thank you. You are all stronger than you know and I would not be who I am without you. I am incredibly proud of you all and so grateful you are in my life.

To Toni, who taught me how much difference one person with a mission can make and what it truly means to have courage. I hope you're dancing wildly with the stars in heaven.

And finally, to Gav, my darling husband, without whom, none of this would've been possible. There is not a day that goes by without me thanking the Universe for having you by my side. Thank you for showing me how powerful true love really is and teaching me magic is real. Xx

About the Author

Helen Rebello is an author, intuitive mentor, self-development teacher, and former tutor at The College of Cranio-Sacral Therapy in London. She has spent over a decade empowering soulful women to find more meaning and magic in their life and unlock the courage to live and work on their terms.

Her drive to empower others led her to train with some of the best teachers in the Western world, such as Sonia Choquette, Barefoot Doctor, Bruce Frantzis, Helen Noakes, Judith Hanson Lasater, and Saul Goodman.

Helen is on a mission to empower 100,000 women worldwide to fulfil their potential; which is why she developed the MAGICAL process; blending her Eastern and Western wellness training with movement, mindfulness, meditation, and mindset tools.

She successfully crowd funded *The Magical Unfolding* book on Publishizer, topping Casey Fenton of couchsurfing.com for the #2 spot, and has already planned her next two books. Helen is an endlessly curious soul, a grounded spiritual yogi, gratitude junkie, a realist who believes in magic, an extrovert introvert, a writer, and lifelong learner. She lives near the magical Malvern Hills in the UK with her beloved husband Gavin. They are never happier than when they are doing what they love, spending time with like-minded souls, teaching together, or exploring different parts of the world.

Her website is www.helenrebello.com

Connect with Helen online:

Instagram: https://www.instagram.com/helenrebelloauthor

Facebook: https://www.facebook.com/helenrebelloauthor

Twitter: https://twitter.com/iamhelenrebello

Printed in Great Britain
by Amazon

35423912R00214